WITHDRAWN

ETHNIC DIVERSITY AND PUBLIC POLICY

Also by Crawford Young

IDEOLOGY AND DEVELOPMENT IN AFRICA

POLITICS IN THE CONGO

THE AFRICAN COLONIAL STATE IN COMPARATIVE PERSPECTIVE

THE POLITICS OF CULTURAL PLURALISM

THE RISE AND DECLINE OF THE ZAIRIAN STATE (*co-author*)

ISSUES OF POLITICAL DEVELOPMENT (*co-author*)

COOPERATIVES AND DEVELOPMENT: Agricultural Politics in Ghana and Uganda

Ethnic Diversity and Public Policy

A Comparative Inquiry

Edited by

Crawford Young

H. Edwin Young and Rupert Emerson Professor of Political Science
University of Wisconsin-Madison

in association with
UNRISD

First published in Great Britain 1998 by
MACMILLAN PRESS LTD
Houndmills, Basingstoke, Hampshire RG21 6XS and London
Companies and representatives throughout the world

A catalogue record for this book is available from the British Library.

ISBN 0–333–65389–0

 First published in the United States of America 1998 by
ST. MARTIN'S PRESS, INC.,
Scholarly and Reference Division,
175 Fifth Avenue, New York, N.Y. 10010

ISBN 0–312–17750–X

Library of Congress Cataloging-in-Publication Data
Ethnic diversity and public policy : a comparative inquiry / edited
by Crawford Young.
p.   cm.
Includes bibliographical references and index.
Contents : Ethnic diversity and public policy / Crawford Young —
Decentralization and the accommodation of ethnic diversity / Yash
Ghai — Electoral systems / K.M. de Silva — Ethnic diversity and
public policy / Jagdish Gundara and Crispin Jones — Indigenous
peoples / Rodolfo Stavenhagen — Public policies towards immigrant
minorities in Western Europe / Sarah Collinson — Preferential
policies for disadvantaged ethnic groups / Laura D. Jenkins.
ISBN 0–312–17750–X (cloth)
1. Multiculturalism.   I. Young, Crawford, 1931–   .
HM276.E77 1997
305.8—DC21   97–24722
                                                         CIP

© UNRISD 1998

This book is printed on paper suitable for recycling and made from fully managed and sustained forest sources.

10 9 8 7 6 5 4 3 2 1
07 06 05 04 03 02 01 00 99 98

Printed and bound in Great Britain by
Antony Rowe Ltd, Chippenham, Wiltshire

Contents

Notes on the Contributors

Sarah Collinson is a Senior Research Fellow at the Royal Institute of International Affairs (Chatham House) in London. Her work focuses on refugee, migration and immigrant integration policies in Western Europe. Her publications include *Europe and International Migration* (Pinter, 1993) and *Beyond Borders: West European Migration Policy Towards the 21st Century* (RIIA, 1993).

K.M. de Silva was Foundation Professor of History of Sri Lanka at the University of Peradeniya, Sri Lanka, from 1969 until 1995. He has been the Executive Director of the International Centre for Ethnic Studies of Kandy and Colombo since its establishment in 1982. His publications include *Managing Ethnic Tensions in Ethnic Societies: Sri Lanka, 1880–1985* (1986) and *Regional Powers and Small State Security: India in Sri Lanka, 1977–1990* (Woodrow Wilson International Center Press, 1995).

Yash Ghai is Sir Y.K. Pao Professor of Public Law at the University of Hong Kong. He has taught at the University of East Africa, Uppsala University, University of Warwick (UK), and has been a visiting professor at the Yale Law School, Toronto University, Melbourne University, the National University of Singapore and Harvard Law School. His principal area of research is constitutional law.

Jagdish Gundara is a Reader at the Institute of Education, University of London, and Head of the International Centre for Intercultural Studies. He is currently a Director of the Commonwealth Values in Education Project, and has conducted research into various aspects of interculturalism and the state, particularly in the European context.

Laura D. Jenkins, a doctoral candidate in political science at the University of Wisconsin-Madison, has recently completed research on affirmative action in India as a Fulbright-Hays scholar.

Crispin Jones is a Senior Lecturer in the Culture, Communication and Societies Group at the Institute of Education, University of London, working in the International Centre for Intercultural Studies. His current major research interest is education, diversity and state form-ation.

Rodolfo Stavenhagen is a member of the faculty of the Colegio de Mexico. Among his many works are *Social Classes in Agrarian Societ-ies* (1976) and *Between Underdevelopment and Revolution: A Latin American Perspective* (1981). In recent years his work has focused on issues of ethnic conflict and the struggles for recognition and rights by indigenous peoples.

Crawford Young is Rupert Emerson and H. Edwin Young Professor of Political Science at the University of Wisconsin-Madison, where he has taught since 1963. He is the author of a half-dozen major books, two of which won prizes (*The Politics of Cultural Pluralism*, 1976, and *The African Colonial State in Comparative Perspective*, 1994). He has also taught in Uganda, Zaire and Senegal.

Preface

Shortly after my appointment in 1987 as Director of the United Nations Research Institute for Social Development (UNRISD) by the Secretary-General of the United Nations, I initiated a wide-ranging programme of comparative research on major social problems of global significance. One of the most important of these research projects dealt with ethnic conflict and development. The decision to launch this ambitious project, comprising 15 country studies spanning all the regions of the world, was fully vindicated by the events that unfolded in the following years. Soon, newspaper headlines and television screens were full of the horrors of violence unleashed by ethnic conflicts in countries around the world. The researchers working on the UNRISD project had constantly to revise their analysis to keep pace with the rapidity of change on the ground. Three of the countries included under the project in 1988 – the Soviet Union, Yugoslavia and Ethiopia – have since disintegrated, at least in part as a result of ethnic pressures.

One of the unforgettable memories I have of the project is that of the final workshop, which was held in June 1991 at the Inter-University Centre in Dubrovnik. The meeting took place there at the invitation of our Yugoslav team which – it is now hard to believe – comprised researchers from Slovenia, Serbia and Croatia. Indeed, ours was the last international meeting held in Dubrovnik before this gem of mediaeval architecture was subjected to barbaric bombardments. None of the meeting's participants can shake off the painful memories of the subsequent destruction of a city that provided such a glorious venue for our deliberations – ironically, on the subject of ethnic conflict and development.

The research project was concerned with the causes, patterns, processes and consequences of ethnic conflicts and the effectiveness of a range of cultural, political, constitutional and economic policies to resolve or manage such conflicts. Specific issues included the historical origins and evolution of ethnic conflicts, the interests and motives of the major social actors, the responsibility of the state, political parties, voluntary associations, religious and other groups, the nature of external interests; and policies and mechanisms to prevent, contain or resolve such conflicts. Numerous volumes have been published under this project, including a synthesis of its principal findings by the project co-ordinator, Rodolfo Stavenhagen.*

The decision to convene the World Summit for Social Development in Copenhagen in March 1995 provided UNRISD with a good opportunity to continue this work but shift its focus to the lessons that may by drawn from relatively successful attempts at accommodation of ethnic diversity. The years immediately preceding the Social Summit were dominated by the eruption of violent ethnic conflicts in a large number of countries. The causes and resolution of ethnic conflicts and attempts at postwar reconciliation and reconstruction are at the core of the theme of social integration – one of three agenda items retained for the Social Summit. UNRISD therefore decided to present to the participants in the preparatory process for the Copenhagen meeting the lessons that may be drawn from the experiences both of countries undergoing violent ethnic conflicts as well as of those which have handled these problems in a relatively peaceful manner. The latter research project, entitled Ethnic Diversity and Public Policies, focused on policies to resolve ethnic tensions and contribute to successful accommodation in ethnically diverse societies. It consisted of several country and thematic studies. These studies have been brought together in two volumes edited by the project co-ordinator, Crawford Young.

The present volume contains essays on key policy issues in ethnically diverse societies. Drawing upon experiences across all regions of the globe, these essays deal with such issues as decentralization and constitutional reform, electoral systems, approaches to treatment of indigenous peoples and immigrant minorities, the role of education, and preferential policies for disadvantaged groups. The second volume seeks to distil lessons from the positive experiences of a number of countries with the accommodation of ethnic diversity. These studies make an important contribution to our understanding of the approaches and policies that foster ethnic harmony. In a world dangerously divided by ethnic conflicts, their importance cannot be overemphasized.

Dharam Ghai, Director
United Nations Research Institute for Social Development

---

* *Ethnic Conflicts and the Nation-State*, UNRISD and Macmillan Press Ltd, London, 1996.

Foreword

This volume originated in a project undertaken by the United Nations Research Institute for Social Development (UNRISD) designed to make a contribution to the preparatory process of the World Conference on Social Development organized by the United Nations in Copenhagen, Denmark, in March 1995. Under the larger rubric of social integration, UNRISD organized a planning conference in Geneva, in October 1993, to define a strategy for inventorying existing policy knowledge and experience relative to issues of accommodating ethnic diversity. 'Ethnic', in this context, is understood in a broad sense to include collective consciousness based upon race and religion, as well as ethnicity narrowly defined. In this venture, UNRISD could draw upon established connections with the global community of specialists on ethnic issues developed in an earlier research project on ethnic conflict, carried out in the preceding several years under the leadership of Rodolfo Stavenhagen of the Colegio de Mexico.

The planning conference decided to employ a dual approach in responding to the challenge. First, a number of major policy issues and themes were identified, concerning which synthesizing papers summarizing comparative policy experience could be commissioned. Secondly, a set of countries from different world regions were designated as illustrative examples of diverse accommodative strategies.

The earlier ethnic conflict project by and large selected for sustained examination the most severely divided societies: for example, Burundi, Yugoslavia, Lebanon. The framing questions concerned the underlying causes and determinants of cultural frictions, tensions and violence. The focus shifted in the present collective undertaking towards the accommodation of cultural diversity and overcoming ethnic conflict.

The driving concern with the therapy of accommodation rather than the pathology of conflict shaped the selection of comparative themes and country case studies. We examine policy domains where unfolding encounters with diversity produce instructive lessons. These comparative essays are assembled in the current volume.

The country studies (Malaysia, Tanzania, Mauritius, Trinidad and Tobago, Spain, Northern Ireland and the United States) will appear in a companion volume. They represent instances where cultural diversity is a basic attribute of civil society, but where (excepting

Northern Ireland) ethnic conflict levels have been moderate. The term 'success' is too fraught with ambiguities to characterize our quest, but we are in search of policy knowledge which points towards effective accommodation of diversity.

An international group of contributors was invited to contribute synthesizing papers on the themes and countries identified. These papers were presented at an international symposium held in August 1994 at UN headquarters in New York. Based upon those discussions, and the critical comments of the anonymous external readers for this volume and others, they have been extensively revised.

I have been privileged to work with the remarkably able UNRISD Director, Dharam Ghai, as principal advisor on the project, on the basis of which role I became editor of this book. I wish to express my deep appreciation to Ghai and other members of the UNRISD staff (Adrienne Cruz, Jenifer Freedman and Jessica Vivian) for their splendid support and assistance throughout. As well, gratitude is due to the several University of Wisconsin-Madison graduate students who provided invaluable collaboration at various stages: Laura Jenkins, Timothy Longman and Cathlene Hanaman. Along with my deep appreciation to all those named comes absolution from any responsibility for whatever deficiencies this volume may have. For these, the culprit can only be the undersigned.

Crawford Young
Madison, Wisconsin

1 Ethnic Diversity and Public Policy: An Overview

Crawford Young

INTRODUCTORY REMARKS

The horrifying tragedies of Rwanda and Bosnia would alone suffice to command attention to the policy challenges posed by ethnic diversity, which is far more ubiquitous in the contemporary world than was formerly recognized. In South Africa, the stunning triumph of policy reason in designing an initially successful transition from apartheid to democracy in a deeply divided society suggests the possibility of carefully reflected and bargained choice being able to transcend communal cleavage – although, of course, only the preamble of the saga of a democratic South Africa has so far been inscribed on the tablets of history. Between these polar examples lies a diversity of situations where identity conflicts challenge statecraft: the former Soviet republics, Northern Ireland, Lebanon, Sudan, Ethiopia, Sri Lanka, India, Canada, United States.

This list could readily be extended. Depending on the threshold of intensity required to secure notice, it could swell to include a substantial fraction of the world's polities. One recent study offers a roster of 233 'minorities at risk' (Gurr, 1994). Other widely read recent publications by influential authors offer a spectre of ethnic Armageddon: pandemonium, the coming anarchy, the clash of civilizations (Moynihan, 1993; Kaplan, 1994; Huntington, 1993).

Ethnic diversity first became a recognized dimension of the world order in the political settlement following the First World War. The doctrine of self-determination, applied initially to the defunct empire-states of Austria-Hungary, Ottoman Turkey, Imperial Germany and Czarist Russia (the latter soon reconstituted in new form), won ambiguous standing as the international norm of state constitution. The issue of 'national minorities' and their rights to protection entered the global agenda, primarily in Europe. At the same time, an implicit assumption of homogeneity as an ultimately normal condition of

1

political society widely prevailed, while the dimensions of the diversity question were shrouded by the colonial thraldom of most of the peoples of Asia, Africa and the Caribbean.

The reconfiguration of global political geography after the Second World War produced a radically altered environment for ethnic diversity. The aftermath of the war produced a large degree of ethnic cleansing (in Eastern Europe, the former Palestine Mandate and India); from Berlin eastwards, ethnic nationalism was contained by centralized autocratic polities (the erstwhile 'camp of socialism'). Normative discourse on rights of national minorities largely evaporated; the United Nations Declaration of Human Rights avoided all reference to them (Kymlicka, 1995: 3). The doctrine of self-determination was redefined as applying essentially to colonized peoples, and was overridden by the higher value of territorial integrity of states.[1]

The newly globalized community of sovereign political units, normatively perceived as nation-states, rapidly grew in numbers as decolonization ran its course. A vocation of nationhood was implicit in stateness; national unity was universally believed to be indispensable to modernity, which imposed upon all states, especially newly independent ones, an imperative of 'nation-building'. Particularly in the early phases of this epoch, the tensions born of communal difference were believed to be difficulties of transition, destined to diminish and even ultimately disappear with the progressive achievement of modernity.

The growing number of ethnic conflicts in the 1970s and 1980s eroded earlier assumptions of a unilinear integrative path to history. The shattering of the (retrospectively) comfortable certitudes of the bipolar world order with the collapse of Soviet-type systems in 1989–91, and the sudden emergence of 20 new states out of their wreckage, dramatically raised the stakes of ethnic conflict. Two other portentous patterns, likewise illuminating the scope and salience of identity politics, altered our basic understandings of world politics. Powerful currents of democratization surged through many parts of the world, sweeping away authoritarian regimes whose claim to legitimacy rested partly on their ability to contain ethnicity by repression while 'nation-building' went forward. And the range of possible political outcomes expanded to encompass a frightening new condition: the dissolution of central state authority, supplanted by warring armed ethnic factions – as in Afghanistan, Bosnia, Somalia and Liberia, whose conflicts remained irresolvable for extended periods.

PREMISES OF THE ANALYSIS

This novel and, in many respects, disturbing world environment is the context for the present volume, which presents studies of comparative focus synthesizing the instruction of policy experience in a number of domains in which statecraft encounters cultural diversity: decentralization and federalism, ethnic preference, electoral systems, education, immigration, indigenous peoples. A companion volume will include a diverse array of case studies: Malaysia, Mauritius, Tanzania, Spain, Northern Ireland, Trinidad and Tobago, United States. This chapter endeavours to extract from these contributions and to draw upon comparative knowledge concerning the politics of cultural pluralism, to take stock of policy options available to accommodate ethnic, racial and religious diversity.

Some fundamental postulates which shape this analysis require statement. The most basic premise – which few believed in 1950, but which most could concede today – is that cultural pluralism is an enduring attribute of contemporary political societies. Closely inspected, the overwhelming majority of the nation-states in our global community have significant internal cleavages based upon ethnicity, race or religion. The significance of these differences in the social and political process varies widely, as does the degree of salience, intensity and politicization of communal segments, both within and between states. But there is no longer any justification for clinging to the belief that the array of processes commonly labelled 'modernization' (expanding communication networks and media, urbanization, rising educational and literacy levels, increasing complexity of economic activity and social structuration) lead ineluctably to deepening levels of attachment to the 'nation' defined by the state of residence, or to the erosion of cultural solidarities of ethnos, race or religion separate from the nation-state unit. Rather, the reverse seems to be the more frequent pattern: social change tends to produce stronger communal identities. In addition, the cultural segments themselves are subject to evolution and change in the crucible of social process and political competiton. At the same time, identities are usually multiple and layered; they are not uniform across ethnic groups and are differently experienced by the individual members.

As a normative premise, cultural diversity requires acknowledgement rather than judgement. A corollary of this postulate is that the earlier presumption that the healthy end-state equilibrium for the nation-state is homogeneity must be dethroned. The spectacle of 'ethnic cleansing' in the contemporary world suggests the deep moral flaw to the premise of homogenization. But no endorsement is intended for the contrary proposition that states have an obligation to promote and enforce difference, as advocated by some messengers of multiculturalism.[2] Rather, the presumption is that cultural pluralism is a natural attribute of a political society. Although states naturally seek to earn the loyalty of their citizenry, this need not – in the contemporary world, cannot – be done by coercive fiat.

We further assume that the value attached to ethnic affiliation by many human communities is a natural condition and not a social pathology. Such solidarities can provide a sense of community in the face of a relentlessly globalizing marketplace. Ethnicity becomes a challenge to broader societal harmony when it is mobilized in hostile confrontation to the 'other'. In such moments of ethnic crisis, the collective psyche is prone to demonize and dehumanize 'the other' in ways that can produce singular conflict intensities and brutalities. The bestial excesses which then occur reflect, above all, profound failures of statecraft – they do not validate a germ theory of ethnicity. Preventative therapy in the form of effective policies of accommodation rather than curative medicine by the extirpation of identity is, we believe, the appropriate prescription.

In exploring the comparative lessons of policies concerning diversity, there is a rich array of experience to survey. Coping with cultural pluralism takes on a new urgency in the present conjuncture, but policy learning in this sphere has a long history. The scope of the topic is so vast, and the range of potentially pertinent information so great, that this volume can make no claim to either definitive conclusion or comprehensive coverage.

Broadly framed policies inevitably have complex impacts and outcomes. Their consequences will often vary over time. Society is in a constant flux and change, and the circumstances which shaped initial policy design will alter in the flow of events. A given formula – affirmative action or federalism, for example – may appear effective in one setting and much less so in another. These stubborn facts militate against categorical judgements.

So also do the multiple measures of policy impact. One is initially drawn to a search for 'success', for a certain prescription for dissolving ethnic conflict. But to a fatally large degree, 'success' is in the eye of the beholder, and there are many different spectators. Policies viewed as beneficial by some communal segments may be seen as discriminatory by others. Outcomes which appear positive to state managers may seem less benign from the cultural or social margins of society. Our evaluative standard is more modest: effective accommodation of ethnic diversity. Conflict – class, interest and ethnic – is a natural aspect of social existence; the heart of the matter is that it be conducted by civil process, by equitable rules, through dialogue and bargaining, in a framework of governance facilitating cooperation and reconciliation.

Only the most incurably visionary analyst would claim that fool-proof, universally applicable formulas for accommodation of ethnic diversity exist. Policy experiences resemble balance sheets, rather than triumphant lists of accomplishments; in all the spheres we investigate, there are liabilities as well as assets. The cultural circumstances of given polities vary widely; the many small, localized ethnic identities of Papua New Guinea, for instance, bear little resemblance to the intensely mobilized ethno-national collectivities in former Yugoslavia.

Further, even if the Holy Grail of universally applicable policy design were discovered, in the real life of polities it would be only partially applicable. Only rarely is there a moment of the covenant when the fundamental political dispensations of a country experience complete transformation, as in South Africa in 1994 or Russia in 1917 or 1991. The realm of policy choice is normally subject to only incremental adjustment.

In the design of policy to conciliate cultural diversity, a given state is constrained by its own circumstances, which are always unique. The course of history creates a powerful path dependency; the range of outcomes and menu of choices is shaped by the parameters set by the past. The configuration of cultural pluralism is particular to a given polity: the number, size, geographic distribution and degree of mobilization of communal segments; the relationship of ethnic diversity to other forms of social differentiation and hierarchy. The cultural definition of the state itself, and the content of its text of legitimation as 'nation', shape the roster of options conceivable. One need only ponder the contrasts between Japan and Indonesia, between Switzerland and France, between Germany and Canada, between Nigeria and Brazil to recognize the central importance of this factor. Here one encounters the contrast between 'ethnic' and 'civic' concepts of nationhood, stressed in recent debates about nationalism.[3]

The agenda of statecraft naturally includes much more than the accommodation of ethnic diversity. The material well-being of society as a whole, and the assurance of basic human needs of all sectors of the populace, are primary state goals. The maintenance of public safety and order, and protection of society and environment, are collective responsibilities. Respect for human rights and the rule of law is the hallmark of a civil state (*état de droit*). Effective governance of the national economy is a measure of the competence of the state. These objectives – and others that might be added to the list – may partly conflict with effective accommodation of ethnic diversity. In our present focus upon the latter aim, we do not intend to argue that coping with cultural pluralism automatically overrides all other policy goals.

The vision informing policy reason in this domain requires a realistic grasp of the nature and dynamics of diversity. Recent debate about ethnicity suggests that it involves three interactive dimensions: primordial, instrumental and constructivist (Young, 1993: 3–35). Ethnic identity often involves deep emotional attachments to group, supplies an internal gyroscope, cognitive map and dialogic library through which the social world is perceived and life routines enacted, and historicizes selfhood in a web of primordial cultural meanings. In everyday political and social interaction, ethnicity often appears in instrumental guise, as a group weapon in the pursuit of material advantage; thus its activation is contingent, situational and circumstantial. Ultimately, all identities are socially constructed, a collective product of the human imagination (Anderson, 1983).[4] Often this occurred long ago and is perceived as a primordial property; in many instances, the construction of the group is very recent or even contemporary (as for the Muhajirs in Pakistan), and thus the dynamics are clearly visible.[5] Social identities are invoked, used and rewoven in the myriad encounters of everyday life at both individual and group level. Combining these three perspectives, we may conclude that ethnicity rests upon a singularly potent set of symbolic resources and affective ties, but operates in a fluid and changing way in the political arena. The units of identity are not themselves timeless, but evolve in social praxis.

With this in mind, we may safely assert that 'ethnic problems' are not 'solved' in some permanent way. Rather, over time, policy choice will face the necessity of periodic readaptations. Through the instrumental use of ethnicity in political competition, the structural relations between groups, and the issues that define them, are in continuous evolution. The unceasing process of construction of identity constantly alters the contours of the ethnic landscape. Thus, the social circumstances to which public policy responds are changing, usually gradually, sometimes swiftly. Statecraft must accordingly avoid the comfortable illusion of permanence of policy formulas.

Policy options vary as a function of the type of cultural pluralism encountered, and its varying configurations. Ethnicity, narrowly construed as shared culture, often language, and its attendant mythology of common descent, tends to involve in particular issues of distribution and domination. Race, defined by the social meanings attached to phenotypical difference, primarily originated in historical forms of colonial conquest and unfree labour recruitment; it was thus hierarchical in its genesis, and leaves as its legacy singularly persistent patterns of inequality.[6] Religious diversity is a distinct sphere, involving for the faithful a comprehensive *Weltanschauung*, which can invest difference with sacred meanings.

Patterns of diversity vary widely as well. A dominant, bipolar division, where the politicization of difference is strong, produces singularly difficult challenges. Many states in Europe and Asia have a dominant, majority group, whose identity defines the state, and minority ethnic groupings (Slovakia, Romania, Russian Federation, China, Myanmar, Thailand, among others); here the issue is cast in the familiar 'national minority' form. Most African states have a multiplicity of ethnic groups, with the state seeking only a territorial and civic meaning. In the Western Hemisphere and Oceania there are indigenous populations, usually small in number, who advance a special set of claims. Most Caribbean states are dominated by the descendants of subordinated imported labour, now identified as racial categories. In North and South America European settlers imprinted their cultural (and racial) personality upon the state system. In Europe, North America and some of the Middle Eastern oil states, new patterns of diversity arise from large recent immigrant populations. Policy formulation encounters, accordingly, a large variation in configurations of diversity and attendant issues and claims.

THE STATE AND POLICY FORMULATION

A final set of postulates shaping our analysis relates to the contemporary world-historical context of identity politics. We start from the premise that, in most of the world, democratic processes – either existing or waiting in the antechambers of the near future – will predominate. Here changes in the last two decades are dramatic. In the early 1970s democracy was rare in Latin America; today it is the norm. With the fall of the Greek military junta and the conservative autocracies of Portugal and Spain in the mid-1970s, Western Europe was uniformly democratic for the first time in its history. Electoral democracy, however weakly institutionalized, swept over the former state socialist world from 1989 on. Africa experienced only one unambiguous democratic succession from 1960 to 1989; from 1990 to 1996, there were 17. Many of the democratic transitions are incomplete and the successor regimes are often fragile. But the international environment is far more hostile to autocratic regimes than has ever been the case previously; respectable status in the community of states, for the near future, necessitates at least a semblance of democracy.

Various definitions of democracy exist, and we have no ambition to increase the number. We simply take as our point of departure the assumption that ethnic diversity policies will be formulated and debated in a context of open political competition in many countries. Constitutional democracy profoundly shifts the balance between state and civil society, to the advantage of the latter. Accommodation policies will thus require reasonable public support. The inescapable link between representative democracy and notions of majority rule will often pose cruel dilemmas. Policy outcomes will be the product of political bargaining within civil society and its communal segments, and not simply the calculus of the state managers.

But the state is more than a passive register of citizen preferences, and in policy deliberation state leadership and initiative is critical. Further, the state apparatus, both administrative and judicial, will necessarily be charged with the implementation of whatever policies may be chosen. Here we encounter another paradox: the state is the arbiter and broker of cultural difference, yet the state is unlikely to be wholly neutral in ethnic terms. States inevitably reflect, in the distribution of power within their structures, the dominance of groups within civil society (by class and interest, as well as ethnic derivation). As noted earlier, many states invest their national personality with the cultural attributes of the leading ethnic community. States are thus asked – figuratively speaking – to leap out of their own skins, to transcend their own cultural nature. Notwithstanding the intrinsic difficulties of this task, and the improbabilities of complete success, we contend that the larger requirements of statecraft – the imperative necessities of stability and comity within the polity – make partial realization possible. As we shall see, there are many policy experiences of ethnic accommodation which appear inconsistent with the narrowly defined interests of dominant ethnic groups (preference for scheduled castes in India, for example).

The capacities of the state to act autonomously in many policy spheres finds new limits in the phenomenal pace of internationalization of capital and communications. The world state system has yet to devise regulatory mechanisms which keep pace with transnationalization of critical economic processes. And the extraordinary pace of change and diffusion of communication technologies creates novel international intercommunicating communities.

The nation-state finds itself challenged from within as well. The 1980s was a painful decade for states, with a state-shrinking neo-liberalism enjoying unprecedented doctrinal hegemony. In many lands one encounters a diffuse malaise, writes Charles Maier (1994: 51), 'rooted in a civil society (actually in structures that are less developed than civil society) that has become deeply distrustful of the state'.

Thus beset by powerful forces of internationalization, especially economic, from above, and disenchanted civil societies and frequently fragmenting communal tensions from below, the nation-state appears far less ascendant than in the very recent past. Yet, even acknowledging a relative decline in its standing, the state remains the ineluctable locus of policy response in terms of ethnic accommodation. The bounded arena of interaction constituted by the state defines the field of encounter and interaction between communal segments.

At the international system level, some capacity exists for articulation of norms concerning ethnic relations which have some impact and thus value: for example, in the spheres of human rights, indigenous peoples, perhaps democratic governance. But the severe limits of international action in specific crises are well demonstrated by the tragedies of Somalia, Rwanda and Bosnia. There is even less reason to believe that ethnic tensions can be regulated by responses within civil societies. Even if diminished and embattled, the state remains the critical agency for policy response.

These reflections upon the contemporary world context serve as a point of departure for our review of major designs and experiences. We shall consider four major policy spheres: constitutional formulas, particularly federal or decentralized alternatives to the centralized unitary state; cultural policies, especially in the fields of education and language; remedies for marginalized population categories (indigenous peoples, immigrants, peripheral minorities) and resource distribution issues (including 'affirmative action' questions). By way of conclusion, we shall return to broader issues of state legitimacy and national identity.

CONSTITUTIONAL FORMULAS

Constitutional engineering undoubtedly offers major opportunities for creating structural frameworks facilitative of ethnic accommodation. Yet precisely because it proposes durable structures embedded in fundamental public, law-defining relations among communal groups, it is contentious and difficult. The centralized, unitary state, by concentrating power and authority at the centre, is susceptible to capture by dominant communal segments. In chapter 2 Yash Ghai reviews the major formulas for averting such outcomes, which include territorial dispersion of power through federalism or decentralization, corporate distribution of power, in some consociational arrangement, or various forms of legal pluralism. Overall, constitutional accommodation of ethnic diversity should foster sharing of power amongst major communal segments, provide incentives for intergroup cooperation and assure voice through reasonable representation.

Federalism in its historical origins was not designed with ethnicity in mind; rather, it was a formula for the unification of territorial units of separate antecedents. In their pure form, federal systems have power and function divided between a national and federated units, with each deriving its authority directly from the electorate; there is a coordinate rather than strictly hierarchical relationship between centre and region. The most visible and influential models came into being by aggregation of related but administratively distinct colonial entities (Canada, Australia, United States), or as an adaptation of loosely united zones of colonial administration too large or ethnically complex for self-rule as a unitary state (Nigeria, India, Malaysia, Papua New Guinea). In a smaller number of instances (Belgium, Spain), once unitary states sought to overcome intense pressures for ethnic autonomy by abandoning centralist constitutions. The unusual Swiss case both reflected the slow emergence of this multinational polity by cantonal agglutination, and the utter failure of a Napoleanic experiment in imposing a jacobin state. Another strain of federalist thought emerged with the appropriation of the concept by Lenin and his heirs as a device for 'solving the national question'. In the Soviet case, and subsequently the Yugoslav and Czech instances modelled upon it, territorial subdivisions based upon 'titular nationalities' were created, while the steel grid imposed by the political monopoly of the centralized Communist Party, command central planning and the pervasive security agencies emptied federalism of most of its content until state socialism itself began to lose its legitimacy. A federation thus conceived could not survive the dissolution of its autocratic institutions, as Ghai shows.

Meaningful federalism presupposes a democratic framework. Autocracy inevitably centralizes power and necessarily denatures regional autonomy. Nigeria, 28 of whose 37 federated years have been under military rule, illustrates the inevitable centralized drift of autocracy. Despite the rhetorical invocation of 'federal character' (and the constant promise of an imminent return to civilian, constitutional rule), army custody of the state is in practice centralized, reinforced by the extraordinary concentration of fiscal resources in the oil sector, tapped exclusively at the centre.

Perhaps the most fundamental argument for the federal system is that, for large and culturally complex countries, no other formula could work. For states of continental scale, such as Canada, Australia and the United States, or societies of extraordinary diversity, such as India and Nigeria, only some form of federal arrangements is compatible with democratic rule. The Russian Federation can survive as a single entity only through federal governance accepting far more real autonomy for the non-Russian zones than its Soviet precedessor. Sudan, since its independence in 1956, has known only a single decade of civil peace, from 1972 to 1983, when a semi-federated system was in place, giving some cultural security to the three southern provinces which do not share the arabophone and Islamic culture of the north (much less the integralist version dominant since 1989). The abolition of southern autonomy in 1983 led at once to a resumption of an unending civil war.

By dispersing power territorially, federal regimes create and empower multiple arenas for representation and participation. Even where communal groups are not territorially segmented, as in Malaysia or the United States, the possibility of voice is increased by the many places it can find expression. Federalism tends to carry with it an ethos of decentralization which applies to echelons of governance beyond the federated units; thus numerical preponderance of racial minorities in the United States can find reflection in the urban institutions, whereas their numbers would not suffice for leadership at higher levels. The diffusion of ethnic interaction in the political sphere over many arenas averts the kind of polarization possible if there is a single, zero-sum struggle for power at the centre.

There are some significant disadvantages to federal systems. Conflicts of jurisdiction are frequent, and require a strong and independent judiciary to resolve. A supportive political culture and leadership skill in bargaining the distributive issues between centre and region are necessary requisites. The regions need a secure fiscal base; if their revenues come simply by federal attribution, their capacity for effective autonomy is inevitably circumscribed.

An abiding fear in many lands where federalism is at times proposed is that such constitutional decentralizing is but a step to secession. The break-ups of the Marxist-Leninist nationality federations give new life to such arguments. Ghai argues persuasively that a refusal of regional autonomy is more likely to catalyse secessionist sentiments than decentralization.

Many forms of decentralization short of full federalism are possible. States have a strong predilection for constitutional symmetry, but perhaps more instances will emerge where an array of differentiated statuses can be available. Ghai lists a number of such arrangements; doubtless they will multiply.

A somewhat different approach to the institutionalized dispersion of state power is proposed by Lijphart (1977), in the theory of consociationalism which he has developed with skill and tenacity. The essence of the scheme is to govern an ethnically divided society through a grand coalition, based upon proportionality, a mutual veto and high autonomy of the communal segments. Its vertebral concept is accommodating cultural pluralism by power-sharing governance. The model is most applicable, Lijphart suggests, for relatively small polities dominated by communal cleavage with a limited number of cultural segments (3–5). The consociational model does not require a federal system; its most critical *locus operandi* is at the centre, where summit diplomacy among segment delegates takes place.

The formula is fully applicable only in a very small number of cases, where political society is entirely defined by self-conscious, long-standing cultural units with relatively homogeneous internal structures. In erecting cultural difference into the central organizing principle of political life, it produces a complete ethnic corporatizing of society. This in turn carries substantial risks that communal segments consociationally empowered will deny cultural agency to their members (Gutmann, 1994: 8). In the many areas where ethnicity is particularly fluid and in flux, the consociation would require arresting the construction dynamic and fixing the units of identity.

If one extracts the critical ethos of power-sharing from the totality of the model, a much more widely applicable orientation towards the management of ethnic conflict comes into view. This brings us to the issue of balanced representation in the national institutions. Here the nature of the electoral system is crucial, and the sizeable menu of choice available needs exploring. Where cultural pluralism is salient, identity politics are very likely to influence electoral choice. The device through which citizen votes translate into representation can facilitate or inhibit power-sharing. Here, the Horowitz (1991) injunction comes into play: preference should be given to electoral systems that provide incentives to contenders to adopt accommodative practices rather than to outbid one another in ethnic extremism, and to those that encourage such accommodation at the stage of political competition, rather than through summit bargaining after representation has been communally defined.

Because electoral system choice does have significant consequences in structuring representation of a diverse society, and also because adjustments in electoral systems are easier to accomplish increment-ally than more fundamental reconfigurations of constitutional state structures, experimentation in this domain is a tempting policy path-way, and is explored in detail by de Silva in chapter 3. Electoral systems are 'the most easily manipulable feature of a political system', write two leading specialists (Taagepera and Shugart, 1989: 2–4).

With the far greater contemporary awareness of the political force of communal identities, the recent debates over electoral system choice give tangibly more weight to calculations about impacts upon diversity and its accommodation than in the past. For countries experiencing a fundamental regime change, such as those of the for-mer Soviet bloc or much of Africa, one of the historically infrequent moments of the covenant was at hand. For a number of long-estab-lished constitutional democracies, important adjustments are in course (more race-conscious districting – now contested – in the United States based on the 1982 Civil Rights Act amendments, pro-portional representation (PR) in Sri Lanka and New Zealand, for example).

The 'Westminster model' plurality system has undoubtedly lost standing in recent years. There are certainly many cultural circum-stances where its impact is perverse; Northern Ireland is an obvious case. If communal voting patterns are preponderant, cultural minor-ities are likely to be disproportionately under-represented.

However, de Silva shows that the evidence is by no means conclus-ive that plurality electoral systems are invariably damaging in cultural plural polities. Much depends on the circumstances, the content of the political culture and the embedded political tradition. There are also some adjustments possible within the system to mitigate negative impacts for given communal segments.

Corrective measures are available to limit the risk of electoral marginalization of some communities. In India, although communal seats were abandoned at Independence, reserved seats were provided for scheduled castes and tribes. In the United States, the 1990 redistricting of congressional and state legislative seats took place under legal mandate to assure reasonable representation of racial minorities (African-American and Hispanic, in practice). The Congressional Black Caucus increased from 25 to 40 as a consequence, and became itself more internally diverse. Application of a 65 per cent black population fraction to generate racially 'safe' seats, and some of the exceptionally bizarre district shapes utilized in congressional districting, have generated sharp controversy and a wave of court challenges. The Supreme Court has invalidated some racially constituted districts, but some degree of race-consciousness in districting is likely to persist.

The major alternative to plurality systems is proportional representation. This can utilize either a national constituency or a number of multi-member districts. Particularly in a number of European countries, PR systems have acquired the familiarity of long usage, and in plural societies such as Switzerland are cited among the factors facilitating harmony. In the remarkably successful 1994 democratic transition elections in South Africa, a PR system created an effective balance of forces which, at least in the short run, has facilitated the extraordinary transition from *herrenvolk* rule to non-racial democracy.

PR has the obvious merit of mirroring in the elected institutions the political demographics, including ethnicity if this shapes voting behaviour and party nomination strategy. However, it also fragments representation, and can give destabilizing leverage to very small electoral formations (as with the tiny religious parties in Israel). It also greatly enhances the weight of the party apparatus in the candidate selection process, thus weakening any link of accountability of the individual representative to a constituency. The system has persuasive advocates, such as Lijphart, but it is difficult to gainsay the conclusion of de Silva that, outside continental Europe, the prospect that PR would provide greater cultural accommodation and political stability in ethnically divided societies remains a matter of conjecture and debate.

There are a number of less widely known variants on these two major systems. In a limited vote system, used in Spain for Senate seats, the voter has fewer votes than the number of seats in a multi-member constituency. A variant of the system, used in Taiwan and formerly in Japan, is the single non-transferable vote, where each voter has a single vote in a multi-member constituency (in practice advantaging the dominant parties). Cumulative voting in multi-member districts gives the voter as many votes as seats, but permits them to be cast as multiple votes for one or more candidates. In theory, self-identified ethnic or racial minorities could assure themselves representation by block voting in such a system. In the United States, it was used in Illinois from 1870 to 1960, but abandoned because, in practice, the two major parties often nominated together only the number of candidates equalling the district size, with the result that many seats were uncontested (Weaver, 1984).

Preferential voting systems offer interesting possibilities, though they have been little used. There are two variants: the alternative vote in single-member districts, or the single transferable vote in multi-member districts. In each case, the voter rank orders candidates. In tallying the votes, if the requisite majority is not attained, the bottom candidate is dropped with these votes redistributed according to the voter's preference ranking. In his brief for this system, Horowitz (1991: 189) argues that the alternative vote system induces parties to 'bid across ethnic lines for the second preferences of voters whose first choice stands no real chance of election'. The alternative vote system has been used in Sri Lanka in presidential elections since 1978, and in a scattering of other places (Ireland, for example, though cultural pluralism is not at issue).

At bottom, what is probably most important in the choice of electoral system, in accommodating ethnic diversity, is the nature of the political competition process it induces rather than the precise ethnic proportions that result from the election itself. The cautionary conclusions of de Silva bear reflection. A systematic tracking of the outcome and consequences of the wide variety of formulas for election representative institutions is necessary before firmer judgements can be made.

CULTURAL POLICIES

In the field of cultural policy, there are both important opportunities and great hazards. Here one most directly confronts the elective affinity between states and the premise of homogeneity as the essence of achieved nationhood. In one way or another, historical practice in such spheres as education and language tend to reflect this inarticulate major premise. If the present world historical conditions invite most states to acknowledge their multicultural nature as a long-term condition rather than merely a transitional stage, then difficult adjustments and painful reappraisals may be needed in a number of domains.

And yet a delicate balance needs to be struck. In some of its more extreme discourse, multiculturalism decants into an assertion of difference as supreme social value. Acknowledgement of diversity is in many settings indispensable. Yet equally vital is recognition of the shared civic values which make of the citizenry a corporate personality with a common interest in the well-being of the polity as a whole. If a political society, to borrow Marx's oft-cited metaphor of the peasantry, is nothing more than a sack of ethnic potatoes, there can be no incentive for the stronger communities to share resources with the weaker. Such concessions are unlikely to be extractable simply by force, nor can bargaining succeed without a sense of shared community.

The field of education is particularly sensitive, as Gundara and Jones argue in chapter 4, both because of the cultural policy choices it poses, and the intimate link between educational opportunity and life-chances. States throughout the modern world assert the right at least to monitor, if not to define, the curricular content, to supervise the operation of the educational system and to set the conditions for the credentialling role of schools. They thereby assume responsibility for the cultural role of the school system.

Delicate issues thus arise as to the portrayal of the diverse segments of the population: their inclusion, to begin with, but also the narrative of their past and future, and their relation to the whole.

There is undoubtedly a large – perhaps vast – potential for a redirected pedagogy to nurture an understanding of diversity in future generations. If didactic creativity and energies comparable to those historically deployed to instil patriotism to the 'nation' were committed to inculcating the values of toleration and empathy towards 'the other' and an understanding of the positive aspects of diversity, the citizenry of the future would be better equipped to respond to the challenges of cultural pluralism.

Language is another critical domain, closely tied to education. As a singularly salient boundary marker, language supplies immediate recognition of difference. Intense emotions can be catalysed by language, when it becomes a core element to ideologies of identity.

Reason of state beckons a choice of a single medium for the conduct of public business; thus language becomes tied to hierarchies of power and privilege. If access and exclusion are measured by mastery of the language of state, then the stage is set for conflict.

In many countries, the primacy of a given language for official purposes is not disputed, but rights are sought for other languages in given spheres. The national minorities in Europe insist on the right to employ their languages in their own regions, and to preserve them through the educational system and other media; Catalonia has been the most successful region in rehabilitating a language the Franco regime tried to repress and restoring it to a dominant role in its region.

For countries with significant immigrant populations, language rights are posed in different fashion. Acquisition of the dominant language of the host country is usually not resisted; the powerful incentives of the marketplace normally suffice to ensure that this occurs. Rights of language preservation within the community are in question, as are the ways in which the educational system meets the special instructional needs of their children. The appropriate implementation of bilingual education programmes and the balance between facilitating transition to the dominant language and nurturing retention and skill in own language remain a matter of debate.

In the multi-ethnic states of Asia and Africa, complex issues of language policy arise. In Asia, politically dominant groups preferred to displace the European colonial languages with indigenous ones. Indonesia was able to transform trade Malay into Bahasa Indonesia and eliminate Dutch without controversy. In former Indochina, Myanmar and even Malaysia, the language of the dominant core ethnic group was an evident choice. But in India and Sri Lanka, Hindi and Sinhala were bitterly controversial. In India, English was finally retained as a link language along with Hindi, with the states promoting the regional languages. Abandonment of the effort to impose a single Indian language as sole official medium has greatly reduced the tensions surrounding this issue.

In sub-Saharan Africa, a pattern seems to be emerging in many countries of gradually extending multilingualism: what Laitin (1992) terms a '3+/-1' pattern. The language of the colonial legacy remains the language of state. One or more lingua francas hold sway as everyday languages of urban, inter-regional and inter-group communication, with or without formal state recognition and promotion. Mother tongues, especially of larger groups, hold their own within the ethnic community for informal communication. The political costs of elevating an African lingua franca into exclusive standing as state language is perceived as too high in many countries; thus it remains an official link language. Citizens seeking upward mobility will therefore need mastery of three languages (their own vernacular, the lingua franca and the official European language). If the lingua franca is the mother tongue, two will suffice; if they move to another lingua franca zone, they may need a fourth (thus 3+/-1). Society collectively internalizes a sense of natural functional demarcations of language roles, and thus a multilingual repertoire appears a normal human attribute, rather than an unstable pathology requiring state intervention to impose a language rationalization (unification) policy. Although some language specialists claim that 'unilingualism is the norm in industrial, urban, literate civilizations' (Laponce, 1987: 25), and that only unusual persons can sustain sophisticated, full command of more than one speech code, the African pattern shows every sign of achieving long-term stability.

Language unification and rationalization strategies in some instances have been remarkably effective. At the time of Italian unification in 1860, only 3 per cent of the population spoke the north Italian version elevated to official status, and no more than 10 per cent understood it; universal command of standard Italian is today taken for granted. In Tanzania, a vigorously implemented language rationalization policy based upon Swahili has had undoubted integrative effects, although some argue at the cost of decline of local vernaculars, some of which may be en route to disappearance. Elsewhere, with levels of ethnic consciousness and mobilization much higher than they were a century ago, policies of linguistic homogenization which could be effective in the past are more likely to foment strong opposition today. Without entering the debate as to whether the preservation of the world's existing stock of languages should be a conscious policy, one may conclude that there are more opportunities than once recognized for states to adjust to a multilingual reality rather than seek by coercive means to end it.

MARGINALIZED CATEGORIES AND PUBLIC POLICIES

An important category of policy challenges comes from the presence in many lands of national minorities, indigenous peoples, peripheral tribal communities or culturally distinctive immigrant populations.

The national minority issue arises in those polities where the state personality – the discourse of nationhood – is tied to a dominant ethnonational group. In such a setting, the minority may appear suspect in its commitment to the state 'nationality'. The recent upsurge in 'ethnic cleansing' practices is a dramatic reminder of the potentially precarious situation of such communities. This issue is particularly acute in Europe from the Volga basin to the Atlantic. The twentieth-century redrawings of the political map in this zone have been rooted in the postulate of 'titular nationalities', to borrow from the Soviet lexicon. Belgium and Switzerland are increasingly the odd exception to 'normal' state-as-nation definitions.

Basic principles for accommodation are simple to state: guarantees of cultural autonomy and security, regional self-rule, adequate representation in the central institutions, assurance of language preservation. Such notions were initially codified as international norms in the League of Nations framework; they are included in the values enshrined by the Council on European Security and Cooperation (CESC) in the 1991 Declaration on the Rights of National Minorities. There are some genuine stories in this respect (the Swedish minority in Finland, or, many feel, Catalans and Basques in Spain). But extremely volatile situations exist in rump Yugoslavia and Macedonia, and only somewhat less explosive national minority questions are found in Romania, Slovakia and the debris of the former Soviet empire. The international normative order, by imperceptible degrees, achieves more influence, but the prospects of effective enforcement machinery for national minority rights are nil. Perhaps more important is the moral pressure of achieving sufficient 'respectability' to earn organic linkages with the slowly enlarging European Union.

Among the more striking developments in the international politics of cultural pluralism is the emergence in recent years of a vocal and increasingly effective international 'indigenous peoples' movement, examined by Stavenhagen in chapter 5. Such groups are found throughout the Americas, along the Arctic rim of Europe and Asia, in Australasia and in scattered 'hill tribe' communities of South and South East Asia. Their shared condition is a history of being conquered and overrun by incoming populations of sharply different cultural orientation. They were driven to the geographic and economic margins of the dominant society, in regions isolated by mountainous terrain or aridity, little coveted by the incoming populations

Particularly in the last two decades, there has been a remarkable rise of self-assertion of many indigenous communities. In striking ways, they have become an inter-communicating international group, drawn together by the 'information highway' of electronic mail and fax communication. Although in the great majority of cases they constitute only very small minorities in the states under whose jurisdiction they find themselves, the broadly similar circumstances they encounter, and a new awareness of shared cultural orientation (shamanism, for example), are providing the basis for common action at the international level. The discourse of sovereignty and self-determination permeates the claims put forward, although as Stavenhagen argues few really expect that full independent nation-state status is achievable (though doubtless many might desire it were it possible). Common themes include demands for full recognition as autonomous communities, an end to assimilative pressures, rights to cultural autonomy, security of community title to their remaining lands, as well as the entitlements of citizenship within the state jurisdictions in which they find themselves. These claims are in part promoted at the international level, through the efforts to codify rights of indigenous peoples Stavenhagen examines.

Important changes have occurred in recent years. Native Americans in the last two decades have generally been successful in litigating treaty rights. In Canada, a large Inuit zone of the Northwest Territories was recently recognized as an autonomous, self-governing unit. In Australia, in recent judicial decisions and federal action, there has been acknowledgement of Aboriginal rights over land which would have been unimaginable a decade or two ago. None of these changes gives complete satisfaction to the indigenous peoples concerned, but they do open space for a continuing policy dialogue which was previously all but nonexistent.

The large and continuing human flows across state boundaries in recent decades have created distinctive immigrant communities in many states. Such migrations encounter the universal distinctions made by states between full membership in civil society as 'citizens', and a much more precarious classification as "immigrants" (or refugees). Migration streams are partly governed by greater opportunity (into Europe, North America, Australasia, or the oil states of West Asia), and partly by grim necessity (ethnic cleansing, drought, famine). In crisis movements, such as the 1994 Rwanda exodus, only neighbouring territories are accessible; African states have generally been hospitable to refugees, though they are normally held in encampments (if swift return is not feasible), with an expectation that their status is temporary. All too often, the displacement is long-term, and refugees can neither return safely, fully integrate into the host community, nor find a third country willing to accept them. Through the United Nations High Commission for Refugees, and a large number of humanitarian relief organizations, the global capacity for crisis intervention wuith respect to refugees is impressive. Much more difficult is the task of finding permanent resolution of the plight of refugee communities. In conditions of involuntary flight, creating the conditions for safe return is undoubtedly nearly always the preferred solution.

Migrants who relocate for reasons of economic opportunity pose different issues. Although such movement occurs throughout the world, diversity accommodation questions have been most visible in Europe, the focus of Collinson's chapter. The substantial labour recruitment in the peak prosperity years of the 1950s and 1960s, and the extra-European origin of a significant fraction of labour immigrants, created novel status issues.

Initially, the expectation was that these 'guest workers' required only temporary hospitality; indeed, for some time policy measures other than those dictated by immediate circumstances were avoided for fear of encouraging the rooting of these populations. The concept of nationhood in Europe was culturally bounded in important respects; though there has been historical incorporation of diverse migrants from other parts of Europe (large numbers in the case of France), the notion of citizenship carried important overtones of the state-defining ethnic community. Legal requirements for citizenship varied, but genealogical dimensions were usually present. In the extreme cases, such as Germany, *jus sanguinis* was rigorously applied, including a 'right of return' to those of German ancestry, and virtual exclusion of residents lacking the genealogical requisite (Brubaker, 1992).

The social and economic benefits of the welfare state have usually been accorded; most have security of residence rights, with deportation occurring only in extreme circumstances. However, effective political voice depends on citizenship; here practices vary, with Germany the most restrictive. As well, in most countries non-European immigrants encounter some degree of animosity, harassment and even violent attack from fringe elements of the dominant society. Cultural practices – particularly for Muslims – may come into conflict with the highly unified jurisprudence of the European state: for example, the 'headscarfs' dispute in France in 1989, involving the right of Muslim girls to contravene school dress codes by wearing head coverings.

These difficulties notwithstanding, European states since the immigrant issue was recognized have made important steps towards defining viable policies. Collinson identifies an emerging official consensus on accepting immigrant permanence, recognition of the valuable contribution they can make, assuming state responsibility for their incorporation into the national society, legislative enforcement of equal opportunity and non-discrimination, and encouragement of an immigrant sense of membership in the national society, in partnership with immigrant leadership. With the door to further legal immigration all but closed, and the non-European immigrant proportion well under 10 per cent, such general policy principles applied consistently over time should have an accommodative effect.

RESOURCE DISTRIBUTION

In societies where communal difference is salient, the prospect that ethnic groups will evaluate their perceived well-being in comparison with others is well-nigh certain. In popular perceptions, such measurements are highly subjective; one may cite innumerable examples where both sides believe they are relative losers. Canada is an obvious example; Anglophones, especially the western provinces, believe Quebec gets far more than its fair share. Those promoting Quebec secession argue the contrary, claiming Quebec could benefit economically by secession.

Although the relationship between economic conditions and communal tensions is incapable of precise definition, few would dispute that it exists (Samarasinghe and Coughlan, 1991). One clear example is Malaysia; the viability of the quasi-consociational Malay-dominant political formula is clearly contingent on an economic expansion which provides the Chinese community offsetting compensation for its relative political marginalization. As a broad proposition, conversely, one may safely assert that sustained economic decline will intensify ethnic conflict. So also will perceptions of gross disparities in ethnic distributions resultant from state policies.

These assertions point towards one of the most intractable challenges to ethnic accommodation policy. Few if any state policies will be absolutely neutral in their distributive effects among ethnic groups. What matters, then, is whether the ethnic distributive effect is widely perceived as a product of deliberate bias towards those groups with favoured access to the state, and whether offsetting or compensating policies are undertaken to redress ethnic imbalance created by a given policy (the location of a major infrastructure project, for example).

Managing the national economy to foster growth is a universal maxim of statecraft. Yet there has often been insufficient recognition of the potential conflict between ethnic harmony and maximization of aggregate growth. Innumerable examples of the tension between the policy claims of economic development and ethnic accommodation may be cited. In Sudan, the renewed civil war was partly triggered by disputes between north and south over two large development projects: the Jonglei Canal and an oil refinery. The former project, begun but not completed to enhance the flow of White Nile water through the *sudd*, was seen as benefiting the north at the expense of pastoral communities in the south; the latter, whose proposed location was in the north, was suspected to serve as a mechanism to syphon the benefits from tapping large petroleum deposits in the south towards Khartoum. Diversion of river flow to huge cotton irrigation projects in the former Soviet Union led to a catastrophic shrinkage of the Aral Sea, and a ruinous impact on the environment of the Karalkapak near its former shores.

The conflict between national macroeconomic goals and ethnic claims also arises when local communities conclude that they absorb all the environmental costs and receive few of the benefits. The Nigerian oil industry is a case in point. The Nigeria delta minorities, Ogoni and others, find that oil development has polluted the tidal estuaries along which their villages are located, but oil revenues accrue entirely to the federal government and are redistributed on a national basis. The anger of these groups is now intense, increased by the execution in 1995 of the Ogoni leader Ken Saro-Wiwa and eight of his colleagues, and their deepening disaffection from the Nigerian federation has become one of the flashpoints of the current impasse of transition to civilian rule.

The strong trend since the 1980s towards economic liberalization and market-based reforms has intensified the dilemmas between optimizing growth and ethnic accommodation. While in the present conjuncture market-friendly development policies are unlikely to be dethroned, a clear recognition of a need to balance liberal economic principles with an acknowledgement of the political costs of deepening ethnic inequality is critical. No one can dispute the importance of overall economic growth as one key policy objective; but there is some truth in the adage that a rising tide lifts all boats. However, metaphorical reasoning has its limits; some ethnic vessels may be stranded as the tide swells, and others may rise at a rate arousing envious resentments.

The range of policies in the economic field is vast, and comprehensive treatment beyond the scope of this volume. Particular attention is warranted for one policy sphere where important experimentation with an explicit ethnic accommodation focus has occurred: ethnic preference measures examined by Jenkins in chapter 7 designed to remedy disadvantage attributable to past state policy or societal prejudice. Many states have historically pursued discriminatory policies in favour of relatively well-situated categories: veterans in the United States, whites in South Africa, men nearly everywhere. At issue here are only very recent policies designed to remedy historically established patterns of ethnic inequality.

Affirmative action policies are designed to compensate for past inequality by guaranteeing opportunities in the fields of education, employment and state contracts to individuals from groups identified as objects of historical inequality. Because they to some degree violate the principle of equality of all citizens of the liberal state, such policies invariably run into several difficulties: defining the beneficiary group and its boundaries; establishing the extent of the preference accorded; justifying the advantage in historical terms; and stipulating a means for determining when the remedy will have succeeded. In the framework of a democratic society, ethnic preference policies must be justified to the dominant society; thus they are always vulnerable and usually contentious.

Jenkins, like other studies (Horowitz, 1985: 653–80), shows that such policies have a mixed record. In Sri Lanka, the policy was designed to favour the Sinhalese ethnic majority. In its own terms it succeeded, but at the price of deepening the disaffection of the Tamil community and igniting an ethnic civil war whose end is not yet in sight. In the case of Pakistan as well, an overall negative verdict seems dictated by the evidence. Ethnic preference, originally to help Bengalis in former East Pakistan, resulted in an increasingly comprehensive quota system for public employment and educational access which particularly disadvantaged the newly 'imagined' Muhajir community (Urdu-speakers from Gujerat and north central India who migrated to Pakistan after the partition of India). An intense sense of deprivation and discrimination has fuelled potent ethnic mobilization, which in turn provokes counter-mobilization by others in the social field. The fatal flaw of the Pakistan system was that it expanded to cover most categories, and ceased to be directed towards clearly targeted disadvantaged minorities.

In the other cases, the balance of evidence is significantly more positive. In Malaysia, the comprehensive Malay preference policy in education, state employment and economic ownership (the 1971 New Economic Plan) adopted after the 1969 communal violence has clearly created a large, more culturally secure Malay middle class. These advantages come at a cost; the alienation of the younger generation of Chinese is palpable, incompletely assuaged by the private sector domains in which Chinese enterprise predominates.

In India, the deeply entrenched social hierarchies created by the caste system create strong arguments for compensatory policies (Galanter, 1984). From the time of Independence, some preferential measures in the fields of education and public employment have been in place for scheduled castes ('untouchables') and tribes (hill peoples); these constitute about 20 per cent of the population. Reservation of educational places and employment for these categories alone do not encounter strong opposition. Much more controversial is the inclusion of 'Other Backward Classes' on the roster. While many in this broad category number among the most hopelessly impoverished rural populations of India, none the less the boundaries of the category are difficult to define, and potentially very large. In some states far more than half the population becomes a beneficiary class, including a significant section of the politically dominant middle classes. Drawing the boundaries of entitlement this broadly generates intense anger and violent opposition among youth of higher castes. Broad definition of 'Other Backward Classes,' argues Galanter, undermines the legitimacy of all preferences to non-beneficiaries by painting 'a picture of unrestrained preference for those who are not distinctly worse off than non-beneficiaries' (1984: 140).

Indian compensatory discrimination policies have helped create a larger middle class drawn from the most underprivileged communities than would otherwise have emerged. Some remedial policy to offset the rigid barriers to equality the caste system creates for the most degraded and stigmatized communities would seem ineluctable. But experience suggests the necessity of limiting application to the most seriously disadvantaged communal categories.

'Affirmative action' in the United States has a complex legal history; its actual meaning slowly evolves through the interplay of occasional legislation, more frequent administrative regulations and constant litigation. Its dilemmas well illustrate the contradictions faced by ethnic preference policies in a liberal state where basic rights are held to be individual. The 1964 Civil Rights Act and subsequent interpretive administrative regulations introduced the premise that historic patterns of discrimination against racial minorities (and women) could only be overcome by setting numerical goals 'to increase materially the utilization of minorities and women, at all levels'. 'Results-oriented' procedures to achieve this end were proposed, but the regulations also (pursuant to the legislative mandate) stipulated that 'goals may not be rigid', nor could they result in 'inflexible quotas'; rather they should be 'targets reasonably obtainable to means of applying every good-faith effort' (Fuchs, 1990: 425–55). However contested its ethos and precise meaning, affirmative action became widespread from the 1970s on, initially targeted on African-Americans, but subsequently expanding to include Hispanics, Native Americans and, to some extent, Asian-Americans, as well as women. The effort has clearly had some beneficial effects for targeted groups, though how much is a matter for heated debate.

The case for remedial action in spheres such as education, employment and public contracting to compensate for pronounced historical inequality, whether a product of state action, societal barriers, or both, is strong. The track record of such policies is uneven, and there are clear limits to their useful scope. Ethnic preference has been subject to a barrage of criticism: difficulty of defining beneficiary groups so that only the genuinely disadvantaged benefit; a tendency to foster rigid group categories with an entrenched interest in defending their allocations; a propensity to advantage the more privileged segment of beneficiary groups; alienation of those who believe their life-chances to be curtailed by affirmative action; difficulty of defining the criteria for determining when such measures, invariably argued as transitional and temporary, are no longer required. These real difficulties suggest caution in embarking on this course. Yet the tensions and discontents fostered by historically structured racial or ethnic inequality, which can only very slowly be dissolved by the operation of the marketplace and purely individual notions of 'merit', may necessitate some carefully crafted initiatives in this domain.

CONCLUSIONS

By way of conclusion, we return to some of the more general issues raised in our opening passages. If any definitive instruction for statecraft is found in the harsh experience of recent decades, the lesson clearly is that 'nation-building' as a vocation of homogenization cannot succeed. Nor, over time, can simple ethnic domination serve as a stable formula for rule.

Thus the content of the discourse of nationhood, which doubtless will continue to be perceived by states as critical to meeting the imperative of legitimation, merits careful reflection. 'Nation' defined as civil community, rooted in values which can be shared by all ethnic components of the national society, offers the most durable framework for accommodating diversity. Accommodation does require the framework, which in turn needs affective attachments by the citizenry at large. Such an ethos of community is best achieved when 'nation' is shorn of any connotations of ethnic exclusivity.

In this often contentious and emotion-laden policy domain, patience and perseverence can be supreme virtues. Frequently, formulas for accommodation will only become acceptable to contending parties after long periods of impasse. Containing violent conflict within tolerable bounds during such a process is an under-recognized achievement of ethnic statecraft. Although the 'time of troubles' began in 1969 in Northern Ireland, with the recurrent if sporadic lethal confrontation, the intensity of the conflict has been contained at a relatively low level of violence; Belfast remains a safer city than New York or Johannesburg. Although Canada has lived under the shadow of Quebec secession threats for two decades, it has coped with an endemic constitutional crisis in resolutely civic fashion. Though no permanent settlement is yet in view in either case, living with crisis in civil fashion is surely a triumph of ethnic accommodation.

The search for effective policies to achieve cultural harmony will continue on a global scale. The world will benefit from a collective learning process, which entails careful observation of the innumerable experimental fields constituted by the 185 odd sovereign units in our global community. The unlimited brutalities which can ensue when the bonds of comity dissolve are a powerful reminder of the importance of an ongoing search for community transcending ethnic difference.

NOTES

1. Most notably in the important 1960 United Nations General Assembly Declaration on the Granting of Independence to Colonial Countries and Peoples, which, after restating the right of all 'peoples' to self-determination, affirmed in its sixth article that, 'Any attempt aimed at

the partial or whole disruption of the national unity and territorial integrity of a country is incompatible with the purposes and principles of the Charter of the United Nations.'

2.   See, for example, the important debate around the seminal Charles Taylor lecture on 'The Politics of Recognition', in Amy Guttman (ed.), *Multiculturalism: Examining the Politics of Recognition* (Princeton: Princeton University Press, 1994).

3.   See, for example, the magisterial though controversial study by Liah Greenfeld, *Nationalism: Five Roads to Modernity* (Cambridge, MA: Harvard University Press, 1992) and the valuable collection in 'Reconstructing Nations & States', *Daedalus*, 122, 3 (Summer 1993).

4.   The debate over identity formation and social construction of ethnicity reflects the important influence of diverse strands of poststructuralist and postmodern theory, with its stress upon the subject, contingency, ambiguity, self-reflexivity and subalternity. Although these approaches have difficulty grappling with essentialized elements of identity, and are refractory to policy reflection, they have enlarged our understandings of the constructivist dimension of identity. See *inter alia* Craig Calhoun (ed.), *Social Theory and the Politics of Identity* (Oxford: Blackwell, 1994); Zygmunt Bauman, *Life in Fragments: Essays in Postmodern Morality* (Oxford: Blackwell, 1995); Anthony Giddens, *Modernity and Self-Identity: Self and Society in the Late Modern Age* (Stanford, CA: Stanford University Press, 1991); Ulf Hannerz, *Cultural Complexity: Studies in the Social Organization of Meaning* (New York: Columbia University Press, 1992); Partha Chaterjee, *The Nation and Its Fragments: Colonial and Postcolonial Histories* (Princeton: Princeton University Press, 1993).

5.   This is particularly the case in Africa: thus the compelling arguments by Vail and his collaborators in Leroy Vail (ed.), *The Creation of Tribalism in Southern Africa* (Berkeley: University of California Press, 1989).

6.   'Race' is a contested concept, and its meanings vary widely in the various societies where it is encountered. I find particularly helpful, for comparative purposes, the treatment by Michael Banton, *Racial Theories* (Cambridge: Cambridge University Press, 1987).

REFERENCES

Anderson, Benedict, 1983. *Imagined Communities: Reflections on the Origins and Spread of Nationalism*. London: Verso.

Banton, Michael, 1987. *Racial Theories*. Cambridge: Cambridge University Press.

Bauman, Zygmunt, 1995. *Life in Fragments: Essays on Postmodern Morality*. Oxford: Blackwell.

Brubaker, Rogers, 1992. *Citizenship and Nationhood in France and Germany*. Cambridge, MA: Harvard University Press.

Calhoun, Craig (ed.), 1994. *Social Theory and the Politics of Identity*. Oxford: Blackwell.

Chaterjee, Partha, 1993. *The Nation and its Fragments: Colonial and Post-Colonial Histories*. Princeton: Princeton University Press.

Fuchs, Lawrence H., 1990. *The American Kaleidoscope: Race, Ethnicity, and the Civic Culture*. Hanover: New England University Press.

Galanter, Marc, 1984. *Competing Equalities: Law and the Backward Classes in India*. Delhi: Oxford University Press.

Giddens, Anthony, 1991. *Modernity and Self-Identity: Self and Society in the Late Modern Age*. Stanford, CA: Stanford University Press.

Greenfeld, Liah, 1992. *Nationalism: Five Roads to Modernity*. Cambridge, MA: Harvard University Press.

Gurr, Ted Robert, 1994. *Minorities at Risk: A Global View of Ethnopolitical Conflicts*. Washington: Institute of Peace Press.

Gutmann, Amy (ed.), 1994. *Multiculturalism: Examining the Politics of Recognition*. Princeton: Princeton University Press.

Hannerz, Ulf, 1982. *Cultural Complexity: Studies in the Social Organization of Meaning*. New York: Columbia University Press.

Horowitz, Donald, 1985. *Ethnic Groups in Conflict*. Berkeley: University of California Press.

—— 1991. *A Democratic South Africa? Constitutional Engineering in a Divided Society*. Berkeley: University of California Press.

Huntington, Samuel P., 1993. 'The Clash of Civilizations', *Foreign Affairs* 72, 3: 22–49.

Kaplan, Robert, 1994. 'The Coming Anarchy', *Atlantic Monthly* (February 1994): 44–76.

Kymlicka, Will, 1995. *Multicultural Citizenship, A Liberal Theory of Minority Rights*. Oxford: Clarendon Press.

Laitin, David D., 1992. *Language Repertoires and State Construction in Africa*. Cambridge: Cambridge University Press.

Laponce, J.A., 1987. *Languages and Their Territories*. Toronto: University of Toronto Press.

Lijphart, Arend, 1977. *Democracy in Plural Societies*. New Haven, CT: Yale University Press.

Maier, Charles S., 1994. 'Democracy and its Discontents', *Foreign Affairs* 73, 4: 48–61.

Moynihan, Daniel Patrick, 1992. *Pandaemonium: Ethnicity in International Politics*. Oxford: Oxford University Press.

1993.'Reconstructing Nations & States', *Daedalus* 122, 3 (Summer).

Samarasinghe, S.W.R. de A. and Reed Coughlan, eds., 1991. *Economic Dimensions of Ethnic Conflict*. New York: St. Martin's Press.

Taagepera, Rein and Matthew Soberg Shugart, 1989. *Seats and Votes: The Effects and Determinants of Electoral Systems*. New Haven, CT: Yale University Press.

Vail, Leroy (ed.), 1989. *The Creation of Tribalism in Southern Africa*. Berkeley: University of California Press.

Weaver, Leon, 1984. 'Semi-proportional and Proportional Representation Systems in the United States', in Arend Lijphart and Bernard Grofman, eds., *Choosing an Electoral System: Issues and Alternatives*. New York: Praeger.

Young, Crawford (ed.), 1993. *The Rising Tide of Cultural Pluralism: The Nation-State at Bay?* Madison: University of Wisconsin Press.

2 Decentralization and the Accommodation of Ethnic Diversity
Yash Ghai

INTRODUCTION

Decentralization typically refers to various forms of territorial devolution or delegation of political and administrative power ('spatial decentralization') (for a recent study see Hannum, 1990). The best known of these is federalism, which gives a high degree of constitutional protection to the constituent units, but less extensive or legally secure arrangements for delegation or transfer of power are more common. Another form of decentralization consists of arrangements for autonomy for one part of the country only (as with Zanzibar in Tanzania, Hong Kong and Macao *vis-à-vis* China after July 1997, Aland Islands in relation to Finland), and in this respect it differs from federalism where in general the devolution of powers is granted to all constituent parts of the state It is, however, possible in a federation to have one part of the country with greater self-government than others (and this arrangement may be conceived of a special case of autonomy, as formally Kashmir in the Indian federation, Quebec in Canada or the Basque country in Spain). Equally a federation, and indeed a unitary state, may contain a territory where the central authorities may enjoy a special and sometimes exclusive jurisdiction (which may be called 'enclaves', as with Indian reservations in the United States and Canada, but which for reasons of space are not discussed here).

Although my primary focus is these territorial arrangements, I use decentralization to refer additionally to other arrangements which recognize the corporate existence of groups or provide for an element of power-sharing among different ethnic groups ('corporate decentralization'), – which themselves can take many forms, ranging from a group's custody of personal laws of its members to the preservation of institutions of internal governance. Sometimes these other arrangements are provided in addition to spatial transfers of power, but

31

sometimes they are established because territorial solutions are not possible (because the different ethnic groups are physically inter-mingled) or are not considered desirable (because a group may be concentrated on a border of an ethnically related state).[1]

In abstract and theoretical terms, it is easy to establish the case for spatial or corporate decentralization for the accommodation of spe-cial ethnic claims. Linked to self-determination, it achieves that with-out the disruption or break-up of a sovereignty. It defuses political conflict by providing alternative sites of power and patronage. It helps to accommodate subnational identities, within a national identity, providing a basis for protection of regional cultures and languages. It can lay the foundations for a more pluralistic and democratic order, the development of regional political parties and a new set of checks and balances. It provides a framework for inter-ethnic bargaining and so converts conflicts into disputes that are susceptible to formal processes. In some ways it gives a political weight to a community that it would not otherwise enjoy and thus it helps to allay fears and anxieties that can alienate it from the national system. Decentraliza-tion is both a way to recognize diversity and to involve all groups in the central state mechanism. Given the variety of forms that spatial and corporate decentralization can take, and combinations there of, it is an extremely flexible instrument, capable of responding to different configurations of ethnic relations. However, spatial and corporate decentralization can be used to disempower a group as well as empower it, as with the previous policy of influx control and bantustans in South Africa, and frequently with indigenous peoples.

Decentralization is often confronted with claims of 'nation-build-ing' or 'territorial integrity' which deny many of its premises. I exam-ine how far decentralization has been used to accommodate ethnic claims and whether these advantages obtain in practice. What are its limitations and drawbacks? Is it a charter for civil disobedience, the setting up of alternative sites of authority, even presaging secession? These questions are not easy to answer as much of the leading literature on spatial decentralization makes only limited (and then mostly superficial) reference to ethnic dimensions, being concerned for the most part with classical federations which, with the exception of Switzerland and the partial exception of Canada, were not con-nected with ethnic factors. I begin my study with an examination of the federal device in three political economies – Liberal, Marxist and Third World.

SPATIAL DEVOLUTION: AN HISTORICAL EXCURSUS

Federalism in Liberal Societies

The older federations were dominated by liberalism and therefore concerned primarily with individual rather than communal rights (for resistance in the United States to the territorial accommodation of ethnicity, see Glazer, 1997).[2] They arose out of considerations of security or administrative or political convenience, and it is these factors which had a primary impact on the structure of the federation and the division of powers and responsibilities (with the partial exceptions of Switzerland and Canada). Switzerland has three principal (German, French and Italian) and one subsidiary (Romansch) languages (of which the dominant is German, being spoken by 65 per cent of the people, followed by French, with nearly 19 per cent). It has also two major religions (Catholics, who constitute just over 47 per cent of the population and Protestants, just over 44 per cent). In addition, the communities that make up the country have strong local traditions and loyalties, fostered by the topography of Switzerland. It is generally acknowledged that it is federalism that has produced a strong and united 'nation' of Switzerland out of such unpromising materials.

For centuries the different alpine communities (as cantons) had lived in a loose form of confederation, with little in the way of a central authority. The absence of a central authority made them vulnerable to predatory neighbours, as in 1798 when the French army invaded. The French imposed a unitary constitution, which was promptly repudiated by the Swiss once the army left. After various short-lived constitutions, the cantons adopted another in 1848 (but not before the Protestants had routed the conservative Catholics in a civil war). The Constitution was a compromise between the smaller cantons, which wanted extensive cantonal autonomy, and the larger ones, which wanted a strong and effective centre. However, it was amended in 1874, matching the increase in powers of the central government with a large dose of direct democracy (in the form of referendums on federal legislative proposals), and introducing a measure of secularism in deeply divided religious communities. The essential principles of the federation have remained constant since then: a three-tiered government, constitutionally protected – federal, cantonal and commune; prescribed legislative and limited executive powers of the centre; proportional representation; the requirement of cantonal and popular support for extension of federal jurisdiction; the use of three official languages; and popular referendums and initiative. To these have been added various conventions designed to give voice to minorities in federal institutions and establish what may be called consociational or consensus government.

Switzerland today has 26 cantons. Although each canton has a majority of one or other linguistic community, there is no direct relationship between territory and religion, or between religion and language. This provides for a measure of flexibility without detracting from the distinctive linguistic orientation of each canton. Nor is exact correspondence of language and territory sought, except in the case of the French-speaking Jura, which separated from the German-speaking Bern to became a new canton.[3] The Swiss manage to preserve local traditions and autonomy not only by means of legislative and executive lists, but also by the entrenched position of communes (the principal focus of identity and loyalty), which carry out key administrative functions and have revenue-raising powers. The centre has to negotiate with the cantons (and persuade the voters) if it wants further constitutional and related legislative powers. Provisions for direct democracy (referendums and legislative and constitutional initiatives) have also affected the relationship between the centre and the cantons (leading to negotiations and compromises on legislative proposals), for these give cantons (and particular interest groups) the power to delay or subvert federal policy.

This style of policy-making and government is reflected in the design and working of federal institutions, and in particular the importance of the legislature. The legislature (the Federal Assembly) consists of two houses, one representing the people, the National Council and the other the Council of State on which each canton has two seats. Each house has equal powers, and in case of disagreement, the matter is not pursued further. The executive, the Federal Council, is elected by the Federal Assembly. It consists of seven members and by a convention, at least two members should come from the French- or Italian-speaking regions, and no more than one from any canton. This reinforces the tendency towards coalition government, and the Council acts as a collegial body, with the annual rotation of its President, thus maximizing the chances of most cantons filling that post. Ethnic proportionality is also maintained in the public and armed forces.

The Swiss system puts a premium on consultation and negotiation and overt forms of power-sharing. While such a system can result in some immobilization, it also strengthens the state, for consent is a stronger cement than coercion. It induces confidence in minorities. It demonstrates that cultural and religious diversity is compatible with single statehood and common patriotism. Unusual as an example of constitutional structures for the accommodation of such diversity in the developed world, it had little influence during the decolonizations of the 1960s, perhaps because it was not itself a colonial power or because its system was regarded as specific to historical factors that limited its portability. However, its appeal is beginning to be recognized with the new search for consensual forms of government.

In Canada the francophone factor had considerable influence on policies of territorial organization from the time that Britain defeated the French. The debates about and the reality of a union or separate governments in lower and upper Canada were coloured by the cultural differences and aspirations of the British and the French communities (so that even in its union form, Canada operated largely as a bicultural political community). When, after various shifts of policy, a decision was made in favour of a federation (1867), the concerns of the French in Quebec dominated the issue of the division of powers. The insertion within the exclusive provincial list of legislative powers of 'Property and Civil Rights in the Province' was to preserve key elements of the French culture, including its civil law system which covers most private, commercial and family law. Canada now has ten provinces and two (federally administered) territories, extending from the Atlantic to the Pacific, and is in many ways a vastly changed place (with considerable European and Asian and Caribbean immigration), but in a fundamental sense its key problem remains the same as at its inception: the modalities of accommodating francophonie in a largely English-speaking country (there are just under 4 million French speakers compared to nearly 17 million English speakers; about 4 million are bilingual, and live mostly in Quebec).

So long as Canada remained a country of Anglophones and Francophones and so long as the centre of gravity was in Ontario–Quebec, the original settlement worked reasonably well. But with increasing multiculturalism and the rising economic power of the western provinces, Quebec became anxious about the future of its special place in the federation and the future of its French culture. In the 1960s it raised demands of greater autonomy and a formal recognition of its distinctive place in Canadian society. At the same time there was a concern to sharpen the national identity of Canada. Thus began a long series of constitutional changes and proposals. The constitutional changes, centred principally around the repatriation of the Constitution from London (and giving Canadians the right to amend it locally) failed to satisfy the Quebec government. In particular, it took exception to the Charter of Rights which ensured to all Canadians equal rights, which was seen as an inroad into provincial autonomy. Two major efforts by the federal and provincial governments were made to accommodate Quebec demands, the Meech Lake Accord 1987 and the Charlottetown Accord 1992. The first focused largely on Quebec's demands, and conceded five major points, including the recognition of its status as a 'distinctive society', veto on constitutional amendments, an independent immigration policy, and the opting out of federal programmes in areas within provincial jurisdiction.

However, the Accord was vetoed by the legislatures of Manitoba, through the intervention of an indigenous legislator and Newfoundland. This not only required the governments to go back to the drawingboard to find a formula less offensive to non-francophones, but also signalled a new interest that the federation had to accommodate – that of the indigenous people. Opposition to the Accord was also based on the manner of its negotiations and conclusion – it was widely seen as a pact between governments, to the exclusion of the people. Consequently the next round had a wider agenda (seeking a resolution of the claims of a range of interests additional to the traditional English–French rivalries) and an extensive consultation mechanism. The Charlottetown Accord was submitted to the people and was rejected, in part because it was seen as inadequate by the francophones and as excessive by the others. This has served to stimulate further Quebec separatism and led to the victory of a party, the Parti Québécois, committed to Quebec's sovereignty. However a referendum in 1995 in Quebec failed by a narrow margin to support secession – and has served to prolonged the angst for all of Canada.

The future form of the federation is in question, and is undoubtedly contingent on developments within Quebec. But the future is no longer a merely Quebec matter. From the time when the Canadian federation was resolved upon by a handful of leaders and given legislative sanction by Parliament in London and to the wide public consultations and the referendum on the Charlottetown Accord, Canadian society has come a long way, and with it have arisen new problems. The Accord (continuing the preoccupation of Canadian politics with legal and jurisdictional matters, in contrast to the more political approach of the Swiss) reflects well these new concerns: new forms of ethnicity and multiculturalism, individual and collective rights, the position of women, social justice and economic rights, a new federal balance based on greater democracy, and above all the status of the First Nations (the Aboriginal people of Canada). Their inherent right to self-government was recognized, defined broadly to protect their culture and develop their resources by themselves. The recognition of the rights of indigenous peoples and their growing assertiveness puts a new gloss on the federal questions, including Quebec's claims to separation, for the larger territory in the province belongs to them.

The recognition of indigenous claims makes up for a glaring lacuna in the older federations of Canada, the United States and Australia, for they did not enter into the calculations of the original constitutional design. Indigenous peoples were not regarded as full citizens and the political and administrative arrangements for their governance did not have to conform to any constitutional rights or principles (in devising 'reserves' for them control and paternalism were the principal considerations, see Asch, 1993; Cassidy and Bish, 1989; Hanks and Keon-Cohen, 1994; Lyons and Mohawk, 1992; Pevar, 1992).

Federations in Communist States

Federations in communist regimes are based on a distinctive philosophy of ethnicity. The principal examples are now defunct: the Union of Soviet Socialist Republics, Yugoslavia and Czechoslovakia. Most other communist states regarded themselves as sufficiently homogeneous to rule out federalism, while China, the remaining multi-ethnic communist state with a clear geographical concentration of minorities, has resolutely set its face against federalism, but provides for regional autonomy for areas where minorities dominate, accepting, although with reservation, Stalin's criteria of a nationality: common language, common territory, common economic life and common culture (Mackerras, 1994: 140–5). Nevertheless a brief account of the theory and practice of communist federations (principally the USSR and Yugoslavia) is instructive for the light it throws on the dynamics of federalism. The other major federation, Czechoslovakia, fits only partially into the general pattern – it was federalized only in 1969 (on the assumption of binationality) after many decades as a unitary state, but even there a defining characteristic was the dominance of the Communist Party (Musil, 1995).

The theory of communist federalism is based upon the Marxist-Leninist principle of national self-determination (Connor, 1984; Roeder, 1990–91: 196–232). The theory was developed during the course of the revolution which overthrew the Czarist regime in Russia, in order to secure the support for the Bolsheviks among the numerous non-Russian peoples in the former empire. It promised them self-determination, including the right to secede if they wished. Those who opted to stay within the new socialist Russia would be granted significant autonomy for their regions to pursue cultural, linguistic and other policies. By according such prominence to ethnic considerations at the expense of the identity of and through economic interests, the theory was in basic conflict with the underlying premises of Marxism. Meant as a temporary concession to what was regarded as a passing force of nationalism, its implementation and practice were fraught with contradictions. Institutional and other policies were employed to attenuate self-determination and federalism, but ultimately they were the undoing of the federation.

Various regions took up the option of secession (contrary to Lenin's expectation, who thought that the very offer of secession would dispel minority anxieties), but they were later coaxed or coerced back. Byelorussia, Ukraine, Armenia, Azerbaijan and Georgia adopted socialist constitutions; the three Transcaucasian republics formed a single federated republic and were united with the others into the USSR in 1922. The Union became even larger with conquests during the Second World War, particularly with the addition of the Baltic states. Eventually the USSR was divided into 15 constituent union republics, and within them, a number of smaller autonomous socialist republics, regions and national districts providing for varying degree of self-rule. The principle for the formation of the republics (and other autonomous units) was the provision of 'homelands' for the major national groups (after which the republic was called, hence 'titular nation'), and generally, but not inevitably, a republic or some other lesser unit for other groups (called 'nationalities') within them.

Yugoslavia was established in 1918 to bring together Southern Slavs – Serbs, Montenegrins, Croatians, Macedonians, Muslims and Slovenes, who had either their own statehood or were freed from foreign rule (Cohen, 1993). Unlike the USSR, the inspiration for the formation of Yugoslavia was a sense of common Slav identity (although it is likely that such identity was confined to a few intellectuals). Yugoslavia became essentially a Serbian kingdom and a unitary state. However, it disintegrated during the Second World War with the German occupation. It was resurrected after the war as a communist federation under Tito, whose partisans beat off the Germans. The wartime resistance was organized largely along the lines of different ethnic groups, and the federation was a reflection of different command structures and the co-operation among them. But it was also a response to Leninist theory on the national question. Thus the borders of the republics were drawn to secure 'homelands' for each of its major ethnic groups – Serbia for Serbs, Slovenia for Slovenes, Croatia for Croats, and Macedonia for Macedonians. The more ethnically mixed heartland, Bosnia-Herzegovina, could not so easily be assigned to one ethnic group.

As with the USSR, the borders did not produce an exact identification of ethnicity with territory. The reason for this is partly the mixed population of the regions, but it is also due, it has been suggested, to the politics of control. In the USSR, for example, significant numbers of Russians were to be found in most union republics, while in Yugoslavia the Serbs were similar dispersed. In the USSR in no union republic did the titular group constitute more than 90 per cent of the population, ranging from 49 per cent to 88 per cent outside the Russian federation. In some instances the members of a titular group (for example, the Armenians) who resided outside its republic exceed those who lived within it.[4] In Yugoslavia, in only Slovenia and Montenegro did the titular groups constitute 90 per cent of the population. In Serbia the Serbs were 74 per cent (while 26 per cent of the total Serb population lived in other republics) and in Croatia the Croats represented 80 per cent of the population, 21 per cent of Croats living outside the republic. In Bosnia-Herzegovina, the population was made of Serbs (44 per cent), Croats (23 per cent) and Muslims (who were treated as a national rather than a religious group, 31 per cent). Within Serbia there were two autonomous provinces, Kosovo, with a majority of Albanians, and Vojvodina, with Magyars as the largest group. It has been suggested that the failure to draw boundaries or to resettle the Serbs affected by expulsions during the war, in Serbia, so that Serbia would be more homogeneous and it would reduce the number of Serbs living in Croatia and Bosnia-Herzegovina, was a deliberate policy to perpetuate a Serbian minority within Croatia as a hedging device against any recrudescence of Croatian secessionist sentiment (Connor, 1984: 331–3). It could also be seen as way of dispersing the Serbs, making them hostages against Serbian attempts to revive their pre-war dominance of Yugoslavia. The carving of Kosovo and Vojvodina out of Serbia had a similar effect.

The notion of a titular nation, the dispersal of significant numbers of its members outside the republic and the mixed population of the republics have been regarded as increasing the prospects of central control over the republics. A titular group was entitled to its linguistic and cultural rights only in the republic, and thus those outside it were subject to pressures to conform to the dominant state practices. The mixed population would increase the dependence of the titular group on the centre. Dependence on the centre was aggravated by the economic system of central planning whereby resources were distributed from the state capital (it is interesting that central control in Yugoslavia weakened considerably when market reforms were introduced in the late 1960s). In the case of the USSR, the large presence of Russians throughout the country also served to enhance central control. At the same time the notion of a titular group would satisfy its desire for a territory of its own. From the perspectives of the centre, it would be easier to implement state policies if the leaders of the local dominant community could be co-opted into the administration.

It was thus necessary to strike a delicate balance between nationalism in the republics and central control. This balance was intended to be achieved by a policy of what was called 'national in form, socialist in content'. Central to this policy was the role of the Communist Party, which in its own organization denied two fundamental assumptions of the federation – ethnicity and decentralization. The party operated on the assumption of democratic centralism, which meant in practice that orders proceed from the centre to lower reaches of state and party. The party was to uphold the 'dictatorship of the proletariat' and thus to be above bourgeois considerations of nation and ethnicity. Since the party controlled the state apparatus as well as party branches throughout the country, it was able to determine policy and implement it without too much regard to republican susceptibilities.

However, in the late 1960s in Yugoslavia the regionalization of the party took place, with considerable weakening of central control. Indeed the tension between regional aspirations and central party control was implicit in both states from the very beginning, and once the legitimizing role of communism (and with it of the party) began to be undermined in the 1970s in Yugoslavia and the 1980s in the USSR, regional (ethnically based) aspirations achieved greater salience (Cohen, 1993; Goble, 1989; Job, 1993; Roeder, 1990-91; Tishkov, 1991). Regional party leaders would either be challenged by members of the dominant ethnic group staking ethnic claims, or these leaders would themselves have to promote these ethnic claims openly. It is thus not surprising that many of the secessionist leaders in both countries were former party activists. The response of the state to allow scope for regional aspirations as a way of keeping the federation intact failed in its aim, and in this failure we learn much about the nature of federalism and communist rule. It is true to say that for much of their existence, the federation did not exist in any practical sense. Although not immune from it, the political process did not reflect republican interests. There was no process of the articulation of republican interests or for their prosecution or compromise. The reality was a highly centralized and undemocratic party. Once that party came under attack and lost legitimacy, there was little to hold the formal state system together. Because the centre had lost all legitimacy, it was unable to co-ordinate and channel the development of increasing regional autonomy in the form of a true federation. Regional leaders mobilized ethnicity, which conferred great legitimacy, particularly in the absence of alternative political ideologies and mechanisms – itself a product of communist rule. The regions could also claim a greater democratic mandate, since many of them held elections or referendums, while obstructing attempts of the centre to hold elections (a tendency which was more pronounced in Yugoslavia).

It would therefore seem that neither in the USSR nor in Yugoslavia was federalism instituted to establish a balanced and decentralized system, or to provide space for ethnic politics and mechanisms for inter-ethnic negotiations. Instead, it was chosen as a device to co-opt ethnic leaders and communities and to minimize tensions arising from their multinational populations. The fundamental incongruity between centralized party rule and the logic of ethnic federalism was held in check so long as the party was able to maintain its control and a measure of legitimacy. While economic failure was undoubtedly a key factor in the collapse of these communist regimes, it was ethnicity, treated in such ambivalent and contradictory ways by the party, which in the end provided a framework for their collapse by offering alternative basis and modes of organization. Here was a true Marxian dialectic, for in the absence of more open-ended politics, the real conflicts were perceived to be those between the centre as represented by the party and ethnic communities which had been provided a 'homeland' by it, for which federation was no longer a solution, but separatism.

Federations in the Third World

Plagued more than other parts of the world by ethnic conflict, the numerous heterogeneous states in the Third World might be expected to have relied on the federal device. However, this has not been the case, despite the special appeal of the concept of federation to the metropolitan powers for purposes of decolonization. Minority groups were apprehensive of independence unless special constitutional arrangements were made for their protection. In the 1960s UN resolutions put a gloss on the principle of self-determination, preventing the fragmentation of the colony into its ethnically constituent parts. The federal idea appealed to metropolitan powers first as a means to bring together colonies that it was considered would be economically unviable separately, as prelude to independence (in French West Africa and the British Caribbean, Southern, Central and Eastern Africa, and Malaysia being outstanding examples). When these collapsed due to resistance from the colonies or specific groups within them,[5] the federal idea attracted them as well as minorities as a device to protect minorities or as a way of coexistence of different ethnic groups, when they were geographically concentrated (as, for example, in Palestine, Ghana, Nigeria, Indonesia, Kenya, Uganda, Sri Lanka, the Sudan and Eritrea), and when groups were not so concentrated, shifts of population were considered.

Federation for this purpose also met with resistance. The majority groups saw in them a threat to the state which they considered was their rightful inheritance. Political and economic ideas of modernization and development popular at the time were also unsupportive of complex spatial arrangements, for they were seen to impede rational planning and national integration. There was some debate as to what arrangements were calculated to promote national unity: the acceptance of diversity and power-sharing or centralization and a new ideology of 'nationalism'. For the most part political leaders opted for the latter route.

The preferences of these leaders were, however, not dispositive of the question. Constitutional orders to be established at independence were the product of negotiations among various parties, in which the initiative often lay with the colonial power, especially as it could delay independence unless a local consensus on forms of governance was reached. While the metropolitan power could dictate, to a degree, the independence settlement, it had no authority and for the most part no inclination to sustain it after the transfer of sovereignty. In numerous instances the spatial arrangements were replaced by the centralization of power. The intolerance of federal or devolution arrangements is driven in large part by the desire to dominate state processes, which provide for many politicians the principal means to economic advancement. Divided powers seem uncongenial to the consolidation of political powers. The centralization of power seldom led to rational planning or implementation, nor did it promote a sense of common identity. On the contrary, it seemed to make both matters worse, and these developments were increasingly ascribed to the centralization of power.

On the whole colonially devised or inspired federations were not distinguished by their longevity (Indonesia, Burma, the federation of East and West Pakistan, Ghana, Kenya, Uganda, Eritrea-Ethiopia). They were introduced at the terminal stages of decolonization, super-imposed on centralized, bureaucratic systems, and it proved easy to claw back, *de jure* or *de facto*, regional powers. These points may be illustrated by the experiences of Uganda and Kenya. The Baganda, relying both on their distinctive ethnicity and historical, legal relation-ship with the colonial authorities, held out for a special relationship with the central authorities in Uganda and a British commission endorsed these demands. The distinctiveness of other kingdoms was also constitutionally recognized, but their status and powers were largely symbolic. This left other parts of the country in a 'unitary' relationship with the centre, thus providing for three gradations of government. This settlement was incorporated in the independence constitution in 1962; indeed it provided the only basis on which all local groups could agree on independence. However, the prime min-ister (Milton Obote) did not approve of the dispersal of power, and when the opportunity arose four years later he destroyed the auto-nomy of Buganda and subsequently of other kingdoms. It proved hard to sustain this centralization of power, in the face of opposition from the former kingdoms, and this provided an opportunity for the army under the control of Idi Amin to take over the government. As is usual with military administrations, power was centralized and exercised in an authoritarian manner. The new constitution (1995) avoids the revival of the federal model, but proposes a significant devolution and facilitates co-operation between districts that would achieve some of the purposes of the older arrangements. In Kenya (Ghai and McAuslan, 1970; Gertzel, 1970), unlike Uganda, the federal units did not have a long colonial history and existence, although to some extent they were based on established local government areas.

The administration in colonial Kenya was also highly centralized. So federalism in Kenya (or *majimbo*, to give its local name) was in both respects an attempt at a major transformation of the system. It was the product of the imagination of European settlers and the British colonial authorities as a means to curb the power of Kenyatta and his political party (KANU), which was seen to represent the interests of the Kikuyu and related tribes. The last two years in the run-up to Independence were largely occupied by working out the details of *majimbo*, which became increasingly more elaborate and complex as the demands of minorities were fuelled by British support. Kenyatta and his party were opposed to it, and accepted it only as the price of independence. Once acceded to power, they went about dismantling it, and within two years of Independence all of *majimbo* was undone (despite the high degree of its constitutional entrenchment). Far from removing ethnic and tribal considerations from politics, the removal of devolution merely accentuated them. As in several other parts of Africa, the one party was wheeled in as a solution to tribalism, but it failed to reflect the diversity of ethnicities and interests, becoming, twice in succession, an instrument of the rule of one particular constellation of ethnic groups.

It is now time to turn to a consideration of some Third World examples of ethnically based federal or devolution arrangements which have been sustained for a period, and to consider how far they were affected by the Third World political economy.

India
Federal arrangements in India were not initially designed for ethnic reasons, but for administrative convenience in disregard of the ethnic factor (though ethnic factor may have become dominant later). In India there were aggregations of territory around the Presidency towns (Bombay, Madras and Calcutta), the centres of British administration and enterprise (Gupta, 1988; Mukharji and Arora, 1992; Shukla, 1994; Srinivasavaradan, 1992). 'Administrative imperatives naturally gave shape to administrative boundaries' (Banerjee, 1992: 43). By the beginning of the twentieth century the provinces were still multilingual and multicultural, and in some instances people speaking one language were broken up into parts of different provinces. This basis of the organization of provinces met early resistance from various groups of Indians. Banerjee (1992) has argued that Indian nation-

alism was the product of the linking of the region to the centre by the emerging elite, who were socialized into a modern and 'Indian' ethos, yet drew their sustenance from local cultures.

> Nationalist politics then began to draw deeper sustenance from various aspects of regional cultures and then in the process threw up a whole range of issues about identity and freedom.... The initial process, then, as it appeared by the turn of the century, was one where a modernised national elite demanded a role in the governance of the colony, and the colonial state was prepared, however, reluctantly and calculatedly, to devolve limited powers at levels below the province.... Simultaneously the democratic urges of the people struck root in the broad linguistic regions and political articulation became interlined with social reform and cultural resurgence. The need to conduct administration in the language of the cultural regions was felt as part of the process of political participation and articulation. Below this double tier of nation and region were groupings of tribal, religions and other minorities at different stages of identity – crystallisation and with complex relationship to the mainstream political process. (43–4)

The consequence was that various linguistic groups demanded that provinces should be reorganized along language groups. The Indian National Congress supported cultural pluralism; and this was indeed a source of its political strength. The principle of territorial organization was also espoused by an important section of the Muslim community – the second largest religious group in India. For the most part this basis of territory cut across the linguistic basis. It was also the more difficult to implement since unlike language groups, religious groups were not concentrated and separated from others. However, federalism along religious divisions had the support of Britain, the imperial power. The Indian nationalist response was to turn to opposition to federalism and to argue for a strong centre. The partition of subcontinental India into two sovereignties established a new context for the federal debate in India and should have led to the earlier consensus on a balanced federation on a linguistic basis. However, by now the Congress party was preoccupied by the problems of administration, the aftermath of the terrible massacres and near-anarchy following the partition, and seduced increasingly by visions of a united and modernizing India. All these suggested the maintenance of existing administrative boundaries and a strong centre (Austin, 1966: ch. 10). This the Indian Constitution of 1950 achieved. The democratization of Indian political life that the Constitution produced reinforced the politics of cultural pluralism, and the resistance of the government to acknowledging the primacy of linguistic identity as a basis of the organization of the state threatened Indian unity. The government eventually gave in to widespread agitation and riots, and in 1956 the map of India was redrawn on the basis of language (and further adjustments to borders since then have reinforced this principle) (J. Gupta, 1975).

The basis of Indian federalism was transformed from administration to ethnicity. But the vision of an India developed and modernized by the state was held on to, and the various constitutional rules that clearly subordinate the provinces (now called states) to the centre were maintained. One of these is article 356, which enables the central government to suspend a state government and take over its administration if it is 'satisfied that a situation has arisen in which the government of the State cannot be carried on in accordance with the provisions of the Constitution' (Dhavan, 1979). This provision has been used 101 times and undermines a basic postulate of the Constitution. It leads to a recentralization of power, along with other developments (Das, 1985). However, these interventions are not driven by ethnic considerations, and the linguistic reorganization has on the whole brought stability to the Indian political system.

Nigeria

The Nigerian federation has a somewhat similar history (Oyovbaire, 1985). In 1939 the territory that comprised Nigeria was divided into three parts, the Northern, Eastern and Western Provinces. Each of them was multinational and multilingual (but in each also there was a dominant ethnic majority), and their existence can be explained in terms of colonial history and administrative convenience. The provinces were unbalanced in size and population, the Northern being alone larger and more populous than the other two combined. At this stage the centre had rather limited powers, so that these disparities did not matter greatly. Various politicians, especially in the southern provinces, demanded a reorganization of the colony which would take greater account of the ethnic distribution of the population, which would have required the establishment of a larger number of provinces (which now began to be called regions). The reorganization was also seen as essential for the protection of groups who were minorities in the existing regions. These considerations became more compelling with the strengthening of the powers of the centre, with the threat of the dominance of one region, while regional powers still remained significant enough to worry regional minorities.

The matter was referred to a commission headed by a British official in 1957, but its terms of reference allowed it to recommend the creation of further regions only if alternative means of protecting minorities were considered inadequate (thus indicating a change in the attitude of Britain towards federations compared to their Indian days). The commission recommended that a justiciable bill of rights would be adequate, noting the difficulties of redrawing boundaries which would not still leave some groups as minorities, and referring to the financial and administrative costs of further political units (Willink Commission, 1958). The independence constitution itself made the creation of new regions a difficult and complex process (in contrast to the Indian constitution which leaves the matter largely to a simple majority of the national legislature, after an opportunity for comment has been given to the legislature of the state/states concerned). As in India, this settlement was unacceptable to a large proportion of the population and the agitation for new regions continued. The imbalance among the three regions gave the Northern Region (predominantly Muslim and Hausa-Fulani) great purchase on federal authority, which by now had been given additional powers. A major reorganization of regions became possible after a military government took charge of the country, following a coup and an attempted secession by the majority group in the Eastern Region which considered that it had been unfairly discriminated against. The first reaction of the army was indeed to try to abolish federalism altogether, seeing a threat to national unity from the demands for the creation of further states. However the abolition of federalism provoked great opposition and led to the fall of the military ruler (Ironsi). His successor (Gowon) was quick to see the potential of the reorganization of states.

Although the government played down the ethnic factor in the reorganization, there is little doubt that it played a key role. A principal concern was that no region (now called state), and therefore no ethnic group, should be able to dominate the centre – seen hitherto as the major threat to stability and legitimacy of the federation. The Hausa-Fulani had used their majority in the Northern Region to dominate the federal government. In practice the ethnic factor was crucial, both in the attempt to provide a state for each major group, and in the need to maintain a balance in the number of states representing the former Northern Region (predominantly Muslim and Hausa-Fulani) and the southern regions (predominantly Christian).

In 1967 12 states were created; the number was increased to 19 following the recommendations of the Commission on the Creation of New States, and is now 36. As in India, the basis of the federation has moved from history and administrative convenience to ethnicity. One effect of the reorganization in both countries, by creating additional states, was to strengthen the centre by reducing the ability of any particular state to challenge it. Another result was to maintain the salience of the ethnic factor at the centre. Nigeria tried to deal with it by a series of provisions in its 1979 constitution (marking the return to civilian rule) to 'federalise' the centre, so that federal institutions would truly reflect the participation of all regions in them (as was evident in the rules for the election of the President and the composition of the cabinet and other public offices, and the registration of political parties). India has not resorted to any formal rules for this purpose, relying largely upon the political process as mediated through political parties.

Malaysia

In Malaysia, in contrast to India and Nigeria, the ethnic factor in federalism has become less rather than more important (at least for its peninsular part) (Safruddin, 1987; Simandjuntak, 1969). But it is ethnic considerations which have throughout influenced the design of political and constitutional system. The Malaya Federation (covering the peninsular) was established after the Second World War in the wake of the retreat of the Japanese administration. Before then there were a number of Malay sultanates (operating under British 'advisers') and a few colonies, administered separately. The first British proposals to amalgamate them in one union met stiff resistance from the Malays, who saw in this the diminution of the status and powers of the Sultans. The Sultans symbolized Malay culture and religion (Islam), and at this time the proposals were interpreted as eroding Malay distinctiveness and their claims as indigenous people. They were also seen as denying the reality of Malay regionalism (based on intense loyalties to the Sultan). The opposition to the proposals became the base for the rise of ethnic Malay nationalism and called into their consciousness their political and economic relationship with other races, Chinese and Indians.

The result was the formation of a Malaya Federation which guaranteed the Sultans their traditional status, dignity, customs and their role as the head of Islam in their states. Penang, which had a Chinese majority and which was a colony, resisted the federation but this was ignored (especially in view of the threat of communist insurgency). However Singapore, which had developed in close conjunction with Malaya and served as its entrepôt, was not admitted to the federation despite the wishes of its people, as this would upset the racial balance within the peninsula. The federation had 49.8 per cent Malay and 37.2 per cent Chinese; with the inclusion of Singapore, the per centages would been 43 Malay and 44.3 Chinese. Further developments show again the force of ethnic factors. Apart from Singapore, Britain had three possessions in Borneo (Sarawak, Sabah and Brunei), which were less well developed than Malaya or Singapore and contained a number of non-Malay 'indigenous peoples'. From the British point of view, a satisfactory way for their decolonization would be their admission to the federation (faced as they were by a rather aggressive Indonesia and proprietary claims by the Philippines). Pressures were building again from Singapore for its admission, as the communist insurgency was seen to intensify and left-wing political forces gaining ascendancy. The simultaneous entry of Singapore and the Borneo protectorates would help in the racial arithmetic, on the assumption that the indigenous peoples in the latter would identify with the Malays, giving Malays and them 46.6 per cent and the Chinese 42 per cent. There was also the fear among the Malays that the federation of Borneo possessions among themselves (which was another option) would lead them into the power of their resident Chinese communities. So the broader federation was consummated (with Brunei, with its considerable mineral wealth, opting out).

That it was a reluctant marriage on the part of the senior partner was evident from the terms on which Singapore was admitted. The normal centre-state relationship under the constitution was not extended to it. It received a smaller number of federal electorates than its population justified and it had a different legislative list (in an attempt to ensure that its entry did not upset the racial politics of the peninsula and the federation). While special provisions in relation to Singapore were to protect the Malays in the federation, special provisions in relation to the Borneo states were intended for the protection of the indigenous people of these states (and included rules about the English language and their religion, and controls over immigration). However, as far as Singapore was concerned, the marriage was troubled despite the pre-nuptial agreement, and Malays felt threatened by the incursions of the leading Singapore party (People's Action Party) into the peninsula (deemed by them to be contrary to original understandings). With the decline in the communist threat, the rationale for this aspect of the federation disappeared, and the dissolution, initiated by the ruling party in Malaysia, duly followed in 1965.

The federation has had relatively little impact on the ethnic factor, especially after Singapore got the marching orders. Ironically, the factor that had promoted Malay nationalism, the threat to their Sultans and Malay regionalism, was superseded by a racial conscious-ness which made them aware of their common cause. If Singapore had remained in the federation, the ethnic mediations through the political structure would undoubtedly have been important; as I show later, they are of some significance in relation to the Borneo states. On the peninsula itself, competition (and co-operation) is between races, not regions, and since races are dispersed throughout and no race is concentrated in any one region, pan-peninsular politics are more important than state politics. This tendency is reinforced by the structure of the federation which establishes a powerful centre, around the capture of which most political activity is organised. Moreover the party (or rather the coalition) in office at the centre has on the whole also controlled state governments, detracting from the federal nature of the system. The real politics of the country, inter-ethnic competi-tion and bargains, are not reflected in the federal nature of the peninsula. Instead, it is reflected in the structure and operation of political parties (as it might be in a unitary state). In recent years, however, the emergence of differences among the Malays on the issue of Islamic fundamentalism has given some life to the federal arrange-ments; for example, the state of Kelantan provides a more hospitable electoral base for fundamentalism than the federation. Otherwise, unlike in India and Nigeria, federalism was not 'ethnicized'; on the contrary, ethnicity denied the imperative and logic of federalism.

Papua New Guinea
By the time decolonization came to the island colonies of the South Pacific (apart from the more homogeneous Western Samoa and Nauru), theories of modernization were being questioned and it seemed less imperative to provide a strong centralizing and integrative state. Nor were the societies of these colonies receptive to a state of this kind. For most of them, independence was imposed rather than sought. There was little development of a colony-wide 'nationalism', people and their leaders identifying principally with their ethnic com-munity or locality. Most constitutional negotiations were devoted to defining the relationship of the state to these largely autonomous

communities, distanced by space and economy from the centre. Partly as a reaction to the colonial denigration of their culture, and partly as a result of unease with state institutions and procedures, there was considerable celebration of indigenous cultures and a desire to see them preserved. The preservation of cultures depended upon, and was a device for, communal autonomy (Ghai, 1988).

Papua New Guinea experienced these demands for provincial autonomy (Ghai and Regan, 1993). There was no special opposition to them, except from expatriate civil servants and Australia, the colonial power. Detail of the devolution of legislative and executive powers to provinces were negotiated and embodied in the draft constitution (which was largely a consensus document). However, at the closing stages, the government secured the removal of the provisions for provincial autonomy, leading to the boycott of the Constituent Assembly by representatives of the Bougainville Province, which had been in the forefront of the movement for decentralization. The Province declared its secession from Papua New Guinea and sought its separate independence. Bougainville was still maintaining its separate existence when independence came to PNG (1975) but eventually agreed to negotiate with the central authorities for a suitable basis for its return.

The basis was found in the slight amendments to the original proposals for decentralization. As a consequence 19 provinces acquired a wide measure of autonomy. Not all of these had their own micro-nationalism, but the establishment of provincial constitutions and flags undoubtedly helped stimulate it. Nevertheless, decentralization did not pose any fundamental challenge to the authority of the centre. Nor did it produce strong local nationalisms; all the provinces contained a large number of small communities, with different languages and cultures. Most leaders looked to the state for resources; colonial practices had concentrated all power at the centre. Nor did ethnicity colour the new arrangements for devolution. The basic conflicts that emerged were not territorially based, but were between the representatives of a province at the national and provincial levels. The representatives at the national level resented the intrusions into their status and authority (and powers of patronage) presented by the representatives at the new tier of government. Nor was the basis of this competition ideological, as there is much of a sameness at all levels. Politicians are motivated by personal advantage and ambition; the promotion of local interests seem less important to political success than patronage. Thus although one of the most extensive schemes of spatial decentralization anywhere in the world was justified in the name of provincial and cultural autonomy, ethnicity has neither sustained it or affected its operation.

However, it is fair to say that the establishment of decentralization did remove resentments in the more politically conscious provinces against central authority and reconciled them to independence. The leaders of these provinces went on to play significant political roles in the national legislature and government. There is a general agreement that decentralization diffused ethnic tensions, but there has been criticism of the expense and inefficiency of the system. In 1995 fundamental changes were made to the structure, but not the powers, of provincial government in order to find a greater role for national parliamentarians in provincial politics and administration – and a greater share of provincial patronage. However, the ability of the system to prevent ethnic conflicts has been questioned in the wake of secessionist attempts in the province of North Solomons (popularly known as Bougainville). The background to these attempts, and the issues they raise are complex (and are addressed in the conclusion).

CORPORATE DECENTRALIZATION

Corporate decentralization sometimes provides an alternative to spatial decentralization, but can sometimes be harnessed to it. In many instances corporate decentralization is used when the geographical distribution of ethnic groups does not lend itself to neat spatial separation. Corporate decentralization aims to provide a measure of autonomy for particular groups. The device is to treat the members of a community as a collective, and vest rights in it. These rights can be personal, cultural or political; they can be entrenched or subject to the overriding authority of the government. They normally consist of positive and substantive rights and entitlements, but they can be negative, as in the form of a veto. They form the basis of the communal organization of politics and policies and of the collective protection of their rights. The following are some examples.

Political Representation and Power

Special forms of representation, like separate seats or electorates, common during the colonial period, are today generally out of favour (except among indigenous Fijian parties). They were rejected on the argument that they are divisive and retard the political and social integration of the different communities. India expressed strong opposition to these forms of representation (blaming its use during the colonial period for the emergence of her communal problems). The rejection of special representation through communal electorates by the Indian National Congress was cited by the Muslim League as evidence of its intolerance of minorities, and in support of its case for a separate Muslim state. Special representation for small minorities (who might not secure representation through the normal electoral process), like the Anglo-Indians, or particularly disadvantaged communities like scheduled castes or tribes may be allowed, either on electoral basis (generally in the lower house) or through nomination (in the upper house) (but these generally provide little prospect of a share in state power or authority over communal affairs).

Special electorates are but a minor illustration of a wider device of communal corporate political rights. The independence constitution of Cyprus (1960) used to provide an interesting example of special representation and communal political rights. The entire constitution was based on the recognition of the Greek and the Turkish communities. Greeks had 35 seats and the Turks 15 in the legislature; these seats were communally elected. For the purposes of legislation pertaining to the particular community, the Greek and the Turks constituted separate chambers. The Greek community was entitled to have one of its member as the President, while the Turks were entitled to have the Vice-President. The Vice-President was not merely deputy to the President, for he was independently and communally elected, had independent powers, appointed all the Turkish members of the Cabinet, and had various vetoes (making him both a part of the government and the leader of the opposition in his role of guarding the Turkish community against a Greek legislative and executive majority). Appointments to public services were to be in the ratio of three Turks for every seven Greeks (similar proportions had to be observed over broadcasts over the radio).

The collapse of the Cyprus independence constitutional arrangements followed from the attempt of the generals from Greece to annex Cyprus (in contravention of treaty obligations to maintain the separate state of the island) and the subsequent intervention of the Turkish army, but it would undoubtedly have been difficult to operate with its rigidities and vetoes. Nevertheless the model of communal corporations has inspired other attempts. The South African constitution of 1983 was based on the corporate existence of three communities (whites, coloured and Indians), each with its own electoral system and legislative chamber for 'own' (i.e. communal) affairs, with a central legislature for other matters. However, the constitution was not intended to provide a real autonomy for the coloureds or the Indians, for it operated under the overall supremacy of the white community. Rather, it was designed to maintain white control over other communities, and to exclude blacks from any participation whatsoever.

A more benevolent use of the model comes from Belgium (which has in turn influenced various constitutions since the collapse of the Soviet Union and Yugoslavia). In 1970, in order to deal with the incipient conflicts between its various linguistic groups, an agreement was reached to establish three linguistic regions, for the French-speaking Walloons, the Dutch-speaking Flemish and a bilingual one for Brussels (a further linguistic community, speaking German, was recognized in 1980). The establishment of Community Councils were authorized with jurisdiction over cultural matters, education, co-operation between the communities, international cultural groups and 'personal matters' in relation to the linguistic region and to institutions in Brussels whose interest or organization are such that they should be 'considered as belonging exclusively to one or the other community'. Here we have a mixture of the spatial and corporate devolution, but a more obviously corporate devolution occurs in relation to the functioning of the national legislature with its 'cultural councils' composed separately of the Dutch and French MPs, with powers to deal with cultural, educational and other matters. Various laws have also to cross the hurdle of the two councils, and thus each community is vested with a veto over certain types of legislation which have a community orientation.

One of the most interesting contemporary general examples of the use of corporate devolution is Fiji (France, 1969; Lawson, 1991; Norton, 1977). Its origins go back to early colonialism, and it was based on the policy of protecting the culture and traditions (and system of governance) of the indigenous Fijians as Europeans settled there and Indians were brought as indentured labour on sugar plantations (the mainstay of the economy). The motive, as is usual with colonialism, was political and administrative control, and in this instance indirect rule was the instrument. In the process, as was also usual, Britain invented tradition and established a system of hierarchy, control and land-holding that suited its purposes. In course of time all this came to pass off as Fijian customs and traditions, and received considerable sanctity. There have been various aspects of this policy. One element was political representation through racial electorates. Another was the prohibition of the alienation of community land to outsiders (which has ensured that over 80 per cent of the land has remained under tribal/clan control). Unusually, these survived into independence, primarily because by now the indigenous Fijians were outnumbered by Indian migrants. A system of racial and mixed electorates was carefully constructed to ensure the political supremacy of indigenous Fijian.

A peculiar dimension of this corporate policy was the establishment of 'Fijian administration', under which the regulation of several aspects of Fijian life were removed from the normal apparatus of the state and vested in an authority which was an amalgam of the 'traditional' Fijian system and the district British administration. Sometimes referred to as 'a state within a state', it provided a wide-ranging system of administration for Fijians under which they had their own provincial and district councils, applied the law and customs of the various local communities in special courts, made regulations to govern life in villages, defined community service and controlled the movement of Fijians. Reinforcing the chiefly system of authority, it provided for consultations with chiefs in what came to be called the Great Council of Chiefs on those aspects of policy which came under state authorities.

Fijian administration was intended to preserve the traditional authority and way of life of the indigenous Fijians, and this was to be achieved by separating it off from the normal state apparatus, laws and procedures. It was continued in force even after independence (in fact, it was entrenched in the constitution), even though power at that time effectively passed to the Fijians. A consequence of this was that the same group of persons became in charge of the state apparatus and the Fijian administration. This brought Fijian administration closer to the state, and indeed it began to be increasingly integrated into it. Fijian administration both dominated the state and became dependent on its resources. The consequence was the inversion of the original purpose, which was to ensure some measure of parity and equality in the formal state laws and administration once the special interests of the Fijians were taken care of through the Fijian administration, and to open up possibilities of a competitive political process for accession to state power. The result of the integration of the Fijian administration, however, was to enhance the stake of the Fijians in the control of the state, for it was increasingly through that control that they controlled their own community and its resources. This aggravated the tension between the two major communities, both of whom aspired to control of the state.

There are other consequences of the corporate treatment of Fijians. To some extent it removed their activities from the mainstream of the economy and, burdened by communal obligations, hindered their participation in the market. It also reinforced the social, economic and political distance between the Fijians and the Indians.

Legal Pluralism: The regime of personal law

Another device for the recognition of the corporate character of an ethnic group is through its personal laws. Before the advent of colonialism, the populations of territories that now constitute independent states were governed by their personal laws. These were largely the customary laws of the localities where they lived, but they also included important principles of the religious laws of their communities. They thus covered matters like marriage and divorce, relations between children and parents, inheritance and succession, and various religious practices (including, particularly in the case of Muslims, criminal prohibitions and sanctions). The validity of these laws depended on the customs of the people (and not official fiat).

Thus these laws (and the application of religious laws to religious property and corporations) ensured a measure of group autonomy, limited the scope of official intervention in the lives of the people of a community, and maintained the values, culture and institutions of the different communities. They ensured a wide measure of religious freedom, for the customs preserved in this scheme were closely connected with religious practices. For the most part these were personal rather than territorial laws, so that a person carried them with him/her wherever s/he moved, even overseas, especially within the British empire (though it has to be admitted that the male gender was more decisive than the female in rules governing the applicable personal laws). This, and the largely unwritten corpus of rules combined with big religious traditions, produced ambiguities that served to reduce conflict by mitigating sharp classifications and distinctions (and helped towards a flexibility and openness not so easy to attain in modern formal state systems).

The preservation of regimes of personal laws moderated the consequences of foreign invasions or changes of sovereignty. In Asia, with the striking exception of the Philippines (where neither the Spanish nor the Americans recognized indigenous laws), the colonial authorities recognized personal laws for the most part (although they were now interpreted and enforced in a different and more formal legal and judicial framework which had an important impact on their development). At Independence the sources and application of laws as provided in the colonial period were continued. Thus legal pluralism was continued after Independence despite the emergence of nationalism and policies to consolidate national unity. The unification of personal laws has its advocates (indeed the Indian Constitution adopted in 1950 has a directive principle of state policy to secure for its citizens a uniform civil code applicable throughout the country), and formal commissions have addressed the question. To some extent there has been an integration of laws, particularly in Africa and parts of Asia (although the trend in the Philippines, with a highly integrated system at Independence, is in the opposite direction, through the formal recognition of the application of Muslim law to followers of that religion and discussions on a similar dispensation for customary law for indigenous peoples; Mastura, 1994). In Africa the progress towards national codes has been hampered by technical difficulties and the lack of resources, and the impetus to convergence has come less as a result of government policies than from the imperatives of economic and social change. On the whole, legal pluralism still reflects the diversity of culture and belief in many parts of the developing world.

Personal laws, based as they are for the most part on customary practices, do change, and as has been hinted above, they changed in important ways during the colonial period through their adjudication and enforcement in formal courts and by being reduced to writing in many instances. They also responded to changing circumstances. It has therefore been possible to undertake some reforms in this area without unduly offending communal susceptibilities. Thus Hindu law in India has been modernized; important legislative initiatives in Malaysia and Singapore have altered many of fundamental rules of family law for non-Muslims (including the abolition of polygamy), bringing about an integration of national laws. In Singapore the application of personal laws (including Chinese customary laws) has been severely restricted. It has, however, been more difficult to bring about changes in Islamic law or practices; nor has it often been tried in fear of the reaction of Muslim leaders (Mayer, 1991). I have already mentioned the Philippines Code of Muslim Personal Law (1977) 'to strengthen all the ethno-linguistic communities in the Philippines within the context of their respective ways of life'. It provides for the application and administration (by the Sharia courts) of Islamic law to Muslims (even where its provision conflicts with the national law), as well containing a codification of the relevant rules of Islamic law. The resistance of sections of the Muslim community to changes in Islamic law is illustrated by the Indian Supreme Court decision in *Shah Bano* (AIR 1985 Sup. Ct. 945), when it held that the rights of a Muslim divorced woman must be decided in accordance with national, not personal laws. It was interpreted by many as an attack on the culture and ethos of the Muslim community, whose support was regarded as sufficiently significant by the government that it passed legislation to overrule the decision. However, in a recent decision the Indian Supreme Court has reiterated the constitutional mandate to unify personal laws and gave the governmen until August 1996 to inform the Court of the steps towards that goal (*Smt. Sarla Mudgal* v *Union of India*, Writ Petition 1079 of 1989, judgment given on 19 May 1995).

In the South Pacific as well each community has been assured the observance of its customs and laws (Ghai, 1994). These communities are relatively less affected by modern change than those in Asia and Africa, and consequently the hold of tradition is stronger. A major demand of most communities during the negotiations for independence was autonomy over their own affairs, land, family and clan – which was readily conceded, as political leadership often came from traditional leadership, in the absence of state nationalism or established political parties. However, in almost all instances, personal laws are subject to legislative amendment or replacement (although the initial responsibility may be with local government authorities more attuned to custom than the central government). Papua New Guinea, Solomon Islands and Vanuatu have attempted to prevent the erosion of custom by requiring custom to be made the basis of national law. Bolder efforts to confront the conflict between constitutional norms (and statutes) and custom are made in the Federated States of Micronesia and Palau. The Palau constitution states that the government shall take no action to prohibit and revoke the role or function of a traditional leader as recognized by custom which is not inconsistent with the constitution, and that statutes and customs shall be equally authoritative (a concept bristling with jurisprudence conundrums and difficulties). The Federated States of Micronesia go even further, seeking to set custom over the constitution itself, through the provision which says that nothing in the constitution is to take away a role or function of a traditional leader recognised by custom or tradition.

No more striking contemporary example of the regime of personal laws exists than that in Israel (Edelman, 1994). Arabs and Jews are subject to different regimes in personal matters, based on their religions. This separation is reinforced by different jurisdictions – Rabbinical Courts for Jews and Sharia courts for the Arabs. The state thus abdicates from the realm of the personal.[6] Such a system not only perpetuates the separation of ethnic groups, but also sharpens the contradictions of the state by emphasizing its skewed cultural foundations. Nor does the system unite the Jews; an abiding source of tension and occasional crises in Israel is the division among religious and secular Jews on the religiosity of the state. The Israeli model has been incorporated in the Israeli–PLO agreement on Palestinian autonomy (1993). The agreement exempts Israelis in Gaza or the West Bank from the 'personal' jurisdiction of the Palestinian Authority. Israelis will continue to be bound by Israeli laws even in Palestine and presumably will also tbe subject to Isreali courts for acts committed in Palestine (art. V).

CONCLUSIONS

It is evident from the above account that it is difficult to generalize about decentralization. Decentralization is both a set of institutions and arrangements as well an attitude of mind. Enough has been said above to demonstrate that somewhat similar provisions have produced quite different results in different countries. Federal arrangements do not by themselves produce federal attitudes, although they facilitate them, if the political forces they liberate are in some balance. Federal arrangements may fall prey to the overarching political and economic system, as it has in Malaysia. It is of some interest to note that it is in the more established countries, in the West, that federal attitudes have been dominant and complex arrangements may work, although it should be noted that there is a federal imperative which arises from certain objective circumstances: India, for example, could hardly be governed through a more centralized system. In developing countries the centrality of the state to accumulation and as a means to personal and group aggrandisement (as well as the need to consolidate independence) has made it hard to sustain federal arrangements, with the imperative of both sharing and transparency. It is in the communist regimes that federalism made the least impact on administration, with little notion of the autonomy of legal and constitutional processes, but paradoxically set the stage for their dissolution. It is therefore useful to try to classify the operation and consequences of decentralization through typologies along the lines indicated in the chapter.

A related distinction which may also yield some insights concerns the origin of the decentralization – whether it has arisen from the coming together of pre-existing sovereignty ('aggregation') – mostly 'liberal' federations – or by the subdivision of one sovereignty ('dis-aggregation') – mostly Third World federations/devolution. The former generally starts off positively and is forward-looking; it represents a willing union, and offers a better chance of negotiating a suitable and balanced settlement. The fact of past separate sovereignties often generates respect for ethnic communities, which is reinforced by the general rule in these federations that the central government is one of prescribed and limited powers. By the same token secession can command a stronger case both morally and politically – which in turn puts a premium on conciliation. A federation by disaggregation often result from various kinds of internal and external pressures, and thus starts off with resentments and suspicions. It can be backward-looking, nursing old grievances. The centre retains key powers and various forms of intervention, compounded by the difficulties of the transfer of power to the new units.

It is also important to make a distinction between the form and consequences of spatial and corporate decentralization. Paradoxically, spatial decentralization, which may involve a greater dispersal of power, may be more congenial to national integration than corporate – its basis is not explicitly ethnic and it clearly identifies some institutions, values and issues as national. Corporate decentralization, based on ethnic markers, tends to enhance ethnic values at the expense of national. Sometimes the regimes of personal laws can be so rigid that they prevent or hinder inter-ethnic mobility or contacts, as under the regime of religious laws, particularly in Israel. Even where mobility is possible, they can generate inter-ethnic tensions since mobility may set off conflicts about the applicability of relevant laws, as in the Shah Bano case, or in Kenya in the Otieno case in which the Luo widow of a Kikuyu lawyer and his family fought over the right to bury him, which turned on the application of competing customary laws, provoked great animosity between the two ethnic communities, reinforcing great national rivalries between them (Ojwang and Mugambi, 1989). The Shah Bano case in India and its legislative aftermath, already referred to, provoked not only divisions within the Muslim community (between conservatives and reformers) but also between the conservatives and sections of the majority Hindu community who felt that the state was unduly solicitous of minority susceptibilities (and commentators ascribe the destruction of the Akbari mosque in Ayoudhya to that resentment). The tendency is towards conservatism which may retard the progress of the community (although the group autonomy of the Ismailis in various lands under the forward looking leadership of the Aga Khan has not only turned it in a highly progressive community but also enabled global solutions transcending particular states where some its members may be living).

In its more political aspects, corporate decentralization obfuscates national institutions – they become bi- or tri-communal institutions; all national decisions have to be ethnically negotiated, so ethnic politics are at the heart of national politics, and the problems of consensus and governance are compounded by mutual vetos which are so often associated with such a system (as in Cyprus and increasingly in South Africa). With the rise in the growth and complexity of state power, the inadequacies of these form of corporate federalism have become obvious – at the same time as this demonstrates the need for ethnic equity.

When one turns to a discussion of how successful the federal or decentralization device is to solve ethnic problems, it is important to note that all forms of decentralization are hard to operate. They require fine balances, constant adjustments and a spirit of conciliation. All these difficulties are aggravated when the ethnic factor is introduced in the equation. But to state the problem in this form begs the question whether a centralized multi-ethnic state may not be even harder to manage than a federal multi-ethnic state. The difficulties of running a federal state have to be weighed against the costs of the refusal to concede the form or reality of federalism in Sri Lanka, pre-Bangladesh Pakistan, Burma, Yugoslavia, Ethiopia – and numerous other countries – years of carnage and bloodshed, the breakdown of administration, the militarization of state as well as society, the disruption of economy and perhaps the eventual fragmentation of the country.

The notion of success itself is problematic. Ethnicity raises complex problems of social harmony, identity, security and equity, while decentralization itself seeks to balance various, sometimes conflicting, considerations. 'Success' has to be judged in part by the immediate crisis that leads to decentralization and in part for the long term. In

Papua New Guinea, for example, decentralization was established to bring the secession of Bougainville to end, and in that sense it was eminently successful, but it did not produce equity or the greater accountability of government. As to long-term goals, the very establishment of decentralization changes the political and constitutional framework and with it the goals that may have been the original impulse behind it.

Spatial or corporate decentralization are not purely instrumental, acting upon social and political forces. Merely by providing a framework for inter-ethnic relations and negotiations, they affect and shape these relations. They may fashion new forms of identity or reinforce old identities. They may enhance or decrease the capacity of particular groups to extract resources from the state. They may provide new forms of contention and dispute. They may reduce the salience of specific problems and issues (e.g. by making them intra-rather than inter-communal). These remarks illustrate no more than that ethnic situations do not stand still and need constant readjustments (the Canadian constitutional proposals of 1992 were sensitive to the need for a continuing dialogue, and perhaps were rejected for that reason, as not being rule-oriented – one commentator called them the first postmodern constitution!). They also demonstrate that the reason for and the impact of these arrangements have to be understood in specific historical and national contexts.

Any assessment of the usefulness of decentralization must take account of these changes. In this context the question may be raised whether, once established, the federal system acquires rigidities, both of institutions and interests; and that therefore what seemed a solution at one point may become a problem later. The issue has been raised in the context of the Indian claims in Canada where the earlier ethnic calculations and preoccupation with specific ethnicities appears to preclude newer accommodations. The Canadian issue is not yet resolved, and in any case would not be conclusive. Modern federal arrangements eschew the institutional rigidities of the earlier forms, although this flexibility may not be sufficient to accommodate new demands of autonomy and incorporation. Likewise it is necessary to make a distinction between the securing of agreement of a federal solution and its implementation, for the very securing of the agreement (which may, for example, be reached under considerable foreign pressure) may serve to demobilize certain forces and work towards the maintenance of the status quo (as may have happened in Palestine). But that this is not an inevitable conclusion is demonstrated by the failure of repeated agreements to demobilize the Tamil Tigers in Sri Lanka.

The success of decentralization is hard to assess since, unlike some other devices which have an explicit ethnic dimension and a specific purpose, decentralization, especially of the spatial variety, is part of a set of arrangements which have other purposes as well (e.g. efficiency, social equity). There is ample evidence, however, that the application of the federal principle has helped to diffuse conflict: the concession of autonomy to Bougainville brought its secession to an end; a series of crises in India have been solved through grants of autonomy, including in recent years the accommodation of claims of federal treatment by the people of Assam, Nagaland and Mizoram, which helped to bring dissidence and rebellion to a close; the grant of autonomy to the south in the Sudan brought peace so long as autonomy was guaranteed; the Spanish recognition of the autonomy of the Basque region defused tensions and effectively marginalized the hard-liners; the dissidence of the Miskito Indians in Nicaragua was dealt with grants of autonomy; and in South Africa the last-minute concession of some form of provincialism and recognition of the notion of 'self-government by any community sharing a cultural and language heritage whether in a territorial entity within the Republic or in any other recognised way' was necessary to break the deadlock which brought both Buthelezi's Zulu-based Inkatha Party and the right-wing Afrikaners into the constitutional process and pave the way for a new order. The reorganization of Nigeria by increasing the number of states is widely acknowledged to have moderated ethnic tensions (whatever other problems may continue to plague that country). On the other hand, the extended federal arrangements have not been allowed to operate except for brief periods, as military rulers, displacing civilian leaders, have run the country in a tight and hierarchical manner.

The more difficult question relates to the longevity of these solutions or the mode and consequences of their operation if they survive. The Sudan terminated southern autonomy, Ethiopia swallowed Eritrea, India has gradually eroded the autonomy of Kashmir. But in many cases decentralization has survived, although its operations may no longer be governed by its original purposes. It becomes part of the wider political system, which determines the salience of the ethnic factor – some, as in Malaysia, transcend or ignore them, while others like Canada seem unable to get out of its incubus (although the adoption of the Charter of Rights has introduced new forms of identity and a new political agenda). In most cases the federal arrangements have established some form of a framework for inter-ethnic dialogue. However, it must be admitted that the federal spirit does not animate many federations in developing countries. Not only are there provisions for the centre to override provincial autonomy in general or specified circumstances (whose use has been liberal, even in India which otherwise has fairly democratic traditions), but the party system which has developed there negates elements of true federalism.

What are the limitations of decentralization? One is obvious. Spatial decentralization is possible only with physical concentrations of groups. A second problem is that spatial decentralization rarely resolves all minority fears, as it may help to create new minorities – the problem of minorities within minorities is well known, and has been used to refuse demands for decentralization (e.g. Nigeria in the 1950s, Sri Lanka now especially in relation to the merger of the Northern and Eastern provinces, the experiences in the former USSR and Yugoslavia) – or to create new states (India, Nigeria). There are, of course, ways to deal with these new minorities through special representation in the region, special consultative councils, local governments, and by vesting special responsibilities in the central institutions for their welfare and protection (e.g. in Canada minorities in any province can appeal to the centre against provincial discrimination). But these methods have seldom been effective.

Spatial decentralization, even when groups are concentrated, may be hard to operate when there are basically two communities (or when as in Canada now, the founding assumption of the federation of two communities has been outlived). A larger number of groups allows for flexibility in arrangements and the establishment of a certain kind of balance (well demonstrated by the Indian experience). A bigger constellation of interests have a stake in the success of the federal arrangements, and the clout to achieve this. Biracial federations with about equal-sized communities have larger possibilities of conflict and limited scope for trade-offs. When the communities are unequal, the federal arrangements become merely a form for the supplication by the smaller community to the larger – in patent negation of the federal principle (as the francophones in Canada often claim).

A further difficulty can arise from the unequal regional distribution of resources, giving a particularly sharp edge to ethnic differences. Federalism may be interpreted merely as a way to ensure for the richer region (and community) the unequal share of that wealth; if it is a minority it may produce resentment (and possible retaliation) by the majority group, and if it the majority group which lives in the richer region, it may lead to the ghettoization of the other. Secessionist groups or those demanding internal autonomy are frequently accused of greed and unwillingness to share their resources with others, as in Katanga, Biafra or Bougainville.

A further limitation, connected to the earlier points about the need for habits of tolerance and compromise, is that federalism may be unable to accommodate communities with very different ideas, beliefs and practices. A classic although simplified case of this was the American civil war (when Abraham Lincoln justified the stance of the northern states by saying that 'This country cannot endure permanently half slave and half free'). In more modern times, this was one (although not the fundamental) reason for the rejection of a federal solution to the Jewish-Arab problem in Palestine under the mandate or the UN schemes (O'Brien, 1986: 228). The Muslim League in colonial India rejected a federal solution for Muslims for the same reason, and it has been claimed that an Ethiopian-Eritrean federation is impossible for the same reason (Tekle, 1991). The position of the French in Quebec is not dissimilar.

An argument which is frequently made against federalizing a multi-ethnic state is the fear that it may be a spring board to secession (or in corporate decentralization, that it will impede national integration). Theoretically, the case would be that by giving a corporate form or a territorial base to a minority, decentralization facilitates secession (this is a reason for the opposition of successive government in Sri Lanka to Tamil demands of autonomy, see Uyangoda, 1994: 104–18: more generally, see Enloe, 1977; Nordlinger, 1972). It increases their resources and strengthens their identities, frequently justifying a claim under the principles of self-determination. In practice the situation is quite different. Few instances of the grant of autonomy have led to secession. What it has led to is the demand from other groups for similar treatment, leading to a kind of dispersal of authority. What this often does is strengthen national unity – the Indian and Papua New Guinean experiences with their linguistic communities are evidence. Secession frequently arises when autonomy is denied or abolished – for which this chapter has provided ample examples.

Instances of secession or attempted secession from a federation reveal on closer investigation that they are not the logical result of federalism. If we take first the case of Bangladesh's break away from Pakistan, it is clear that the central authorities in Islamabad had in fact refused to treat East Pakistan as an equal partner (despite its larger population) (Young, 1976: ch.12). It tried to impose Urdu upon a Bengali-speaking people, banned the broadcast of the songs of the leading Bengali poet, Tagore; drained off economic resources to the West; discriminated against Bengalis in state services (particularly in the armed forces), and in the end denied its major party, the Awami League, the fruits of its electoral victory. The crisis was precipitated by the refusal of the centre to accept Mujib Rahman's proposals for a genuine and equal federation. It was not the infrastructure of federalism which enabled East Pakistan to secede – it had none, but the intervention of India in the face of atrocities of the Pakistani army. The denial of its federal rights may have added to the moral case for autonomy, but even in a unitary state the case for secession in these circumstances would have been overwhelming.

The break-up of the federations in the USSR and Yugoslavia was also the result of the failure to implement a genuine federation. This is less true of Yugoslavia; the federation there had tried to bring together people who had a long history of enmity, but provided relatively little opportunities for the development of a real Yugoslavian identity. Both federations relied heavily on the Communist Party to hold them together, preventing an organic unity. Also the central authorities used ethnicities in opportunistic ways, not calculated to promote good inter-ethnic relations. In any case, the situations in the USSR and Yugoslavia is more correctly analysed less as secessions but as the explosion of the federations. Perhaps less so in Yugsolavia, the separation of constituent parts followed rather than caused the breakdown of the central authorities. The break up of Czechoslovakia is different from these two. It was consensual (at least elite consensus) – therefore, not secession. It does not appear to have been connected with the nature and operation of the federation, for this was effectively negated by the dominance of the Communist Party. After the 'velvet' revolution, there appears to have been a vague feeling on the part of each community that it was getting less than the other from the federation, and that it would be better off without the other. But fundamentally, the federation became a prey to the general salience that ethnicity achieved elsewhere in the wake of the collapse of communist regimes.

I turn finally to Papua New Guinea, where parts of Bougainville are in rebellion and want secession. The settlement of 1976, which established a wide-ranging decentralization, appeared to solve the problems of Bougainville. An elected provincial government was established, responsible to an elected local assembly. With its human and physical resources, it quickly built an enviable reputation for efficiency, and was assessed by various enquiries as the most effective and account-able of provincial governments. Regular elections were held, and its leaders played a full role in national politics. The troubles of 1989 originated in the inequitable distribution of the income from the copper mine, but unlike 1976 it was not a provincial-wide protest but was linked to disputes among the community which owned the land on which the mine was located and concerned the internal dis-tribution of royalties (Ghai, 1994). One of the first acts of the 'rebels' was to destroy the institutions of provincial autonomy, the provincial government and the local civil service. They command little support in the province, who do not share their desire for a separate statehood. The local, democratic forces to which decentralization gave rise were as much the victims of their anger and violence as the central author-ities. Decentralization cannot be held responsible for the attempts at secession. Rather, the rebels couch their claims in the language of self-determination, ignoring the significant autonomy that the province enjoys and which it has not been fully able to use due to constraints of administrative ability. As in so many modern instances, the villain of the piece is not decentralization, but self-determination. The earlier grant of autonomy to Bougainville helped to strengthen its links to the rest of the country, for it eliminated some genuine grievances, and established a democratic order internally connected to the national system. There is little doubt that without the 1976 autonomy, the rebellion of 1989 would have garnered more support in Bougainville – so decentralization has prevented rather than promoted secession.

These case studies point to the need to distinguish secession from the termination of a federation. There may be little to mourn in the second case – it suggests that ethnic communities have decided, mutually, to lead separate lives. Decentralization is important for ethnicity because it represents a compromise, a balance between those who want a tight, unitary system of government and those who may prefer separation. It helps to overcome the oppression of one group by another. It suggests a way in which different ethnic groups, with certain specific interests and traditions, are able to live together to achieve benefits of scale and to affirm that the ultimate values are higher than the ethnic, and that a person's vision is not limited to narrow ethnic gains. These values lose their salience if the wish to separate is mutual and the separation is achieved without strife or recrimination.

NOTES

1. The reluctance of Croatians to allow Serbs autonomy in Krajina and Knin is explained by their nearness to concentrations of Serbs in Bosnia-Herzegovina and Serbia, while Sri Lankans have opposed Tamil autonomy in Jaffna for its nearness to South India with a Tamil majority.

2. Speaking, for example of Puerto Rico, he writes, 'If Puerto Rico were to become a state it would break the general pattern. This would have to be a Spanish-speaking state. It would be inhabited almost entirely by a single ethnic group. There would be little likelihood once it became a state that its dominant population would be diluted much by migrants from other parts of the United States, as happened in California, New Mexico, and Hawaii. Undoubtedly the fact that Puerto Rico would be such a state, distinguished in these respects from all other states of the Union, would weigh heavily with Congress in accepting it as a state' (p. 76).

3. The establishment of the Jura canton is instructive for a variety of ways, not least the Swiss's sympathetic consideration of minorities and the democratic procedures followed in deciding on the form and extent of separation, topics which cannot be pursued here. I am grateful to Jill Cottrell for a translation of the relevant pages from Jean-François Aubert (1983). A brief account in English may be found in Wolf Linders (1994: 65–8).

4. Details of what has been called 'gerrymandering' may be found in Connor (1984: 302–22). He suggests, for example, that in the Central Asia area the authorities feared that excessively large and unmanageable, self-aware groups might evolve through the growth of a Bukharan, Turkic and/or Muslim national identity. Therefore, its borders were drawn so as to divide the inhabitants into a number of units and thus encourage a sense of separate national identity on the part of the Kazakhs, Kirgiz, Turkmen and Uzbeks. By contrast in the Caucasus the authorities were confronted with the Armenians and the Georgians, each of which had a developed sense of national consciousness that had already manifested itself in separatist movements. Consequently, they were, along with the Azerbaijanis, grouped into a single Transcaucasian federated republic. This situation lasted until 1936, when the unit was broken into three union republics, but without any special regard to the prevailing distribution of ethnic groups (pp. 302–3).

5. In Central Africa the opposition was also connected with the ethnic factor, since the federation was widely perceived by Africans as a device to extend white settler control from Southern Rhodesia (now Zimbabwe) to Northern Rhodesia (now Zambia) and Nyasaland (now Malawi). It is said that the discussions on federalism in East Africa were aborted by the Kenyan authorities because it would have diluted the dominance of the Kikuyu by the combined strength of the Nilotic people.

6. The Israeli model approximates in important ways to the scheme suggested by Karl Renner through the recognition of 'organic' groups, their personal laws and a high degree of cultural autonomy (Theodore Hanf, 1991).

REFERENCES

Asch, Michael, 1993. *Home and Native Land: Aboriginal Rights and the Canadian Constitution.* Vancouver: University of British Columbia Press.

Aubert, Jean-François. 1983. *Exposé des institutions politiques de la Suisse à partir de quelques affaires controversées.* Lausanne: Payot.

Austin, Granville, 1966. *The Indian Constitution: The Corner Stone of a Nation.* Oxford: Clarendon Press.

Banerjee, Ashish, 1992. 'Federalism and Nationalism: An Attempt at Historical Interpretation'. In N. Mukarji and B. Arora (eds.), *Federalism in India: Origins and Development.* Delhi: Vikas Press.

Burgess, Michael, 1993. 'Constitutional Reform in Canada and the 1992 Referendum', *Parliamentary Affairs*, 46, 3.

Cairns, Alan, 1977. 'The Governments and Societies of Canadian Federalism', *Canadian Journal of Political Science*, 10, 5.

——1992. *Charter v. Federalism: The Dilemmas of Constitutional Reform.* Montreal: McGill-Queen's University Press.

Cassidy, Frank and Robert L. Bish, 1989. *Indian Government: Its Meaning in Practice.* Halifax: The Institute for Research on Public Policy.

Cohen, Leonard, 1993. *Broken Bonds: The Disintegration of Yugoslavia.* Boulder: Westview.

Connor, Walker, 1984. *The National Question in Marxist-Leninist Theory and Strategy.* Princeton: Princeton University Press.

Das, Bhagwan D., 1985. 'Federalism or Patrimonialism: The Making and Unmaking of Chief Ministers', *Asian Survey*, 25, 5: 793–804.

Dhavan, Rajiv, 1979. *President's Rule in the States.* Bombay: Tripathi Ltd.

Edelman, Martin, 1994. *Courts, Politics and Culture in Israel.* Charlottesville: University of Virginia Press.

Enloe, Cynthia, 1977. 'Internal Colonialism, Federalism and Alternative State Development Strategies', *Publius*, 7, 4.

France, Peter, 1969. *The Charter of Land: Custom and Colonisation in Fiji.* Melbourne: Oxford University Press.

Ghai, Yash, 1988. 'Constitution Making and Decolonisation'. In Ghai (ed.), *Law, Politics and Government in the Pacific Island States.* Suva: Institute of Pacific Studies.

——1994. *Reflections on Self-Determination in the South Pacific.* Hong Kong: University of Hong Kong Law Working Paper Series.

Ghai, Yash and Patrick McAuslan, 1970. *Public Law and Political Change in Kenya.* Nairobi: Oxford University Press.

Ghai, Yash and Anthony Regan, 1993. *The Law, Politics and Administration of Decentralization in Papua New Guinea.* Waigani: The National Research Institute.

Gertzel, Cherry, 1970. *The Politics of Independent Kenya.* Nairobi: East African Publishing House.

Glazer, Nathan, 1977. 'Federalism and Ethnicity: The Experience of the United States', *Publius*, 7, 4.

Goble, Paul, 1989. 'Ethnic Politics in the USSR', *Problems of Communism.* (July–August).

Gupta, Jyotinindra Das, 1975. 'Ethnicity, Language Demands and Traditional Development in India'. In Nathan Glazer and Daniel Moynihan (eds.), *Ethnicity, Theory and Experience*. Cambridge, MA: Harvard University Press.

Gupta, U.N. (ed.), 1988. *Indian Federalism and Unity of Nation*. Allahabad: Vohra Publishers.

Hanf, Theodore, 1991. 'Reducing Conflict through Cultural Autonomy: Karl Renner's Contribution'. In Uri Ra'anam, Maria Mesner, Keith Armes and Kate Martin (eds.), *State and Nation in Multi-Ethnic Societies: The Breakup of Multinational States*. Manchester: Manchester University Press.

Hanks, Peter and Bryan Keon-Cohen (eds.), 1994. *Aboriginals and the Law*. Sydney: Allen and Unwin.

Hannum, Hurst, 1990. *Autonomy, Sovereignty and Self-Determination*. Philadephia: University of Pennsylvania Press.

Job, Cvijeto, 1993. 'Yugoslavia's Ethnic Furies', *Foreign Policy*.

Lawson, Stephanie, 1991. *The Failure of Democratic Politics in Fiji*. Oxford: Clarendon Press.

Linder, Wolf, 1994. *Swiss Democracy*. London: Macmillan Press.

Lyons, Oren and John Mohawk (eds.), 1992. *Exiled in the Land of the Free: Democracy, Indian Nations, and the US Constitution*. Santa Fe: Clear Light Publishers.

Mackerras, Colin, 1994. *China's Minorities: Integration and Modernisation in the Twentieth Century*. Hong Kong: Oxford University Press.

Macrae Kenneth, 1983. *Conflict and Compromise in Multinational Societies: Switzerland*. Waterloo, Ont.: Wilfred Laurier University Press.

Mastura, Michael, 1994. 'Legal Pluralism in the Philippines', *Law and Society Review*, 28, 3: 461–75.

Mayer, Ann E., 1995. *Islam and Human Rights: Tradition and Politics*. Boulder: Westview Press, 2nd edition.

Mukarji, N and B. Arora (eds.), 1992. *Federalism in India: Origins and Development*. Delhi: Vikas Press.

Musil, Jiri (ed.), 1995. *The End of Czechoslovakia*. Budapest: Central European University Press.

Nordlinger, Eric A., 1972. *Conflict Regulation in Divided Societies*. Cambridge, MA: Harvard Center for International Affairs.

Norton, Robert, 1990. *Race and Politics in Fiji*. St Lucia: University of Queensland Press, 2nd edition.

O'Brien, Conor Cruise, 1986. *The Siege: The Saga of Israel and Zionism*. New York: Simon and Schuster.

Ojwang, J.D. and J.W.K. Mugambi (eds.), 1989. *The SM Otieno Case: Death and Burial in Modern Kenya*. Nairobi: Nairobi University Press.

Oyovbaire, S. Egite, 1985. *Federalism in Nigeria*. London: Macmillan Press.

Pevar, Stephen, 1992. *The Rights of Indians and Tribes*. Carbondale and Edwardsville: Southern Illinois University Press.

Roeder, Philip, 1990–1. 'Soviet Federalism and Ethnic Mobilisation', *World Politics*, 43.

Reppard, William, 1936. *The Government of Switzerland*. New York: Van Nostrand.

Safruddin, B.H., 1987. *The Federal Factor in the Government and Politics of Peninsular Malaysia*. Singapore: Oxford University Press.

Shukla, V.N., 1994. *Constitution of India*, ed. Mahendra Singh. Lucknow: Eastern Book Co., 9th edition.

Simandjuntak, B., 1969. *Malayan Federation 1945–63: A Study of Federal Problems in a Plural Society*. Oxford: Oxford University Press.

Srinivasavaradan, T.C.A., 1992. *Federal Concept: The Indian Experience*. Delhi: Allied Publishers.

Simeon, Richard, 1980. 'Inter-governmental Relations and the Challenges to Canadian Federalism', *Canadian Public Administration*, 23, 1.

Russell, Peter, 1993. *Constitutional Odyssey: Can Canadians Become a Sovereign People?* Toronto: University of Toronto Press, 2nd edition.

Tekle, Amare, 1991. 'Another Ethiopian-Eritrean federation? – An Eritrean View', *World Today*, 47: 47–50.

Tishkov, Valery, 1991. 'Inventions and Manifestations of Ethno-nationalism in and after the Soviet Union'. In K. Rupesinghe and P. King (eds.), *Ethnicity and Conflict in a Post-communist World*. New York: St. Martin's Press.

Uyangoda, Jayaveda, 1994. In Sunil Bastian (ed.), *Devolution and Development in Sri Lanka*. New Delhi: Konark Publishers.

Vipond, Robert, 1985. 'Constitutional Politics and the Legacy of the Provincial Rights Movement in Canada', *Canadian Journal of Political Science*, 18, 2.

Willink Commission (UK), 1958. *Report of the Commission Appointed to Enquire into the Fears of Minorities and the Means of Allaying Them*, Cmnd. 8969. London: HMSO.

Young, Crawford, 1976. *The Politics of Cultural Pluralism*. Madison: The University of Wisconsin Press.

3 Electoral Systems
K. M. de Silva

UNIVERSAL SUFFRAGE

The general tendency to view the debate on electoral systems as part
of the problem of good governance diverts attention from two inter-
related issues. First of all, despite the contemporary prevalence of
universal suffrage as an essential aspect of democratic government,
its comparatively recent origin is often ignored. Second, in all societies
electoral systems of some sort, but with the franchise limited by
education, income and gender, if not such factors as race (colour) as
well, are much older than universal suffrage. Electoral systems are, of
course, linked to extensions of the suffrage and the eventual emergence of universal suffrage.

The white settlement colonies of the British Empire, especially those
in the southern hemisphere, the Australian colonies and New Zealand,
set the pace in the expansion of the electorate to the point of virtual
universal suffrage.[1] Australia has had its own problems of ethnicity,
not merely in the barriers in force up to very recent times on non-
European settlement, the 'white' Australia policy, but also in the
effective exclusion of the aborigines from the franchise. New Zealand,
no less exclusively white than the Australian colonies, nevertheless
incorporated the native population, the Maoris, as part of the
electorate.[2] New Zealand has, in fact, the right to claim the title of
pioneer in the establishment of universal suffrage as an essential
feature of its democratic government.[3] In Britain, in contrast,
the democratization of the electorate was a long struggle. Among
the principal landmarks are the Great Reform Bill of 1832 and
the electoral reforms of 1867 and 1884 (Blake, 1978: 450–77; McKib-
bin, Pellin 1967; 1974; Taylor and Johnston, 1979). There restrictions
based on property, education and gender continued, and were
eventually eliminated over a 45-year period from 1884. The first
British general election under universal suffrage was held as late as
1929. Plural voting based on property rights continued till 1945, when
it was eliminated. The United States took pride in being more democratic than Europe, but the fact is that in many of the southern states
of the country – and not only there – Afro-Americans were generally

excluded from the voting registers by a combination of factors until well into the 1960s.

In Europe, New Zealand's counterpart would be Sweden. The origins of parliamentary government in Sweden go back to 1917 and were closely linked to extension of the suffrage. There were two stages in this latter process: male suffrage in 1907–9 and universal suffrage in 1919–21. This was nearly two decades after New Zealand's electoral reforms. After the first of these extensions of the suffrage in 1907–9 proportional representation (PR) was introduced (Madsen, 1987). Sweden, like the rest of Scandinavia, was well ahead of most parts of Europe in introducing a wide suffrage and in the concern shown for electoral reform from the early part of the twentieth century.

In many European countries – France, Switzerland and Belgium, for instance – there was strong resistance to the granting of voting rights to women. In France women received the right to vote only in 1945; in Belgium limited female franchise came in 1920; the franchise was extended to *all* women only in 1948. It took even longer for the Swiss to grant women a similar right. Women in Sri Lanka had the right to vote at the age of 21 from 1931. But Sri Lanka, as we shall see, was always a special case.

Universal suffrage, naturally, is of even more recent vintage in the ex-colonial world. Generally, its introduction goes back to the post-Independence period, whenever that may have been. One exception is Sri Lanka, where universal suffrage came in 1931, 16–17 years before Independence through the recommendations of the Donoughmore Commission. Indeed, Sri Lanka's first general election under universal suffrage was in 1931, just two years after Britain's first general election under universal suffrage (de Silva, 1981). India's first election under universal suffrage came in 1952, five years after Indian Independence, and 21 years after Sri Lanka's first general election under universal suffrage.

ELECTORAL SYSTEMS

Electoral systems had a long history in the British Empire. In most cases the franchise was restricted in terms of wealth, education and gender, or where British rule was established in territories with an ethnically-mixed population or where there was a religious divide, electoral systems were designed either to recognize, or to protect, foster and nurture these distinct identities. These were, to use the jargon of the last phase of colonial rule, communal electorates. Two principles were at work, and in conflict: the principle of territorial electorates – which the mainstream nationalist movement in British India and British Ceylon insisted on – and communal electorates – which the minorities agitated for.

Separate electorates for Muslims were incorporated in the Indian Councils Act of 1909. From that time onwards the nationalist agitation against the British came apart on this issue of the recognition of distinct communal identities in the electoral system. The differences on this issue reached a dénouement in the bloody partition of the Raj in 1947 (Phillips, 1962). The most coherent defence of communalism came from the poet-philosopher Muhammed Iqbal on 29 December 1950 in India – a defence which culminated in the demand for a homeland for India's Muslim population (Dobbin, 1970: 97–8).

It would be true to say that the British generally supported the principle of communal electorates in India, and even when as in the case of the Montagu-Chelmsford Commission's report of 1917 communal electorates were strongly condemned, the implementation of the recommendations showed a clear reluctance to abolish them. On the contrary, in the inter-war period the principle of communal or special electorates was extended beyond the Muslims, for whom they were originally designed, to other groups in British India's diverse population. These included the so-called untouchables, for whom euphemisms such as scheduled castes and Harijans were later used (Coupland, 1944). There were echoes of this same debate in other multi-ethnic and multi-religious colonies. Only in the case of Sri Lanka were decisive measures taken to move away from communal electorates.

In general, pre-Independence electoral systems in colonies, including the British Raj, operated on a restricted franchise, often excluded women, but incorporated special representation for minorities either through communal electorates or through a system of nomination by the governor of the colony.

The British colonial administration in Sri Lanka endorsed the views of the Donoughmore Commission, and in implementing the reforms that emerged from its report constructed an electoral system based essentially on territorial electorates. Recognizing, however, that representatives of the smaller minorities could not secure election without communal electorates, provision was made for special seats for them in which the representatives were nominated by the Governor of the colony.

The classic case that illustrates the complexities involved in devising electoral systems which recognized if not embodied the diversity of a colonial population comes from a French protectorate – the Lebanon. The National Pact of 1942–3 was a crucially important feature of the Lebanese political system for over 40 years. Despite its vital import- ance in sustaining the stability of the Lebanese constitution for several decades, the terms of the pact were never set down in writing. It was, in essence, an informal agreement, and although this informality gave it a measure of flexibility, the ambiguity that was part of the pact proved to be a fundamental flaw during periods of tension in the country's political life. The pact was an unconventional bargain, through which the legitimacy of a sovereign Lebanese entity was accepted by the Muslim leadership, while the Christian groups in turn agreed to share power with the former, as well as to give a measure of recognition to the Arab character of the Lebanese polity. The central feature of this national compromise was a careful distri- bution of power among the component elements of the Lebanese population based on their presumed numerical strength. Thus the demographic profile as it existed in 1942–3 was reflected in the man- ner in which the political spoils were shared (Cobban, 1985: 70; Lijphart, 1980: 147–50).

A two-tier structure developed, of which the electoral system was one part and the other a complicated division of offices at the legis- lative, executive and administrative levels. In 1943, the French, who had ruled Lebanon on their own since 1920, supported a move to give the Christian sects 32 seats in the national legislature as against 22 for the Muslim sects. The British, who by this time had much greater influence in the Middle East, insisted on a division of seats that would be slightly more favourable to the Muslim sects: a ratio of 30 seats for the Christian sects as against 25 for the Muslims. This ratio of 6 to 5 in favour of the Christians became an essential feature of the National Pact, and was eventually incorporated 'at every given level of govern- ment' (Cobban, 1985: 71). South Asian politicians and publicists would have recognized these as communal electorates. In accepting the election of a Maronite as the powerful president of the Lebanese state and in establishing a ratio of six Christian deputies to every five Muslim deputies in Parliament, the principle of Christian dominance if not supremacy in the state was underlined. Throughout the next four decades the total number of legislators in the Lebanese parlia- ment was always a multiple of 11, divided in these proportions (Cob- ban, 1985: 71). In a sense this distribution of power embodied a practice that had grown up under the French Mandate, where it was established that the presidency would go to a Maronite, while the Prime Minister would be a Sunni Muslim. The National Pact merely made this division of governmental and legislative power more elaborate. Thus it was agreed that the Speaker of the House would be a Shi,ite; and while the commander of the army would be a Maronite, the Chief of Staff would be a Druze (Cobban, 1985: 70). Professor Itamar Rabinovich sums up the structure emerging from the National Pact as 'a unique political system, which acknowledged the primacy of its religious communities and vested them with political power, [and] came to be dubbed *confessional*' (Rabinovich, 1985).

Rabinovich explains that:

> The Muslim Establishment's willingness to accept Christian hegemony in Lebanon, when the Christian numerical strength was clearly declining, was induced by a number of factors whose influence continued in later years.... Yet not all Muslims and Christians accepted the 1943 compromise, and segments of the major communities continued to harbour dreams either of an Arab union or of a purely Christian Lebanon.   (Rabinovich, 1985: 25)

While this 'system had important merits – not the least of which was that it was based on an awareness of the fundamental conflict in Lebanon and attempted to come to grips with it –' there were serious flaws in it from the outset.

> The Lebanese parliament thus reflected the web of relationships among the traditional foci of power in the country. And moreover it was for a rather long period virtually closed to new contenders. Furthermore, in upholding the principles of confessionalism and playing down the notions of nation and class, the Lebanese political system acquired an archaic complexion, and from the mid-1960s it found itself challenged by the political attitudes prevailing in most of the outside world.   (Rabinovich, 1985: 26)

If the electoral and political structure of Lebanon was unusual in its complexity, there were other states too in which, either after Independence or at the transfer of power, extraordinary electoral arrangements were incorporated as salient features in the constitution in an attempt to mitigate the harsher features of violent ethnic conflict and regional divisions (e.g.Nigeria and Uganda) or 'to ensure safe and adequate representation' for all sections of 'the...community' (e.g. Mauritius).   (Dinan *et al.*, 1994)

In Nigeria an unusual electoral formula for the presidency was adopted in the late 1970s in an effort to encourage multi-ethnic parties after the political turbulence of the previous decade, the breakdown of governmental structures, military rule and civil war. A successful presidential candidate was required to obtain not merely a majority of votes nationwide, but also to secure at least 25 per cent of the votes in two-thirds or more of the 19 states in the Nigerian federation (Horowitz, 1985: 635–6). Since the country's multitude of ethnic groups was unevenly distributed in its various constituent states, this new requirement was expected to ensure that a candidate would have broad multi-ethnic support (Horowitz, 1985: 635–6). In Uganda a proposal was adopted in 1970 for 'every candidate for parliament [to] stand in one basic and three national constituencies. The basic constituency would be the candidate's home region and the three national constituencies in the three other regions of the country. The percentage of votes won in each constituency would count as electoral votes, and the winning candidates would be those with the highest totals for their four constituencies...' It was expected that such a scheme would avoid representation of parochial interests and encourage national unity, and that the electoral system would be a 'device to induce national integration' (Mittelman, 1975: 125). Neither of these proposals – the Nigerian and the Ugandan – served the purpose it was intended for, as the subsequent history of the two countries would show, but they are nevertheless serious and extraordinary attempts at mitigating the dissensions stemming from ethnic and regional divisions.

The electoral arrangements drafted at the time of the transfer of power from British rule in the island of Mauritius have been altogether more successful. They are also unique and intended quite explicitly to ensure ethnic harmony in a country of immigrants where the Indian community was numerically dominant. Mauritius and the tiny island of Rodrigues were divided into 21 constituencies of which 20 returned 3 representatives to the legislature. There are 62 'directly' elected members. In drawing the boundaries of the constituencies, great care was taken 'to ensure adequate representation of the two most important [groups] – namely the Hindus and the General Population'. The unique feature of the system were the eight additional seats allocated to the 'best losers'. The first four of these seats are allocated to the 'appropriate community', i.e. the community most under-represented, regardless of party affiliation, provided, of course, that the candidates belong to a political party. The first four seats are therefore awarded on a purely community basis. The second of the four 'best loser, seats is awarded to the appropriate party and the appropriate community, i.e. on a party and community basis (Dinan *et al.*, 1994: 43–46).

THE PLURALITY SYSTEM AND PROPORTIONAL REPRESENTATION

Electoral systems have been described as 'the most manipulative instrument of politics' (Sartori, 1968: 273). Over the past two centuries, electoral institutions have come to play an important role in the governmental structure and political process of most nations of Europe and North America. Our concern in this chapter is with democratic systems and democratic forms, and not with totalitarian or authoritarian systems which claimed to operate a structure more genuinely democratic than the traditional ones. There have been three major influences on the contemporary world's electoral systems: the British, the United States and European. As the only superpower for much of the nineteenth century and the metropolitan centre of a world-wide empire, Britain's electoral practice and tradition have had a profound influence on electoral systems and practice on the member nations of that empire. One practice and tradition that was transferred to former member states of the empire was the first-past-the-post system of electoral politics, based generally on single member, and a few multi-member, constituencies. Post-colonial nations have readily accepted this system. Indeed, it is the most prevalent system in the modern world. The United States political system of presidential government has had ready acceptance in Central and South America, and, of course, in the former United States colony of the Philippines. Elsewhere it has had greater acceptance in Africa than in other parts of the world, whether these former colonies had belonged to the British or other European nations.

While the British and US systems are divergent in regard to the form of the executive power, they converge as regards electoral structures. The US system is a federal one, but its electoral structure at the national level (i.e. at elections to Congress) is much like the British single-member constituencies in which the election is determined on the first-past-the-post, or plurality system as it is sometimes called. They both differ from the proportional representation (PR) systems in operation in many parts of Europe. PR systems are now beginning to influence practice in many parts of the ex-colonial world, although admittedly that influence is still rather limited. We have had Sri Lanka turning to PR in the 1980s after over five decades of experience in the Westminster-inspired first-past-the-post electoral system (de Silva and Samarasinghe, 1980: 16–39). Sri Lanka also adopted an executive presidency in 1978 after thirty years, experience of prime ministerial government (Wilson, 1980). In this instance the change was effected partly at least to mitigate the effects of ethnic tensions that have bedevilled the politics of the country since the mid-1950s. Then again there is the case of New Zealand, which adopted PR in 1993 after over a century of experience of the British-style first-past-the-post system, a decision in which the protection of ethnic diversity was not a factor – despite its relaxation of the restrictions on non-European immigration. New Zealand is a bi-ethnic state with a homogeneus white population of largely British origins and a Maori community, mostly Polynesian in composition.

In New Zealand, unlike in Sri Lanka, the pressure for the introduction of PR came from a minor party, or a combination of minor parties – the Alliance – and not from one of the traditional parties of government, the Labour Party and the National Party. Indeed, both these parties were strongly opposed to the introduction of PR, but the Alliance, which had secured 14 per cent of the vote nationally in 1990 and won only one seat in the 97-member legislature, kept up the pressure for a system of PR. The National Party, prior to the election of 1990, had given an undertaking to hold a referendum on PR. At the election of 1990, the National Party had won 48 per cent of the vote but secured 69 per cent of the seats. As in Sri Lanka in 1978, one of the arguments in favour of PR was the tendency of the existing electoral system to exaggerate the swing of the electoral pendulum.

When the referendum was held in September 1992, the electorate voted overwhelmingly (85 per cent) in favour of abolishing the simple plurality single member system. Of the four alternatives offered, 70 per cent voted in favour of a mixed-member PR form modelled on that currently operated in Germany. The New Zealand version of this would have 60 MPs elected on a constituency basis and 60 elected on a party list, with the seats being distributed in accordance with the proportion of the vote won by each individual party.

A second referendum was held on 6 November 1993, to coincide with the general election of that year, at which voters were asked to make a straight choice between the mixed member PR system and the existing Westminster-type constituencies operating on the first-past-the-post basis. On this occasion the vote in favour of the PR system was 54 per cent, substantially lower than it had been in 1990.

The new rules have been implemented since the general election of 1996. Under the German system a political party would have to win at least 5 per cent of the vote nationally or win a minimum of three constituencies, to secure membership of the legislature. In addition a special provision is made for national minorities. The Maori representation would be protected by these provisions, and of course by nomination to electorates on a party ticket or on the party list. The new PR rules, as classical theory world predict, led to some party fragmeatation, and the inability of any party to win a majority of seats for the first time in decades. The capacity of the uncertain coelition to govern effectively remains to be demonstrated.

The Anglo-American preference for the first-past-the-post system of electoral choice has significant differences in the organization of electorates. Since the electoral divisions are generally based on either a fixed number of seats in the legislature, as in Britain and the United States, or population growth is reflected in an increase in the number of seats in the legislature, shifts of population are accommodated in the electoral system through regular delimitation of constituencies. In the British system, which has been transferred to the democracies of the former colonial empire, the delimitation is left to independent commissions, which generally adopt a formula based on population and area for this purpose. Quite often there is a tendency to give some sort of weight to rural populations or regions with a concentration of minorities. This does lead to distortions of some sort, especially to the disadvantage of parties dependent on urban and working-class support. But these have generally avoided some of the distortions prevalent in the United States where the delimitation of constituencies after a census is left to state legislatures, which in the past tended to over-represent rural areas. With the Supreme Court decision in *Baker* v. *Carr* in 1962 this was fundamentally changed, with the requirement that districts should equally reflect population. Thereafter, in the last three decades, a wholly new pattern of electoral demarcation developed, based partly on partisan advantage and partly on protecting the interests of incumbents. The Civil Rights Amendment Act of 1982, requiring race-conscious redistricting, resulted in the creation of some grotesque electoral districts (the notorious salamander-shaped electorates) in states such as Texas, Georgia, Louisiana and North Carolina. This amendment is now involved in litigation. The British-type independent commissions have generally a more wholesome record in this regard, even where the number of seats in the legislature increases with each delimitation, keeping pace with population growth (Taylor and Johnston, 1979: 335–434).

In general, majority or plurality voting systems create higher thresholds for legislative representation than does PR.

In the not too distant past and in countries which claimed to be operating on democratic principles the franchise was restricted on the basis of property, education and gender. In the United States, and perhaps Australia too, there were racial restrictions as well. It would be true to say that the composition of the electorates was regulated to dilute the emerging strength of groups regarded as undesirable or a threat to the established order. In the former category would be recent immigrants in British colonies. During the nineteenth century, property requirements and weighted voting schemes were employed throughout Europe. In the United States even today, unusually cumbersome registration requirements help to inhibit voting by the poor and the uneducated, many of whom happen to be Afro-Americans. Registration is relatively simple in some states, but in every state registration is the responsibility of the voter, and is a state responsibility, not a federal one. In contrast, under the British tradition, registration of eligible voters is the responsibility of the state, and once an individual reaches voting age (18 or 21 as the case may be) registration is virtually automatic.

There are two views about the origins of PR in Europe. One view is that entrenched groups, if not parties, generally preferred majority and plurality voting rights as a means of retaining power, and also of reducing the representation of the emerging working class. However, as parties representative of or supported by the working class gained in strength and seemed likely to win electoral majorities, PR was seen as a means of curbing the strength of working class or radical parties. The second view is that with the proliferation of political parties representing specific groups in late nineteenth- and early twentieth-century Europe, groups based on class and religious identity no less than ethnicity and region, the prevailing plurality system tended to distort the electoral will. Thus, in a sharply divided electorate in which a large number of political groups fared equally well, it was quite conceivable that a group which secured 25–33 per cent of the total vote could secure an overwhelming majority of seats in a national legislature. The resulting distortion would lead to an aggravation of existing tensions in society since such a government would be seen as representative of a minority imposing its will on the majority.

Whatever the origins of the system, it came to be adopted in a number of European countries, large and small. One of the main arguments in its favour was that it would generally heal rifts in sharply divided societies, whether they be rifts based on religious differences, class tensions, ideological conflict or even ethnic identity (Rokkan, 1970; Taylor and Johnston, 1979). PR was expected to help establish a governing coalition, and that coalition would seek amelioration of tensions through policies based on a consensus.

There are important variations in PR systems. A useful distinction could be made, following Arend Lijphart, between *extreme* PR, which poses few barriers to small parties, and *moderate* PR, which limits the influence of small parties through such means as applying PR to small electoral districts rather than large districts or provinces, or nation-wide balloting. Also a minimum percentage of the vote could be required in order to gain representation. The threshold in Germany is 5 per cent while in the Sri Lanka system it was as high as 12.5 per cent until 1988, but has since been reduced to 5 per cent. Sweden too falls into this category of a nation with a moderate PR system, with a threshold of 4 per cent. Other countries – Israel and the Netherlands, for instance – have minimal (1 per cent) thresholds, producing large numbers of political parties. Until very recently the Italian system did so too.

There are also variations on how candidates are chosen. In the more commonly used list system the intention is to provide for political parties to have more or less the same ratio of seats in the legislature that these parties acquired in an election. The much less widely used Hare system (named after the nineteenth-century British political reformer, Thomas Hare) is a complicated mechanism where individual candidates can be ranked by voters in order of preference. In the current Sri Lankan system each voter has three votes in an electoral district, but cannot give more than one vote for any single candidate in the list of the political party of his or her choice.[4] The voter can choose to cast just one vote, or two or three, as he or she prefers. Germany uses a combination of single-member constituencies and proportional representation, but the allocation of seats on the party list in the Bundestag depends on the percentage of the vote that the parties obtain at the general election.

Our main concern in this chapter is PR in ethnically divided societies. Since the major purpose of PR is to facilitate minority representation, it should be more suitable for such societies than the first-past-the-post-system. Lijphart claims that this is indeed the case and cites

Belgium and Finland as examples (Lijphart, 1993). The evidence from Sri Lanka, one of the few post-colonial nations emerging from the British empire to adopt PR, is ambiguous at best, as the results of the two general elections under PR held so far, in February 1989 and August 1994, would indicate. The fact is, as Lijphart himself points out, because there are so many different kinds of ethnic or religious minorities in democracies, it is difficult to measure the extent to which PR succeeds in providing more representation for minorities than does the first-past-the-post system (Lijphart, 1993).

Two points are clear, however. First, PR systems have not been as readily transferable to non-European settings as the Anglo-American plurality or majority system. Nor have they been as readily accepted in the post-colonial systems of the former British Empire, save in Sri Lanka (1978) and New Zealand (1993). Pakistan is a potential entrant to the small PR club, if the government ever summons the political will to get parliamentary approval for legislation for this purpose.[5] Secondly, even in Europe and North America not all ethnically divided societies have adopted PR systems. Thus Canada still maintains the British system at both the federal and state level.

Switzerland and Belgium are important cases of PR in culturally divided societies. Like Canada and the United States, Switzerland is a federal state, with a bicameral legislature. In the 200-seat *Nationalrat* every canton or half-canton is represented according to its population, with each guaranteed at least one member. Elections are held every four years under a rather complicated list system on the PR principle. In the 46-member *Ständerat* every canton has two seats and every half-canton one. Methods of election and length of term are left to the discretion of each canton.

Lists of candidates for parliamentary elections are developed in each canton by the individual parties. Although as many as 15 or 20 different lists may be presented at any given election, most of them have no chance of election. Four major parties dominate both houses of parliament (Kohn, 1980; Schmid, 1981). In effect the system amounts to a permanent coalition. The great stability this provides compensates for any defects in the system, such as the exclusion of groups outside the coalition.

The Swiss example is unique (Schmid, 1981) – indeed, the national experience is *sui generis* – and so provides no general support for the contention that PR on its own helps reduce ethnic dissonance in ethnically and religiously divided societies. Belgium, on the other hand, like Switzerland, has a unique, decentralized governmental system. But the system itself is far more fragile than the Swiss one, and the sharp divisions in the Belgian polity are barely kept in control by a complex consociationalism (Covell, 1981, 1993; McRae, 1986; Hooghe, 1993) with elaborate post-sharing and compromise arrangements which bring to mind Lebanon's well-known National Pact of 1943. If one leaves Switzerland out of the reckoning because of its unique historical experience, the cases of Canada and Belgium point to a not very comforting conclusion on the utility of electoral systems in reducing ethnic tensions. The effects of sharp divisions based on religious, linguistic and regional differences are mitigated more by competitive democratic politics and increased prosperity than by the electoral system adopted by these countries. Whether a PR system would improve the situation in ethnically divided societies thus remains very much a matter of debate (Lardeyret, 1993; Lijphart, 1993). The unusual electoral system of Mauritius has been defended very recently on the grounds that 'It is, undoubtedly, an achievement that this 'adequate representation' has been made possible without the imposition of a Proportional Representation system which would probably have polarized the divisions along communal, caste and linguistic lines and thus rendering the process of nation building more difficult' (Dinan *et al.*, 1994: 43). As against this we have the phenomenon of a PR system being adopted by every one of the new democracies emerging from the collapse of the communist system in Central and Eastern Europe (Benoit-Rohmer and Hardeman, 1994: 91–111). Thus the debate goes on, and will continue.

An essential element of any such debate would be an examination of a recurrent theme in discussions on PR, namely its essential purpose. Is a PR system meant to reflect the ethnic and cultural divisions in society, or does its essence lie in the provision of incentives for co-operation in such divided societies? The current Western European and Scandinavian experience, save in the case of Germany, would appear to provide evidence of the operation of the latter as a principal factor. (Unlike most of the other states which have adopted PR, Germany is a homogeneous society.) There the PR system goes back to the days of the Weimar Republic during which the principal consideration was the secure establishment of a democratic tradition.

In other parts of the world, especially in post-colonial states of the former British Empire, such PR systems as exist often reflect the operation of the first principle: the need for an electoral system to reflect the ethnic and other divisions in society. Pre-Independence electoral systems in ethnically divided states – including states in which the division was based on religion – of the former British Empire generally incorporated the principle of communal representation. When a PR system was introduced in Sri Lanka, for instance, minority groups in the country regarded it as a substitute for the system of communal representation which operated up to 1931. Although there is no specific reservation of seats for ethnic or religious communities the distribution of population is such that the reflection of the ethnic and religious profile of the country is an important consideration.

The PR system of the post-colonial states of Central and Eastern Europe generally reflect the operation of the first principle. Nevertheless, there is also an obvious anxiety that the PR system should help to establish firm democratic principles of government through co-operation across ideological and ethnic/religious divisions.

CASE STUDIES

The discussion in this part of the present chapter deals with electoral systems in ethnically divided societies. In some of these – Sri Lanka, for example – rivalries and conflicts are largely between indigenous populations; while in others ethnic diversity has been complicated by the transfer of populations from outside, e.g. Indians and Chinese to Malaysia. The case studies chosen here range from Guyana and Trinidad and Tobago in the Caribbean and the South American coast, to Sri Lanka and Malaysia in South and South East Asia, and Fiji in the South Pacific. All of them are former colonies of the British empire. In all of them the debate on electoral systems as a means of mitigating or ameliorating ethnic conflict formed an integral part of the negotiations on the transfer of power. In all of them save Sri Lanka the electoral system introduced at the time of Independence has remained more or less intact. Guyana and Caribbean nations such as Trinidad and Tobago have accommodated immigrant communities in such large numbers that the immigrants are today the overwhelming majority of the population. But that majority is itself ethnically divided and the rivalries between them keep these societies in a state of tension, real or incipient, real in the case of Guyana and incipient in Trinidad and Tobago. The indigenous populations in these countries are now marginalized to the point of being minuscule minorities. In Fiji the indigenous population is now a bare majority, and its relations with the descendants of the immigrant Indians keep these islands in a state of acute tension. The electoral systems introduced range from weightage for minorities in the delimitation of electorates; reservations of seats for minorities in the national legislature; multi-member constituencies; to PR – in the case of Sri Lanka; and a complex system of electorates to bolster the indigenous population as in Fiji.

Sri Lanka

The first of our case studies is Sri Lanka. From 1931 to the present day Sri Lanka has adopted a whole range of electoral devices, culminating in PR in 1978. It has changed the structure of its democratic system from a parliamentary form (1947–8 to 1978) to an executive presidency (from 1978) and is now scheduled to revert to a parliamentary system. Almost all the changes were devised to cope with the conflicting demands of its diverse population at the time of Independence, and with episodes of violent conflict which began in the mid-1950s, and erupted again from the mid-1970s onwards.

We begin with the negotiations on the transfer, a unique case in British colonial history prior to the Second World War, where a colony seeking the status of an independent nation already had an electorate based on universal suffrage at the time of Independence. A detailed examination of electoral systems was an integral part of the transfer of power negotiations (Jennings, 1949: 33). The principal feature of the electoral system adopted on Jenning' recommendations was a structure based on South Africa's experience – weightage in favour of rural areas.[6] The advantages of such a scheme were many: it was acceptable to the majority Sinhalese because of its avoidance of communal representation; the sparsely populated areas, which were also the areas where the minorities were strongest, received increased representation, while the rural areas in which the Kandyan[7] section of the Sinhalese population was dominant, also benefited from increased representation; and there was also the added advantage that by reducing the size of the constituencies, the prospects of increased minority representation through constituencies which were not specifically communal could be ensured, and finally, it gave weightage to the backward areas of the country as against the more populous and prosperous areas. The actual distribution of seats was to be effected by an independent Delimitation Commission.

The Soulbury Commission, which drafted both the terms of the transfer of the power and the constitutional framework for it, approved this scheme. It also widened the discretion of the Delimitation Commission. The province was the unit adopted for demarcation of constituencies, and there were to be one constituency for each 75,000 of the population in each of the island's nine provinces, ascertained to the nearest 75,000 (Soulbury Report, 1945). The weightage came in the provision that there would be an additional constituency for every 1000 square miles of area. The weightage varied from a minimum of one in the densely populated Western Province to four each in the Northern Province with its largely Tamil population, the Eastern Province with its mixed (Tamil, Muslim, and Sinhalese) population and the North Central Province, a backward, sparsely populated Kandyan area.[8]

In addition there were to be six nominated members to represent minorities who could not secure election even under the weightage system. The Soulbury Commission made one other important recommendation, the creation of multi-member constituencies, in response to a suggestion made to the Commission that:

> minority representation would be strengthened by the creation of multi member constituencies on the ground that the only chance of representation for small communities depended on their concentrating all their strength on candidates of their own choice in a multi-member constituency.   (Soulbury Report, 1945)

It must be noted that the system of delimiting constituencies survived the supersession of the Soulbury Constitution in 1972, passing almost unchanged into the new constitutional structure of the first Republic (1972–8). At the end of every decade, a Delimination Commission was required to revise the constituency boundaries.[9]

One of the first political initiatives of the first post-Independence Sri Lankan government was a unilateral decision on the status of the Indian minority in the island. Negotiations on this in 1947 with Jawaharlal Nehru had collapsed. The Ceylon Citizenship Act No. 18 of 1948 restricted the status of a national of Sri Lanka to those who claimed it by descent or registration. Both involved a complex procedure, especially the latter. The application of these conditions to Indians in Sri Lanka was defined in The Indian and Pakistani Residents (Citizenship) Act No. 3 of 1949. The requirements were much the same that had been offered to Nehru in 1947. A third piece of legislation, The Ceylon (Parliamentary Elections) Amendment Act (No. 48 of 1949) removed the voters of Indian origin from the electoral rolls (Weiner, 1993: 1737–46). The immediate effect of all this was to distort the electoral balance even more markedly than before in favour of the rural Sinhalese and to make them the arbiters of the country's politics. With each fresh delimitation of constituencies thereafter that distortion became more pronounced (de Silva, 1981; Wilson, 1981).

Sri Lanka, the pioneer in the implementation of universal franchise in a pre-Independence colonial setting, became, in the 1980s, the pioneer in the transition from a 'first-past-the-post' electoral system to a form of PR. Elections to the national legislature for 46 years since the first general election of 1931 had been fought under the former system.

The system had developed two major drawbacks: first, there was the inevitable distortion in an electoral system from which a sizeable 'Indian' Tamil population was excluded because they had no votes. Thus the weightage given to an area and the calculation of seats according to the number of inhabitants benefited the Sinhalese majority to the disadvantage of the minorities. Second, after 1970 the winning party or coalition tended to get distorted majorities. In 1970 the SLFP and its allies with just 48.0 per cent of the vote obtained 76.7 per cent of the seats, while in 1977 the UNP with 50.9 per cent of the votes won 83 per cent of the seats. The eventual result of such large parliamentary majorities has been a weakened opposition. Thus in 1970 the UNP with 37.9 per cent of the vote gained only 11.3 per cent of the seats, and in 1977 the Sri Lanka Freedom Party with 29.7 per cent of the votes won only 4.8 per cent of the seats.

The second of these drawbacks rather than the first was the major factor in the decision to abandon the Westminster electoral system.[10] In the system as it was in the 1970s, with the Indian Tamils left out, and with the distribution of population in which the Tamil minority was concentrated into the north and to a lesser extent in the east of the island, elections could be, and indeed were, fought in the Sinhalese areas of the country with little or no consideration of minority views (save perhaps those of the Muslims).

The PR system incorporated in the 1978 constitution was the Hamilton Method, first proposed by Alexander Hamilton in 1792, and was also known as the method of the Largest Remainder. Under this system the whole country was divided into a number of multi-member electoral districts by a Delimitation Commission appointed by the President of the Republic from among persons not actively engaged in politics. The Delimitation Commission divided the country into 22 electoral districts, of which 21 coincided with existing administrative districts, and one consisted of three administrative districts.[11]

The constitution lays down that the total number of seats in Parliament shall be 196 and 36 of them are so distributed that each province has four. The Delimitation Commission was also charged with the function of distributing the rest of the seats equitably among the electoral districts. Neither the distribution so made nor the boundaries of these electoral districts can be altered save by constitutional amendment.

The Hamilton Method is used for the apportionment of the remaining 160 seats. At every election these seats are reapportioned among electoral districts according to the electoral register used for the election in question. The total number of qualified voters (or electors) is determined, and this total is divided by 160. The result is brought to the next higher integer and forms what is known as the qualifying number of electors. Every electoral district is entitled to one member for each qualifying number of electors registered for the district.

One feature of the Sri Lanka PR system that came in for considerable criticism was the requirement that a party or group seeking election through an electoral district had to secure a minimum of 12.5 per cent of the poll in an electoral district. This was regarded as too high and has since been reduced to 5 per cent (Mauzy, 1993: 112–13).

We need to look at the change to PR in terms of ethnic divisions in the island. With the 1978 constitution there came a change in the system of allocating seats on an area basis; each of the nine provinces now received four seats. The old system (1947–77) had given the Tamils of the north and east a significant if gradually declining weightage on an 'area' basis. Of the 25 'area' seats, the Northern and Eastern Provinces had eight; under PR they still had eight but it was eight out of 36. Nevertheless because of a vitally important change in determining the voting strength of electoral districts, from 'population' to 'registered electors', the advantages hitherto enjoyed by the Sinhalese rural voter since the general election of 1952 were substantially reduced. The stateless Indian Tamils and those who have opted for Indian citizenship were no longer counted as part of the population for the demarcation of electoral districts. One result was that the minorities in the north and east were slightly better off in the number of legislators they could elect, but more importantly the prospects of members of minority groups in the Sinhalese areas, both Tamils and Muslims, securing election to parliament improved substantially, especially that of the Muslims.

There are other advantages stemming from the operation of PR. A repetition of the distorted majorities gained by the victorious parties at the general elections of 1970 and 1977, majorities which deprived the minorities and the Tamils in particular of any prospect of acting as a balancing force in Parliament, will almost certainly not be repeated under the new system. The operation of PR – as seen in the parliamentary elections of 1989 and 1994 – has eliminated distortions of this sort. And the representatives of ethnic minorities, especially the Indians and the Muslims, are already in a stronger bargaining position than they were at any time since the 1960s. PR is potentially an effective safeguard against the amendment of the constitution without due regard being paid to the interests of the minorities.

Even more important than PR for its implications for ethnic relations in the island is the new system of direct election of the executive President of the country. The election is on the basis of a single transferable vote system under which if no candidate secures 50 per cent of the votes, all other than the first and second in terms of the votes secured are eliminated and the second and third preferences of the votes polled by them go to the first two in the list. In the presidential elections of 1982, 1988 and 1994 the winning candidates secured a clear majority, but should the election, at some future occasion, be determined by the second and third preferences the minorities could determine the fate of the rival Sinhalese parties far more decisively than in the past. It had become increasingly evident in the general elections since the mid-1950s that there was little or no disadvantage in a subtle or even blatant anti-Tamil campaign in the Sinhalese areas; indeed previous elections were won or lost in the Sinhalese areas, and the major parties could ignore the north of the island. This situation has changed since the 1980s, and the experience of the two presidential elections held so far shows that no party or individual aiming at the presidency could afford to alienate the minorities, or fail to campaign in the Tamil areas of the north and east, as well as among the Indian plantation workers and the Muslims and Roman Catholics.

The Sri Lankan experiment with PR has one other unusual feature, the introduction of PR to local government elections at all levels – from village councils, urban councils and municipalities, to District Councils (from 1981 until their supersession in 1987) and Provincial Councils. From the experience gained in these elections the mechanics of the PR system in which the parties effectively determined the composition of the slate in rank order, a change was made to give voters three votes each, which could be used on behalf of three candidates on a party list. The voter had to choose one party list in preference to another or others, but within that list could determine the fate of individual members. This change, first used in local government elections, was introduced in elections, to the national legislature as well at the general election of February 1989. Currently the Sri Lankan legislature is reviewing the PR system, and there is considerable pressure for the introduction of a version of the mixed-member PR system that prevails in Germany.

Malaysia

When the focus shifts from Sri Lanka to Malaysia we see a change from a record of experimentation and reform in electoral systems, and forms of governmental authority, to one in which the key factor is the retention of the structures established at the transfer of power: federal, monarchical and parliamentary forms of government, as well as an electoral system based on the first-past-the-post system of constituencies. For Malaysia (or Malaya as it was before Independence) the time of troubles started before Independence, not after (with the single exception of the riots of 1969), as was the case in Sri Lanka. It began, of course with the Japanese invasion and Japanese rule in the 1940s, and was followed after the defeat of Japan and the re-establishment of colonial rule with the long years of the Chinese-led communist insurgency. Like Sri Lanka, Malaysia is a multi-ethnic society in which the component elements of ethnicity increased under colonial rule with the immigration of Chinese and Indians. At Independence the Malays, unlike the Sinhalese, formed only a bare majority. As in Sri Lanka, so in Malaysia, one of the principal issues that came up for discussion and settlement prior to the transfer of power was the question of the citizenship rights of immigrants, Chinese and Indians in this instance, and not merely Indians as in Sri Lanka.

After the Second World War the British introduced the concept of federal citizenship as part of its proposal to establish a Malayan Union. This was to be a change from a system in which persons in the various Malay states were subjects of the rulers of these states while those who lived in the Straits settlements were British, to one in which they all had a common British citizenship.

The Malayan Union concept was strongly opposed by the Malays who feared that they would be submerged by the non-Malays. Their opposition to the Malayan Union proposal and the citizenship provisions was so great that the British government felt constrained to abandon these. In their place the Federation of Malaya Agreement of 1948 was adopted. The citizenship regulations in this agreement were later incorporated with only minor alterations in the 1957 Malayan Independence constitution and the post-Independence constitution of 1963. Nevertheless the citizenship question has remained a divisive issue in Malaysian politics – the Malays resenting the grant of citizenship to the non-Malays and the latter seeking even more relaxed conditions for acquiring citizenship (Rachagan, 1978: 253–93).

Universal suffrage and a common register for all communities were introduced in 1955 two years prior to Independence, on the recommendations of an Election Committee appointed in 1954. That Committee did consider proposals for communal rolls and communal electorates, but rejected these in favour of a common roll. Following on the recommendations of this Committee the 1957 and 1963 constitutions decided in favour of territorial rather than communal electorates. The latter were rejected because it was felt that they would strengthen communal feeling and act as formidable constraints to the objective of national integration (Rachagan, 1978: 261–63).

The electoral system devised in 1954 was modelled on the British prototype, i.e. the Anglo-American first-past-the-post system based on single-member territorial constituencies with a common electoral vote. The committee did consider the possibility of a PR system, but rejected it because it feared that it could result in a multiplicity of small parties and intrinsically unstable coalition governments that would shy away from the introduction of long-term policies or radical but necessary measures which sections of such a coalition would not support. Ironically enough, since 1957, the Malaysian governments have been coalitions, but pre-election coalitions rather than coalitions necessitated by the results of an election. The committee of 1954 did concede that the electoral system they recommended would tend to benefit large parties and thereby compromise the principle of fair representation, but this disadvantage was seen as less consequential than the problems that could stem from a large number of small parties attempting to form a coalition government (Rachagan, 1978: 256–7).

In Malaysia as elsewhere the effect of the first-past-the-post system has been to exaggerate the relative strength of the ruling coalition, the Alliance Party and its successor, the Barisan National. Except in the first election in 1955 the Alliance's share of votes never reached two-thirds of the votes polled, and in the 1969 election its share dropped to less than half 48.6 per cent. But in every instance save 1969 when it dropped to 63.5 per cent its share of seats in the legislature was well over the two-thirds mark. Opposition politicians have often urged the introduction of some form of PR, in particular the system in operation in the Federal German Republic, in order to make the government reflect more genuinely the views of the electorate (Rachagan, 1978: 257–61).

Following the British practice the delimitation of constitutions has been assigned to an independent commission. Originally assigned to the Election Commission, these powers on delimiting constituencies were withdrawn in 1962, when the Alliance Government found the Commission's 1960 delimitation of constituencies unsatisfactory. Thereafter the Commission could merely recommend changes, and Parliament, which in effect meant the government, became the final arbiter of any delimitation proposals. These new provisions were incorporated into the Malaysian constitution of 1963. Here we need to note the contrast with Sri Lanka, where the recommendations of a Delimitation Commission are binding on the government.

The Malaysian experience is often treated as evidence that the first-past-the-post single-member constituency system is conducive to long-term economic growth and political stability and the amelioration of ethnic tensions. While it is true that Malaysia as an ethnically divided country has avoided conflict since 1969, this has less to do with the electoral system than to a strongly held belief in political circles that the government's electoral victory is inadequate unless it secures the two-thirds of the seats in Parliament that would enable it to amend the constitution if that were seen to be necessary. To achieve such a margin of victory, the political support of Chinese voters is absolutely essential for the Malay political leadership within the government. It is purely a matter of coincidence that this exercise in political manipulation has been successfully pursued under the existing first-past-the-post system. A PR system could serve this purpose just as effectively.

It must be remembered that the Malaysian constitution does not state that a two-thirds majority in parliament is needed to change or amend it. But the dominant Malay group regards this ability to change the constitution through a two-thirds majority as vital to the perpetuation of their political dominance. From their point of view a two-thirds majority affords them a security they regard as essential to meet any threat posed to their interests at some future date. Despite the entrenchment of Malay dominance in the country's constitution, the non-Malays themselves believe that the same constitution protects their vital interests and they themselves have a stake in maintaining the system.

The Malaysian voters themselves appear to accept this need for the government to secure a two-thirds majority in Parliament. On the one occasion – May 1969 – when the Alliance fell short of this, the political system very nearly crumbled in the face of political tensions and communal rioting, although the Alliance did have a secure majority.

Since the Malays are unlikely to obtain a two-thirds majority on their own, it is essential for them to work hard to ensure that their non-Malay coalition partners are elected. And it is in the interest of UMNO, the dominant Malay component of the Alliance Party (the others being the MCA (Chinese) and MIC (Indian)) to secure non-Malay support in as many constituencies as possible because the latter often constitute swing votes when UMNO is seriously challenged by its rivals. Because of a significant difference in the geographical distribution of minority groups within the country in Malaysia, in contrast to Sri Lanka, the non-Malay vote is more important to UMNO than the vote in the north of the country was to the Sinhalese under the first-past-the-post system which prevailed in Sri Lanka until 1977. Although Malay-majority constituencies are slightly less than 100 out of 133 in Peninsular Malaya and currently 180 in the nation overall, including Sabah and Sarawak, the number of mixed electoral constituencies are almost certain to increase with every future delimitation, and with that the need for non-Malay votes for UMNO's continued dominance of Malaysian politics. While it is possible that Malay-based parties may resort to even more strident ethnic appeals than be concerned about non-Malay voters, nevertheless the presence of the non-Malay minority in an increasing number of constituencies may act as some kind of restraint on UMNO and its rival Malay-based parties. Non-Malays in the ruling coalition have a similar inducement to racial moderation. In many of the constituencies with a non-Malay majority there is a substantial Malay vote – generally in the range 33–40 per cent (where the non-Malay percentage is very high, say 60 per cent or more, non-Malay parties could win without the Malay vote, but such constituencies are few in number). The fact is that non-Malay candidates generally do not win many Malay votes on their own. As a result the non-Malay candidate supported by the governing coalition is at an advantage in that a very substantial proportion of these Malay votes would be available to him. In such circumstances he does not need the majority of the non-Malay vote to win the seat.

There are many reasons for the relatively peaceful operation of the Malaysian political system. Among the most important of these is the existence of a bargain between the two principal ethnic groups in the country, Malays and the Chinese. This bargain is more implicit than explicit, but it acts as a powerful restraining influence on both. Its basic principle is that the Malays would treat the Chinese economic interests as the engine of the national economy, and agree to absorb the young Chinese into the political system, while the Chinese, for their part, would accept Malay political dominance and an increasing share for the Malays in the economic life of the country in return (Mauzy, 1993: 112–3). The origins of this bargain go back virtually to the time of Independence, and while it has been reinterpreted particularly after May 1969, this bargain has lasted to the present day. Malaysia's electoral and parliamentary system which encourages multi-racial co-operation, particularly among the racially based component parties of the ruling coalition is a second factor, while the rapid expansion of the economic wealth of the country is the third. In addition – and this is the fourth factor – there is the structure of race relations in Malaysia, which also acts as a restraint against any abandonment of the bargain. Generally, the third factor, the nearly continuous economic growth and development of the country since 1957 has been emphasized more than the others. Undoubtedly, this has given the ruling coalition greater leeway in keeping all ethnic groups more or less satisfied with their lot (Ali, 1991: 96–118; Goh, 1991: 74–95). Even so, the demographic pattern of the country with its almost even balance[12] between the Malays and non-Malays at the time of Independence has also contributed substantially to the maintenance of this political bargain and has acted as a powerful deterrent to any radical attempt to change the ethnic composition of the ruling Alliance for fear of the possible devastating consequences of a national racial conflagration. This point the ruling Alliance has always emphasized in its appeal to the electorate just before elections. By and large the electorate seems to endorse the argument.

Then again there is the geographical distribution of the population. While there is a greater ethnic mix than in Sri Lanka, for instance, there is also no large territory with a non-Malay or Chinese majority. The nearest to such a situation is the island of Penang (a state in the federation) where there is a Chinese majority. But there is a general recognition that an independent Penang is not a viable proposition and there has been no serious attempt at establishing a Chinese 'homeland' based on Penang. The federal nature of the Malaysian political system and the readiness of the Alliance to let a non-Malay coalition party dominate the state legislature in Penang have also helped to abate Chinese resentment of the relative lack of political influence in the centre.

Guyana and Trinidad and Tobago

Our concern here is with the political consequences of the demographic transformation that occurred in some of the Caribbean islands and states off the coasts of South America in the same region from the transfer of people from Africa as slaves to work on the plantations, and subsequently the transfer of people, in the beginning almost entirely males, from the territories the British ruled or controlled in the Indian subcontinent to British colonies in other parts of the world. The second of these movements was a process governed almost entirely by economic considerations, a response to the operation of market forces, the demand for a reliable supply of labour in British owned sugar and other plantations in the wake of the abolition of slavery.

The push of poverty and the pull of opportunity resulted in a massive change in the ethnic composition of many of these receiving territories. This same combination of forces, poverty at home and opportunity in the plantations overseas, converted what was intended to be no more than a temporary period of service into semi-permanent and, later on, permanent residence. The indenture system[13] as this was called lasted several decades and operated in regard to every colonial territory to which Indian workers were sent, with the exception of Sri Lanka where the distances to be traversed were short enough for more informal methods of recruitment to be used. There were, on the whole, two main regional centres of labour recruitment in India. One, and perhaps the bigger of the two, was the Madras Presidency; and the other was Bihar. The vast majority of the Indians transferred overseas under the indenture system never went back. They settled in the host territories.

When the colonial empire was moving towards self-government in the 1950s and 1960s, the sugar colonies in the Caribbean and the South American coast, no less than in the Indian ocean, tended to lag behind. In almost all of them the Indian population was either a dominant majority (Mauritius), a clear majority (in Guyana) or a substantial minority (Trinidad). Trinidad and Tobago, where the Indians then were well short of a majority, was the first to gain Independence (in 1962). The electoral system introduced was an uncomplicated first-past-the-post form of territorial constituencies with no communal roll. The distribution of population in the two islands was such that the people of African descent gained a majority in the national legislature and retained it till the general election of November 1995, when the Indians secured a bare majority.

In Guyana the situation was more complicated because the political leadership of the nationalist movement was dominated by a leftist political group under a dual leadership of Dr Cheddi Jagan, an Indian, and regarded as a Marxist, and a Creole, Forbes Burnham. The People's Progressive Party they led was formed in 1950: it won the general election of 1953, the first under universal suffrage, sweeping to power with a two-thirds majority in the colonial legislature. The new government held office for less than six months. It was toppled from office by the British government, with the active support of the government, which did not wish to see a left-wing regime in power in South America. Soon the party split in two, one section under Jagan and the other under Burnham, whom the Colonial Office and the United States saw as a moderate politician and one who could be trusted to keep the radicals out of power. Nevertheless at the 1961 elections too Jagan's party won a clear majority (nearly 57 per cent of the seats) under the prevailing first-past-the-post system while Burnham's People's National Congress could secure only 31 per cent.

At this point it was decided that future elections would take place under a PR system. At the elections of 1964, the PPP won 46 per cent of the votes while Burnham's share was 40 per cent, and a third group – mainly supported by the Amerindians of the interior – received 12 per cent. The distribution of seats was as follows: PPP 24 seats; PNC 22, and the third group seven seats. Burnham was installed as Premier, and controlled the government when Independence came in 1966.

In power Burnham manipulated the PR system further by granting the vote to Guyanese residents overseas (in the United States, Britain and elsewhere in the Caribbean). Over one third of Guyana's population lived overseas, and the ethnic divide in the home country – Africans and Indians – was also reflected overseas. Burnham retained power till his death and his party controlled the government till 1993, when a general election gave Jagan the chance to take power as Prime Minister after nearly three decades in opposition.

The Guyanese experiment in PR is a unique case, a PR system devised to keep a majority out of power. It did succeed in doing so for over 30 years, until the regime it was designed to help eventually collapsed as a result of catastrophic economic decline and the decay of political institutions. PR was introduced at a time of ethnic conflict of near civil war proportions (1963–4) but far from ameliorating ethnic tensions it did little to encourage ethnic accommodation in Guyana (Milne, 1981; Premdas, 1992).

Fiji

The transfer of power negotiations in Malaya and Fiji had one common feature: in both a concerted attempt was made to protect and consolidate the political dominance of the indigenous leadership as against immigrants. It was easier to do this in Malaya because the Malay population was a clear majority in the country and the Chinese, who were a dominant minority, were nowhere near overtaking the Malays in numbers; in Fiji the Indians were already close to being a majority. Thus a complex electoral system was devised to protect and guarantee the political dominance of the Fijian leadership.

The roots of Fiji's current crisis go back to the year 1874 when the islands were annexed by the British under Governor Sir Arthur Gordon, through a deed of cession which, over the years, assumed the status of a fundamental document protecting not merely the rights of the indigenous population, but embodying a doctrine of Fijian paramountcy. In the same year Gordon took the decision to bring in Indian indentured labour to work on Fiji plantations. This was intended to be a means of preserving the integrity of Fijian villages and to shelter the Fijians from white exploitation, in contrast to the role of Indian plantation workers in Guyana who were used as the planters' weapon in a emerging class struggle with Africans (Norton, 1981: 314).

The assumption on which indentured labour was brought in was that they would eventually go back whence they came. In practice this had not happened in any of the countries to which Indian indentured labour had been brought, and Fiji did not prove to be an exception. On the contrary the Indians stayed and their population grew. By 1946 they had surpassed the native Fijians in numbers, and within 20 years of that they were a clear majority of the whole population.

As in other British colonies an electoral system based on nomination by community and a limited franchise came before Independence, and long before universal franchise. There were two nominated Fijians in the legislature (out of 18 members, the rest of whom were European). In 1916 Indians were granted one member in a new and enlarged council. But 'native' and Indian representation continued to be on the basis of nomination by community. The Indians, however, raised the question of a 'common roll', i.e. election on a non-communal basis. This has remained one of the principal demands of the Fijian Indians. Once Indians became a majority of the population – and even earlier – this demand was seen as an attempt at Indian domination in Fiji. The response to this was a Fijian assertion of 'paramountcy' described by a recent scholar as 'an assertion of Fijian political pre-eminence' (Premdas, 1992).

In the early 1960s political change came rapidly to Fiji. Universal suffrage was introduced in 1963, and for the first time Fijians were allowed to elect their representatives. In 1966 a new legislative council with an elected majority and semi-responsible government was installed, prior to a transfer of power. The Fijians, however, were reluctant to press for Independence for fear that they would lose out to the Indians. It took an unexpected but decisive victory for the Fijian-dominated Alliance Party at the elections of 1966 to bring the Fijians around to accepting the inevitability of Independence.

A new constitution was required for Fijian Independence and negotiations conducted between August 1969 and March 1970, under British mediation, sought to reach an understanding as a means of reconciling the Indian insistence on a common electoral roll with Fijian claims for 'paramountcy'. A compromise was reached under which the two sides agreed that some time between the first and second elections after Independence a Royal Commission would be appointed to examine these conflicting issues of a common roll and a communal roll. In the meantime a complex electoral system embodying elements of both but with a greater emphasis on the communal roll was established. The core of the system was the principle of a parity of seats in the legislature under which the Fijians and Fijian-Indians would have 22 seats each, while the others – general electors as they were called – would have eight. Twenty-seven seats would be elected exclusively by each race or group, and 25 seats on a system of cross-communal voting. Under this system each voter was given four votes; but no matter which party formed the government, the ethnic composition of the legislature remained fixed. The cross-communal voting was expected to lead the way to a common roll in the future. As regards the Fijian claim for 'paramountcy' the Indian-dominated National Federation Party agreed that additional 'weightage' be given to Fijian interests through a second chamber, the Senate.

In the Senate there was a clear and entrenched Fijian majority. The entrenchment was given greater emphasis by requiring the consent of the Fijian Great Council of Chiefs to any changes in matters relating to Fijian land and custom. This was done by a provision that a two-thirds majority in each chamber was required for altering the constitution. Since the Fijian Great Council of Chiefs had 8 of 22 seats in the Senate, it had the capacity on its own to block any constitutional change that it did not approve.

While it was hoped that a new electoral system would have been introduced by 1975, the Fijian-dominated government was vehemently opposed to the changes in the representational system recommended by the Royal Commission appointed under the terms of the 1970 agreement. As a result the political bargain of 1970 collapsed, and both parties to the deal had a sense of grievance, the Fijians because the changes envisaged by the Commission were seen to threaten the political dominance the Fijians sought, and the Indians because the rejection of the recommendations of the Commission meant that there was less prospect than ever before of establishing an electoral system based essentially on a common roll. And then there was the problem of land 'seen as a scarce resource and competition for it ... regarded in ethnic terms. The symbolic significance makes it more than just an ordinary issue' (Milne, 1981: 65).

The results of the election of March–April 1977 came as a shock to the Fijians. Because of divisions within their ranks an Indian-dominated government won a narrow victory. But it could not consolidate its position, and another election in September 1977 gave the Fijian-dominated Alliance Party an overwhelming victory, this time because of divisions in the ranks of the Indian-based National Federation Party. Attempts at establishing a government of national unity failed. In 1982 the Alliance Party managed to retain power, but in 1987 it was defeated as a result of a fundamental change in Fijian politics, a coalition between the Federation Party and the newly formed Labour Party. The latter caused a small shift in the Fijian vote, enough to give the new coalition a narrow victory.

Soon thereafter the Fijian-dominated Royal Fijian Armed Forces overthrew the newly elected government, and imposed a new constitution, the central feature of which was a consolidation of Fijian political paramountcy. The structure of the electoral system remained as it was in 1970, but with the difference that in both houses of Parliament Fijian domination was entrenched much more securely than in 1970. It was an unilateral shift from the principle of an ethnic balance to one of unmistakable Fijian hegemony.

Under the new constitution Fijian representation in the House of Representatives would increase to 53.6 per cent while that of the Indians would drop from 42.5 per cent to 39.1 per cent. The reduction in the representation of the General Electors was even more marked: it fell from 15 per cent to 4 per cent. It was argued that with a rapid depletion of the Indian population through emigration,[14] Fijians would soon become more than half the population, thus justifying the allocation of 53.6 per cent of the seats to them. The Prime Minister would be elected by the House of Representatives, and it was laid down that he or she must be a Fijian, while Fiji was declared a Christian state.

In the Senate, the Fijians numbered at least 24 out of 35, or 68 per cent. The President of Fiji had the right to appoint nine 'prominent citizens'. The net result is that the Indians will be only marginally present in the Senate. Unlike the Prime Minister who is elected by the House of Representatives, the President is appointed by the Great Council of Chiefs. Thus the Head of State too is almost certain to be a Fijian. The new constitution confers on chiefs a vitally important role in the making of the Presidency, in protecting Fijian lands and customs, and in influencing appointments to the Public Service and Police Service Commission. To Fijians, the issue that appeared to concern them most was the prospect of domination by an Indian population whom they saw as outsiders if not intruders. As a recent scholar explains, they saw Indian political pre-eminence as the means to their subjugation in their own land and their permanent marginalization akin to the fate of other indigenous populations in the world. Hence they supported the military coup that enshrined their paramountcy in the new constitutional order: they argue that it is intended to prevent their culture and community from being marginalized in the manner experienced by the Maoris in New Zealand, the Aborigines in Australia and native people in North America. The reality of an ethnic seizure of power by the Fijian nationalists came in the wake of the breakdown of a formula for inter-ethnic accommodation (Premdas, 1992).

This brief survey of the Fijian crisis and that nation's electoral system brings us to the point that the latter is unusual in the survival of a form of communal voting which has virtually disappeared throughout the democratic world except in so far as the protection of small minorities is concerned, such as the Maoris in New Zealand. Communal representation of this sort, through separate seats or electorates, still survives in India and Pakistan. In Pakistan there are both separate electoral registers and seats for minorities such as the Hindus, the Christians, the Parsees and even the Ahmadhiya sect, while in India in an effort to provide representation to groups such as the Anglo-Indians and to redress the position of the so-called scheduled castes and the tribals, a system of reservation of a prescribed number of seats in Parliament and through nomination in the state assemblies has been made. These electorates are, however, mixed and not confined to members of the scheduled castes or tribes.

CONCLUSION

Our review of electoral systems in ethnically diverse societies has taken us from industrialized Western nations to poorer countries around the world which have attained Independence in the last four decades or so. In all societies questions relating to the suffrage and electoral systems are essentially debates on the exercise and manipulation of political power. Our principal concern has been with the utility of electoral systems – majority/plurality and PR – in mitigating tensions in ethnically divided societies or in the maintenance of a measure of stability in situations of incipient or actual violence. The fact is that elections have a multiplicity of roles in a poly-ethnic state and as a result there is no simple answer to the question that has concerned us most in this chapter, the identification of the most appropriate electoral system for the maintenance of harmony in such societies. Electoral systems on their own are inadequate for this purpose unless they are linked to a democratic ethos and a political system based on regularly conducted, peaceful competitive politics. An expanding economy and the spread of prosperity, throughout all sectors of the population, will help, but one cannot lay too much stress on this because prosperity is just as likely to aggravate tensions as it is to assuage them. In any event there are as many examples of PR systems helping to mitigate the effects of ethnic dissonance as there are of PR systems which have conspicuously failed to do so. This is also true of the first-past-the-post electoral systems modelled on Anglo-American practice. Thus the search for, and the debate on, the most appropriate, if not the ideal, electoral system for maintaining ethnic harmony will continue for years to come.

ACKNOWLEDGEMENT

The author wishes to gratefully acknowledge the assistance of Professors Crawford Young and A.J. Wilson in the preparation of this essay. In addition Ms Lynn Daniel, editor of the *Far East And Australasia* (published by Europa Publications Ltd, London) generously provided information on New Zealand's preparation for the change to a PR system in 1996.

NOTES

1. In some of the Australian colonies, New South Wales for instance, agitation for the lowering of the qualifications for the franchise, distribution of seats in representative assemblies on the basis of population, and for voting by secret ballot arose as early as 1848–9. In Victoria, property qualifications for members of the Assembly were abolished in 1857, and in November that year manhood suffrage was conceded.

2. As early as the 1860s special seats were introduced for Maoris in the New Zealand legislatures.

3. The secret (or 'Australian') ballot was adopted in New Zealand in 1869, and manhood suffrage in 1879. In 1889 plural voting was abolished, although property owners could still register in several electorates and chose where to vote. In 1893 this privilege was abolished. In 1893 women were enfranchised. The crucial landmark in this democratization of the electorate was the victory of the New Zealand Liberal Party in the general election of 1890.

4. Under article 99 of the Constitution of 1978 there was a requirement of a poll of 12.5 per cent of the votes cast in an electoral district to qualify a party or independent group to a seat in the legislature. The 15th amendment to the constitution sec. 4(1) substituted for this the requirement of 5per cent of the total vote in an electoral district.

5. General Zia ul Haq advocated the introduction of PR on the list system in 1979 for the elections scheduled for that year. Once the elections were postponed the scheme was abandoned. In early January 1993, President Ghulam Ishaq Khan came out in favour of PR on the list system with Germany as the model.

6. The Jennings Mss (Institute of Commonwealth Studies, University of London); W. I. Jennings, *The Road to Peradeniya* (typescript of his autobiography) (n.d.) The reference is at p. 134.

7. A section of the majority Sinhalese population resident in the central hills of the island, and the north-western and north central plains which formed part of the Kandyan kingdom, the last of the independent kingdoms of the island. It was ceded to the British in 1815.

8. This was increased in 1975 to 90,000 under the first amendment to the constitution of the First Republic.

9. Only two delimitations were held between 1947 and 1977. These were in 1959 and 1976. A constitutional amendment of 1959 limited the discretion of the Delimitation Commission in respect of the creation of multi-member constituencies by specifying that such constituencies could be created only if the composition of the population in a province was such that it was possible to provide for the representation of a minority racial group there. This could be Sinhala, Tamil or Muslim. Thus, after 1959 it was not possible to consider the creation of multi-member constituencies to provide for representation for religious minorities or caste groups.

10. See *Parliamentary series No.14 of the Second National State Assembly, Report from the Select Committee of the National State Assembly appointed to consider revision of the Constitution*, (The Government Press, Colombo, 1978), p. 214.

11. This high cut-off point was criticized as one that placed small parties at too great a disadvantage. The government's intention quite clearly was to discourage the proliferation of small parties, one of the problems associated with PR. The 12.5 per cent margin was the same as the vote required of all candidates under the first-past-the-post system in order to secure a return of the monetary deposit they had to pay to enter the contest.

12. At the moment Malaysia's population of 17 million is composed of 58 per cent Malays, 32 per cent Chinese, 8 per cent Indians, Kadazans, Ibans and other indigenous groups.

13. An indenture was generally a contract in which the costs of transport to the colony requiring the services of an immigrant would be borne by the recruiting agent, in return for a specified term of service, generally two or three years, after which the migrants could go back home on a passage provided by the contractor.

14. By 1989 the number of Indians in Fiji had fallen below the level of the Fijians – 46.4 per cent to 48.4 per cent. Given the current political situation in Fiji, the chances are that this decline in the number of Indians would continue and the Fijians would soon become a clear majority in the country.

REFERENCES

Ali, S. Hussein, 1991. 'Development, Social Stratification and Ethnic Relations. The Malaysian Case'. In S.W.R. de A. Samarasinghe and Reed Coughlin (eds.), *Economic Dimensions of Ethnic Conflict: International Perspectives*. London: Pinter Publishers.

Benoit-Rohmer, Florence and Hilde Hardeman, 1994. 'The Representation of Minorities in the Parliaments of Central and Eastern Europe', *International Journal on Group Rights*, 2, 2: 95–111.

Blake, Robert, 1978. *Disraeli*. London: Methuen.

Ceylon: Report of the Commission on Constitutional Reform, 1945. Cmd 7667, Colonial Office. London: HMSO (The Soulbury Report).

Ceylon: Report of the Special Commission on the Constitution. 1928. Cmd 3131. London: H M Stationery Office (The Donoughmore Report).

Coakley, John (ed.), 1993. *The Territorial Management of Ethnic Conflict*. London: Frank Cass.

Cobban, Helena, 1985. *The Making of Modern Lebanon*. London: Hutchinson.

Coupland, R., 1944. *The Constitutional Problem in India* (in three parts). Delhi: Oxford University Press.

Covell, Maureen, 1981. 'Ethnic Conflict and Elite Bargaining: The Case of Belgium', *West European Politics*, 4, 3: 197–218.

———1993. 'Belgium: The Variability of Ethnic Relations'. In John McGarry and Brendan O'Leary (eds.), *The Politics of Ethnic Conflict Regulation*. London: Routledge.

Crouch, Harold, Lee Kiam Hing and Michael Ong (eds.), 1978. *Malaysian Politics and the 1978 Election*. Kuala Lumpur: Oxford University Press.

de Silva, C.R., 1981. 'The Electoral System, 1947-1978: An Overview'. In K. M. de Silva (ed.), *Universal Franchise, 1931–1981: The Sri Lankan Experience*. Colombo: Government Press.

de Silva, C.R. and S.W.R.de A Samarasinghe, 1980. 'Which PR? A Critical Examination of the System of Proportional Representation Adopted in the 1978 Constitution of Sri Lanka'. In *Preliminary Documents: Seminar on Parliamentary Process in Sri Lanka*. Colombo: Marga Institute.

Diamond, Larry and Marc F. Plattner (eds.), 1993. *The Global Resurgence of Democracy*. Baltimore: Johns Hopkins University Press.

Dinan, Monique *et al.*, 1994. 'Mauritius Country Paper'. Presented at the United Nations Research Institute for Social Development, Conference on Ethnic Diversity and Public Policies, New York, 17–19 August.

Dobbin, Christine E. (ed.), 1985. *Basic Documents in the Development of Modern India and Pakistan, 1835-1947*. London: Van Nostrand Reinhold Co.

Goh Ban Lee, 1991. 'Restructuring Society in Malaysia: Its Impacts on Employment and Investment'. In S. W. R. de A. Samarasinghe and Reed Coughlan (eds.), *Economic Dimensions of Ethnic Conflict: International Perspectives*. London: Pinter Publishers.

Hintzen, P.C., 1989. *The Costs of Regime Survival: Racial Mobilization, Elite Domination and Control of the State in Guyana and Trinidad*. Cambridge: Cambridge University Press.

Hooghe, Liesbet, 1993. 'Belgium: From Regionalism to Federalism'. In John Coakley (ed.), *The Territorial Management of Ethnic Conflict*. London: Frank Cass.

Horowitz, Donald R., 1985. *Ethnic Groups in Conflic*. Berkeley: University of California Press.

—— 1991. *A Democratic South Africa, Constitutional Engineering in a Divided Society*. Berkeley: University of California Press.

Jennings, W.I., 1949. *The Constitution of Ceylon*. Delhi: Oxford University Press.

Kohn, Walter S.G., 1980. *Governments and Politics of the German-Speaking Countries*. Chicago: Chicago University Press.

Lardeyret, Guy, 1993. 'The Problem with PR'. In Larry Diamond and Marc F. Plattner (eds.), *The Global Resurgence of Democracy*. Baltimore: Johns Hopkins University Press.

Lijphart, Arend, 1980. *Democracy in Plural Societies*. New Haven: Yale University Press.

—— 1993. 'Constitutional Choices for New Democracies', and 'Double Checking the Evidence'. In Larry Diamond and Marc F Plattner (eds.), *The Global Resurgence of Democracy*. Baltimore: Johns Hopkins University Press.

—— 1994. *Electoral Systems and Party Systems*. New York: Oxford University Press.

Madsen, Hendrik, 1987. *Policy and Politics in Sweden: Principled Pragmatism*. Philadelphia.

Mauzy, Diane, 1993. 'Malaysia: Malay Political Hegemony and Coercive Consociationalism'. In John McGarry and Brendan O'Leary (eds.), *The Politics of Ethnic Conflict Regulation*. London: Routledge.

McGarry, John and Brendan O'Leary (eds.), 1994. *The Politics of Ethnic Conflict Regulation*. London: Routledge.

McRae, K., 1986. *Conflict and Compromise in Multi-lingual Societies, Belgium*. Waterloo: Wilfred Laurier Press.

Milne, R.S., 1981. *Politics in Ethnically Bipolar States: Guyana, Malaysia and Fiji*. Vancouver: University of British Columbia Press.

Mittelman, James H., 1975. *Ideology and Politics in Uganda: From Obote to Amin*. Ithaca: Cornell University Press.

Norton, Robert, 1981. 'The Mediation of Ethnic Conflict: Comparative Implications of the Fiji Case', *Journal of Commonwealth and Comparative Politics*, 19, 3 (November): 309–328.

Pelling, Henry, 1967. *The Social Geography of British Elections*. London: Macmillan.

Phillips, C.H. (ed.), 1962. *The Evolution of India and Pakistan, 1947–1958*. London: Oxford University Press.

Premdas, R., 1992. *Ethnic Conflict and Development: The Case of Guyana*. Geneva: United Nations Research Institute for Social Development.

—— 1994. 'Balance and Conflict in Fiji'. In John McGarry and Brendan O'Leary (eds.), *The Politics of Ethnic Conflict Regulation*. London: Routledge.

Quade, Quentin L., 1993. 'PR and Democratic Statecraft'. In Larry Diamond and Marc F. Plattner (eds.), *The Global Resurgence of Democracy*. Baltimore: Johns Hopkins University Press.

Rabinovich, Itamar, 1985. *The War for the Lebanon, 1970–1985*. Ithaca: Cornell University Press.
Rachagan, Sothi, 1978. 'The Development of the Electoral System'. In Harold Crouch, Lee Kiam and Michael Ong (eds.), *Malaysian Politics and the 1978 Election*. Kuala Lumpur: Oxford University Press.
Rokkan, Stein, 1970. *Citizens, Elections, Parties: Approaches to the Comparative Study of the Process of Development*. Oslo: Universitetsforlaget.
Samarasinghe, S.W.R. de A. and Reed Coughlan (eds.), 1991. *Economic Dimensions of Ethnic Conflict: International Perspectives*. London: Pinter Publishers.
Sartori, Giovanni, 1968. 'Political Development and Political Engineering'. In *Public Policy* Vol. 17, John D. Montgomery and Albert O. Hirschman (eds.), Cambridge, MA: Harvard University Press.
Schmid, Carol L., 1981. *Conflict and Consensus in Switzerland*. Berkeley: University of California Press.
Taylor, P.J. and R.J. Johnston, 1979. *The Geography of Elections*. London: Croom Helm.
Weiner, M., 1993. 'Rejected Peoples and Unwanted Migrants in South Asia', *Economic and Political Weekly*, (21 August): 1737–46.
Wilkinson, Steven I., 1993. *High Conflict/Low Conflict: Six Case Studies of Ethnic Politics*. Washington: Woodrow Wilson International Center for Scholars.
Wilson, A. Jeyaratnam, 1975. *Electoral Politics in an Emergent State: The Ceylon General Election of 1970*. Cambridge: Cambridge University Press.
——— 1980. *The Gaullist System in Asia: The Sri Lanka Constitution of 1978*. London: MacMillan.
———1981. 'General Elections in Sri Lanka, 1947– 1977'. In K. M. de Silva (ed.), *Universal Franchise, 1931–1981: The Sri Lankan Experience*. Colombo: Government Press.
Yelvington, Kevin A. (ed.), 1993. *Trinidad Ethnicity*. Knoxville: University of Tennessee Press.

4 Ethnic Diversity and Public Policy: The Role of Education

Jagdish Gundara and Crispin Jones

INTRODUCTION

As is well known, state education policy in general reflects rather than leads state social policy. However, the power of an appropriate education should never be underestimated. In the context of this chapter, it is asserted that the contribution that intercultural education can make to the social and economic development of all ethnic groups within a state is a considerable one. The term intercultural education is derived from three decades of work in this area undertaken under the auspices of the Council of Europe within a range of European states (e.g. Batelaan, 1983; Jones and Kimberley, 1986). As defined in that specific context, intercultural education was seen as an education that seeks to examine and promote the dynamics of cultural exchange within pluralistic educational systems and institutions which are within states that are already multicultural. As such, the definition has a wider validity and is the preferred term used in this chapter. At this point, it is important to make clear that ethnic diversity does not axiomatically mean minority/majority relations. In the UNRISD Research Guidelines which were used in the preparation of this chapter, a helpful distinction is made between ethnic, racial and/or religious *diversities*, rather than *minority/majority* relations, the distinction that is more usually made in educational discourses within North America and the European Union (EU) but which makes less sense in other contexts, such as South Africa.

However, to meet such developmental needs in relation to intercultural education effectively, a state's education provision has to look at a wide range of more general social policy issues. Thus in this chapter the educational debates are, of necessity, placed in such a social policy context to facilitate the educational discussion. Thus, following upon such a discussion, the remainder of the chapter falls into six sections, namely:

(a) The educational context
(b) Educational policy issues
(c) Education performance and achievement issues
(d) Curriculum issues
(e) Teacher education issues
(f) General conclusions

Most contemporary societies are socially diverse on a range of indices, which may include language, religion, social class, territorial or geographical origin. States' responses to such elements of diversity have often been to ignore them or to devise policies to assimilate such groups within the existing apparatus of the state.

As schooling has become an international phenomenon and young children as well as adults are educated, the role of education and training to ensure that such diverse groups feel that their interests and voice are represented within the mainstream of society becomes critical. As groups become literate, their ability to understand better both how they are included or excluded becomes manifest to them. Therefore, public policy provision as such ought to ensure that individuals and groups have a sense of well-being in a polity which ensures that they can pursue their vocations and aspirations. In the socially diverse societies of most modern states, where socio-economic inequalities are extended by discrimination, proactive public policy measures ought to ensure that such divisive issues are reduced.

However, it is often the most marginalized in the poorest countries who are the ones most negatively effected by failures in such policy provision (Sen, 1992). Their civic entitlements are continually being denied. Unfortunately, the quandary in which many governments are caught is that if they do not implement the World Bank's recommendations on structural adjustments, they do not receive any of the aid essential for the sort of social policy that is most appropriate for the socio-economic development of such marginalized ethnic groups. This has particularly detrimental effects on their children, despite proclamations and protestations to the contrary. Furthermore, where there are such marginalized groups, the stability of the state is jeopardized even further if their legitimate aspirations are denied or ignored (Glyn and Miliband, 1994).

Almost in counterdistinction to such economistic perspectives, the UN Convention on the Rights of the Child stresses the holistic rights of children, which include nourishment as a social right, education (a social and cultural right), shelter from arbitrary detention (a civil right) and freedom from exploitation (a social and economic right). These rights are clearly of particular importance to children from disadvantaged or oppressed ethnic minorities. Furthermore, the exploitation of adults from disadvantaged or stigmatized ethnic communities also has negative consequences for their children (Ginsburg, 1992: 1–29).

This holistic approach is particularly important because, unless there is adequate provision for health and other life-sustaining mechanisms, the right to develop through education, through access to information, play, leisure and cultural activities and through freedom of thought, conscience and religion all become of less importance. In the last few years, the threats to ethnic minority (and in some cases ethnic majority) children's rights have included not only the routine denial of basic rights but the humiliation of total communities in situations of civil disorder and violence. Under such circumstances, the educational rights of the most vulnerable groups, themselves often within the most vulnerable states in the international system, cannot be guaranteed by these states themselves, a point that is gone into in more detail later.

It is also important that different interpretations of the human rights of ethnic groups are subject to close scrutiny. The objections to the establishment of human rights groups cannot be construed as a genuine cultural argument for the denial of such rights, as was suggested at the 1993 UN Human Rights Conference in Vienna by certain member states. Such objections and the policies that potentially could flow from such an interpretation of the concept of rights could be used as a pretext to persecute certain ethnic groups, and deny them, among other things, appropriate educational provision.

Within this larger context of human rights, states can deny that certain ethnic groups exist, and such non-democratic features of states that practise such policies are a major impediment to the protection of such groups' rights. Even those states which have experienced external invasion and colonization, or imposition of foreign military control, upon liberation may return to exclusive policies, not accepting the ethnic diversity within their own societies. The impact of such excluding practices and policies on educational provision and outcomes is self-evident. Thus, the whole process of state maintenance and/or nation-building all too frequently raises issues that are beyond the resources of a particular state. To make 'one out of the many' ought not to be allowed to negate the interests of the diversity of ethnic groups that make up the state. This poses a much more complex issue for national education systems in terms of their helping to sustain a unitary state which is inclusive of diverse groups, in particular their values, epistemologies, knowledges, languages, rights and cultures. In the absence of this happening, such groups may demand educational autonomy, setting into motion alternative and separatist educational systems that may lead to the disintegration of the state itself. As an example of this, the recent rise of religious fundamentalisms, particularly when religious groups have been persecuted within states, both raises the need for the protection of religious rights and raises complex issues for education.

A further factor is that such stigmatized groups are often poor, and as such are particularly vulnerable because of illiteracy, making them often unaware of how the state undermines their human and civic rights. The education of children from such communities becomes a complex issue, sometimes placing them in a Catch 22 position in that, in some cases, parents are prevented from sending their children to government schools because they are too distant, while, on the other hand, they are often so poor that they cannot afford to pay private school fees. Hence, the illiteracy of their parents is passed onto their children.

The indigenous peoples, however defined, are often the most voiceless of such minority groups within many modernizing states. (The concept of original autochthonous, indigenous or aboriginal group is difficult. As the seventeenth-century English writer Sir Thomas Browne put it, 'There was therefore never any autochthon but Adam'.) Genocide and rapacious exploitation is a contemporary phenomenon, which has similarities with the other, historically documented extinction of indigenous peoples in the Americas, Africa and Australasia. Their lands are seen as being the last frontier for development in what is represented by states as 'empty' land, or, as Julian Burger states, 'wild, untamed, unknown, unowned and unclaimed' (Burger, 1987: 13). As in the past, this land is seen as suitable for conquering and exploitation and since dominant ruling groups rarely have democratic consultations with the existing indigenous peoples, the resultant subordination of groups is not very different from the earlier, historical exploitation, displacement and colonization of such peoples.

To implement unilaterally measures which sustain the unequal power relationships with such marginal and increasingly hyper-marginalized peoples only weakens the state's ability to maintain its integrity, because force and domination often breeds resistance. Also, to integrate them forcibly into the mainstream economy means that they become heavily disadvantaged and frequently discriminated against. It should be possible for a state to accept small groups of self-governing communities who have autonomous lives which do not constitute a threat to its integrity. Such groups can also be provided with education appropriate for their needs, needs defined by agreement between the parties concerned, at the state and at the local community level. Should such autonomy of groups be allowed, certain groups may wish to remain aloof from the modernizing and national development and educational processes. Others may wish to choose to modernize for their own reasons and on their own terms. This is particularly the case if very few of them are formally well educated or possess reading and writing skills. However, educational provision for minorities only becomes meaningful if it is part and parcel of a whole range of social policy provisions necessary for living. Primary health care (PHC) as well as shelter and gainful employment are necessary if educational initiatives like literacy work are to be successful. Their lack makes the provision of effective education an almost impossible task.

Integrated social policy provision which takes into account the varied socio-economic divisions in society should be perceived as inclusive by all such divisions and groups within the state. In many areas of the world, where poverty is prevalent, the provision of basic education and levels of literacy remain very low, and, more recently, appear to have got worse. The intergenerational impact of these negative features, which may lead to early mortality because of the inability of parents or the state to provide the appropriate, effective and complex infrastructures necessary for survival, really requires assistance from the international agencies. Community education on preventative health measures within minority communities is essential to ensure that these children survive to become further educated and thus help to break the cycle of continual disadvantage. Pioneering work by the Child-to-Child Project is an excellent example of the potential effectiveness of this kind of education (Child-to-Child Trust, 1993; Hawes and Scotchmer, 1993). Such integrated provision not only saves children's lives but helps improve and change their lives for the future.

However, as was just mentioned, many states have failed, or are unable to deal equitably with the ethnic diversity within their borders. This has meant many of the international agencies, including the

United Nations, the Council of Europe, the European Union and other regional organisations have had to articulate positions with reference to ethnic diversity. At the present time also, the historic exclusions of groups in the so-called developed countries are surfacing and the educational attainments of such groups are often fairly low, meaning that international interventions are needed there as well. A good example of this is the current position in Europe. The issues in relation to many states of former Eastern Europe are well known as are the tragic events in former Yugoslavia. But former Western Europe is not without problems in this area also. Thus, 50 years after the defeat of fascism in Europe, not only are neo-Fascist groups taking root but the phenomenon of 'ethnic cleansing' is on the increase.

At this point, statements of intent, aspiration or rights by international agencies may demonstrate their value. Two particular instruments should be mentioned in the context of this chapter:

1. Article 5.1(c) of the UNESCO Convention Against Discrimination in Education, 1960 states:

> It is essential to recognize the right of members of national minorities to carry on their own educational activities, including the maintenance of schools and, depending on the educational policy of each State, the use or the teaching of their own language, provided however:
> (i) That this right is not exercised in a manner which prevents the members of these minorities from understanding the culture and language of the community as a whole and from participating in its activities, or which prejudices national sovereignty;
> (ii) That the standard of education is not lower than the general standard laid down or approved by the competent authorities; and
> (iii) That attendance at such schools is optional. (UNESCO, 1993.)

2. Article 30 of the UN Convention on the Rights of the Child, 1989 states:

> In those States in which ethnic, religious or linguistic minorities or persons of indigenous origin exist, a child belonging to such a minority or who is indigenous shall not be denied the right, in community with other members of his or her group, to enjoy his

or her own culture, to profess and practise his or her own religion, or to use his or her own language. (Brownlie, 1992: 182)

Such documents form a basis for providing a more effective state social policy and for a more just and effective education system in particular. However, exclusions of groups by political parties and ill-thought through educational policies continue to bedevil the process of policy formulation. Ethnic groups, whether they are minority, majority, migrant, national or indigenous, present educational challenges which require sustained political and policy effort, if the educational rights of such groups are to be enhanced. Educational policies which deal with these issues not only need to be permanent but also need to be dynamic, to ensure that such groups are able to identify with the state at large.

THE EDUCATIONAL CONTEXT

State educational measures only become meaningful if they are tailored to the needs of the various diversities that make up the state. Yet, in Malaysia, the Malays refer to themselves as the 'Bhumiputra' (sons of the soil), while they at the same time discriminate against the real sons of the soil, a contradiction in terms in any case, the Orang Asli. Educational provision for this group is totally inadequate (Minority Rights Group, 1993). These people are forced to learn the Malay language, while the Chinese and Indians are discriminated against in all sectors of education to privilege the needs of the dominant Malay Bhumiputra population. If education is to play a significant role in the lives of such a diversity of people and assist in their development, then the education of the dominant group cannot be imposed upon them in this manner. As Burger puts it:

> What the dominant culture does is to undermine the overt bounds of unity. The indigenous language disappears with the introduction of bilingual and then unilingual education; traditional dress vanishes as the raw materials become less available and western norms are imposed in schools and at the workplace.   (Burger, 1987: 31)

An overall appraisal of educational systems in the context of modernization processes at a time when the politics of recognition are to the fore is important. Such an appraisal has to include an evaluation of the needs of the total population, which includes the needs of indigenous and other ethnic minorities. It is only through such a thorough appraisal that not only will the educational outcomes and career prospects of minorities improve, but also that societies themselves will become more stable. For example, in the United States, the average educational level of all Native Americans who go to school is extremely low. To illustrate, of the 40,000 or so Navajos, one third are functionally illiterate. The dropout rates of children from these communities are twice the national average. This is not an isolated example. The situation of children from indigenous groups in Australia and Canada is often no better in terms of educational performance.

Obviously, the low levels of literacy amongst certain minorities in Latin America and Asia are partly a result of little or no primary school education. However, even when compulsory educational provision is made, it is too often made on the basis of the modalities and languages of the dominant groups. As an example of this, the Miskito, Sumu and Rama peoples of Nicaragua presented a petition to the Government which stated:

> That our children receive instruction in their mother tongue in accordance with our culture and traditions. To do this we want our own people to be trained sufficiently in order to teach our languages and customs and also to teach the Spanish language.
>
> (Burger, 1987: 239)

A comprehensive educational provision, if it is developed, has to be adapted to the needs of such local and minority groups and communities. Often, a clear picture of need is difficult to obtain and subsequently plan from. For example, the languages and cultures of resistance like 'Isotsi' and 'Taal' in Soweto and 'Fanagalo' in the mines of South Africa are probably not amenable to being developed as school languages, partly because they are languages of resistance in specific contexts which are likely to change as the South African polity becomes more democratic. Nevertheless such a situation poses a fundamental values dilemma and may lead to schools not developing meaningful language policies. A more considered and accurate recognition of minority educational needs would not only improve the life-chances of children from minority communities, but would also strengthen the positive contribution such groups can make to the social, cultural and economic life of the state in which they live.

In most states such actions are not given the serious consideration they need in order to ensure that competence in both the first and national languages is enhanced. Yet, for the modern state to survive in its current form, the fears by groups that their cultural, religious and linguistic identities are being, or would be erased through education, means that there is a need for the state, in its own interest, to protect the educational rights of such groups.

Such serious consideration is important, because both the dominant and subordinate groups need to establish, through education, a legitimation of their ethnic, religious or cultural identities. Education also gives the skills, knowledge and understandings to enable them to build a broader solidarity within the state. Such a solidarity needs to acknowledge all the diverse identities within the state and should also help establish greater commonalities and equalities.

A critical area within this aspect of education relates to gender issues. Particular attention needs to be paid to the literacy of women, because many of them are still illiterate and a larger share in the nurturing and pre-school education of children is undertaken by them. Women within ethnic minority communities and their children are often more vulnerable if educational provision where they live is weak or inadequate, and if generally there is little modern social infrastructure. As a consequence, all too frequently, their access to adequate primary education is poor as is their entry to secondary and vocational education. And to make things worse, their dropout rates are higher than average

At the same time, a disproportionate share of nurture in most contexts is still expended on boys, while the higher incidence of discrimination against girls in minority socio-economic structures continues. While it could be argued that parents and cultural groups ought to retain autonomy in relation to the bringing up of their children, neither customary nor state institutions ought to be allowed to be used to suppress the educational aspirations of girls. Resolution of this paradox is all but impossible. However, the state, through clearly thought-out educational policy and anti-discrimination legislation, can ensure that girls and women receive a greater share of their educational entitlement than is often the case at present. Neither communities nor states should be allowed to use cultural arguments for denying primary, secondary and higher education to girls, the more so as educational success is likely to improve their life-chances as well as the development of their communities.

To achieve any of these laudable aims, however, at least two critical preconditions have to be met. The first is adequate resourcing, often but not always an expression of political commitment; and the second is an adequate and clear set of educational policies at all levels of the education system, whether at regional, national or local level.

EDUCATIONAL POLICY AND ADMINISTRATION

If much of the conceptualization of multiculturalism in its individual state context has been oversimplified, as the earlier sections of this chapter indicated, it is not surprising that much educational policy, administration and practice in relation to societal diversity has been equally oversimplified. Often, it has been ineffective, partly as a consequence of this failure in adequate conceptualization. And this ineffectiveness is visible whatever the political stance that has been taken by the government of a state in respect of population diversity.

Furthermore, many of the taxonomic frameworks for the analysis of education and ethnic diversity put forward in North America and Europe, although useful in their time, need revision, both in terms of current circumstances and in terms of rescuing them from simplistic utilization. Put briefly, such taxonomies (for a British example, see Street-Porter, 1976) evoke a range of potential educational (and more general societal) responses to ethnic diversity which range from assimilation, through integration to (cultural) pluralism. Revision is needed for three significant reasons:

1. Such taxonomies are too often used as if states had suddenly and recently become multicultural; this clearly is not the case, as even a cursory examination of the evidence reveals.
2. Too frequently, they also ignore broader debates within education about educational disadvantage generally. This has meant that these taxonomies tend to be used as stages towards a state of societal ethnic social justice, with education tagging along behind in a well intentioned vacuity.
3. Finally, taxonomies such as this can be used in a unilinear way, as if there is a progression from one mode of educational or other social response to another in an inexorable or deterministic manner. Thus assimilation is often seen as the starting point and pluralism as the end-point of educational or other social development. One consequence of this has been the too rapid rejection of the work of scholars writing on assimilation such as Gordon (1964, 1978).

However, such taxonomies do contain valuable elements, most noticeably the recognition of the range of potential educational policy response to diversity, and their potential to help unpack and understand the seeming confusion that often attends any analysis of policy in this area.

One way in which such taxonomies can be given greater clarity is by looking again at their internal dynamics. This may be done by developing the taxonomy into a series of *oscillating polarities*, in other words, educational policies that are in a constant state of movement, reflecting political and other changes and decisions within the wider state. Two examples of this movement are first, between policies advocating educational pluralism (even separation/segregation) and those advocating assimilation, and secondly, between educational policies supporting free market-driven 'efficiency' and policies supporting social market 'just distribution' in relation to educational resource allocation. Such a model is one on which educational policy and practice can be better located, as it allows for the contested, backwards and forwards nature of such policy and practice in this area, both in terms of time and place.

A further aspect of such policy oscillation is the way in which educational systems have to address the issue of ethnic diversity as such diversities are defined by the individual state. This question operates at two overlapping, operational levels, namely the academic and the political. Academic definitions of a state's ethnic diversity, may, to some politicians, lack political reality. Some political definitions, according to the academics (and of course to some politicians as well) lack reality altogether. For example, if ethnic groups, whether minorities or not, by a state's own laws have to have educational rights, politicians (particularly if they are in power) can deny such rights by denying the very existence of the ethnic group in question, or defining them in such a way as to diminish or change their status. A state does not need special provision for those who do not officially exist. If redefined or divided to suit the dominant politicians' perceptions, the state can then decide on the appropriate educational provision. In both cases, a state could claim that no educational rights were being refused, save those refused to any other of its citizens.

As a result, over time, the acceptance of differing forms of appropriate educational provision may frequently lead to the policy oscillation that has just been described. If the changes are dramatic, so will be the educational consequences. And rapid educational change is seldom beneficial to pupils, whether or not from non-dominant ethnic groups.

However, how the state defines such diversity can rarely be disputed within the education service save at the margins of educational practice. In other words, education cannot be a major element for reform or change unless the government of the day wishes it, although it does maintain a degree of relative autonomy. Of course, states with forms of regional or local devolution in relation to education may attempt to introduce practices in relation to diversity which differ from those of the central government. However, with few exceptions, in reality, educational policy and practice at regional and local levels is seldom dramatically opposed to the policy orientations of the central state. But there will be exceptions and there will be policy oscillation. Educational policy and practice may be assimilationist in some parts of the system while it is more pluralistic in others. In states with politically significant ethnic groups and/or minorities, or with highly devolved federal structures, educational practice may vary considerably between regions. Indeed, such oscillation can occur within a single institution, reflecting individual teachers mind sets in relation to issues of ethnic diversity.

Such policy oscillation was seldom recognized by most states in the 1960s and 1970s in relation to the education of their full range of ethnic groups. Until the 1980s, educational policy in relation to societal diversity within many education systems in North America and Europe appeared, in the main, to follow the model of progressive social development referred to earlier, in which there appeared to be a slow move in both general social policy, and in educational policy in particular, towards an acceptance of certain (and varied) aspects of cultural pluralism and an acknowledgement of the xenophobia in the wider society that schooling was doing all too little to prevent. It was not a steady movement towards a more open and plural educational climate, of course. Indeed, much educational policy in states has remained assimilationist, in practice if not in terms of policy.

However, from the 1980s onwards, the effects of what some commentators have called postmodernity has dramatically changed perspectives on educational (and other) responses to diversity. The breakdown in confidence in relation to the modern agenda has been as profound in education as elsewhere, as the complex consequences of modernity have become more apparent. As Bauman notes:

Postmodernity may be conceived of as a modernity conscious of its true nature – *modernity for itself*. The most conspicuous features of the postmodern condition: institutionalised pluralism, variety, contingency and ambivalence – have all been turned out by modern society in ever increasing volumes; yet they were seen as signs of failure rather than success...   (Bauman, 1992: 187–8)

The rise of fundamentalism in many major religions has been one significant response to this change in the perception of the modern agenda. When accompanied by a greater expression of feelings of ethnic exclusion and particularism rather than pluralism, this has led to dramatic changes in educational perspectives on diversity in many states and rapid policy change. One possible consequence of these sorts of changes is that educational policy can appear even more internally inconsistent than is usual, extolling certain national and/or religious aspirations in the schools, while at the same time, attempting to foster tolerance and resist xenophobia.

Policy oscillation also relates to *levels* of administrative authority within a state's educational system. Many states are seeking to decentralize certain aspects of administrative policy in relation to education, although most states still attempt to maintain control over key aspects of educational practice, most noticeably the curriculum and teacher training. Such decentralization can often be intended to meet ethnic group demands for greater control of their educational futures although few states are yet prepared to move beyond the educationally less significant in relation to such demands. However, devolution of policy authority poses grave questions for national-level policymakers. Accept devolution and the unity of the state, not just its education system, may be threatened; enforce central control and the unity of the state may also be threatened if ethnic groups feel that their rights and aspirations, in education as elsewhere, are not being met or are being threatened. There is no simple answer to this issue and each state usually attempts to resolve the issue in ways which best secure the stability of the state rather than the educational needs of the ethnic groups concerned.

A similar set of issues relate to financing special provision for ethnic groups and minorities within a national system of education. In general, much financial policy in respect of ethnic groups more usually reflects the group's (or groups') political power or potential political power. Ethnic groups *per se* may have political power within an individual state, particularly if they are affluent and can make tactical arrangements with other groups, as happens, for example, in Australia. More usually, however, it means that generally disadvantaged ethnic groups are frequently educationally disadvantaged as well. Of course, many governments attempt to provide special provision for minority and/or disadvantaged ethnic groups, particularly in relation to issues of language and access, but such funding is seldom seen as a core funding element in an educational budget. To complicate the issue further, funding policies, like educational policies generally, have to be looked at against a backcloth of community concern. In other words, have the educational policies proposed (or implemented) got the support of the ethnic groups involved? Which, of course, raises a further set of issues in relation to group representation and legitimation. Educational policy-makers, in general, would prefer to formulate, adopt and implement policies that both met the needs and had the approval of the ethnic groups concerned. In practice, this rarely happens for complex reasons. Some of these would be inherent to the process of educational policy formulation, adoption and implementation, some to the conflicts and misunderstandings that arise so often between elected politicians, appointed officials and the range of ethnic group opinion and its representatives. And in a sense, as the policy-makers fiddle, the educational Rome of many ethnic groups' achievement levels continue to burn.

ACHIEVEMENT ISSUES

Central to any discussion of the educational issues associated with ethnic groups in any education system has to be the issue of achievement. Leaving the precise meaning of achievement on one side for the moment, it needs to be made clear that educational achievement is usually differentially distributed, with some students being more successful than other students. (Common measures of educational achievement that are used include literacy and numeracy levels, drop-out and repetition rates, public examination results, access to secondary and tertiary education and successful entry to the job market.)

Even where criteria referencing rather than norm referencing is the measure of the achievement or attainment, students will still achieve at different levels. In this context, these terms need some clarification. Norm referencing is when a proportion of the group in question is judged to have reached an appropriate level. Such levels mean that a proportion of the students 'have' to fail and is often associated with traditional public examinations. Criteria-referenced achievement suggests that successful demonstration of a skill or a capacity is the main criteria used. Such referencing is often associated with vocational education assessment and in theory could lead to all students being successful. A simple example of this would be the attainment of a craft skill such as the making of a screwdriver. Either the tool works or it does not. If all the class make effective screwdrivers, all have 'passed' the examination (if there was one), or have achieved at the required level.

However, measuring the individual achievement levels of students is relatively less complicated. Variation is both accepted and expected. Measuring the individual achievement levels of groups of students is, however, a much more complex task. The groupings and variations most frequently examined in educational contexts are variations in achievement levels between girls and boys, between working-class and middle-class students and between differing minority groups, often defined in ethnic or 'racial' terms. ('Racial' is placed in inverted commas to indicate its problematic nature.) Human 'races' have no basis in contemporary biology, but clearly have social science significance. Such analyses reveal very complex patterns of unequal educational performance. Most frequently, but *not* axiomatically, socially and/or economically disadvantaged ethnic groups have low levels of educational achievement in general, whether norm- or criterion-referenced.

Such low levels of performance indicate, at the initial level of analysis, that to the social and/or economic disadvantage suffered by many ethnic groups has to be added a further disadvantage, namely educational disadvantage. This in turn feeds on and sustains the two larger forms of disadvantage. This is because of the power of education in terms of its role in vocational selection through academic qualification. Thus low levels of educational achievement by a particular ethnic group helps to ensure their continued marginalization within the state the group resides in, the fate of many of the autochthonous.

Low levels of educational achievement are therefore at the core of debates about intercultural education. Thus the concern over the curriculum explored in the following section has as its principle focus the enhancement of educational achievement for ethnic groups. However, as was indicated earlier, such underachievement has many forms and many causes.

In relation to form, the most obvious concern is that academic achievement is most commonly expressed in terms of public/national examination results. Many stigmatized ethnic group students do badly in such examinations, or more commonly fail to take them, having dropped out of schooling prior to the examination year or years. Ethnic groups whose members consistently do badly in such examinations are clearly disadvantaged, whatever the causes of such poor performance. Such failure in relation to public examinations often has immediate impact on subsequent life-chances, maintaining the disadvantaged position of both the ethnic group in question as well as the individual student.

There are other forms of underachievement. Students from disadvantaged ethnic groups tend to drop out of school earlier and in disproportionate numbers, again perpetuating disadvantage and also discontent. Saying this is not to reassert a direct link between economic growth and educational investment, as clearly this is not the case. However, educational investment in relation to disadvantaged ethnic groups probably does have significance, the more so if the groups in question are currently economically marginalised.

Less tangible are the consequences of an inadequate education on such ethnic groups' children's spiritual, cultural, aesthetic and moral development. It is a powerfully held belief of educators that education has a significant contribution to make in these areas of a young person's development. How it is done and how it is measured is a much more difficult issue. What may be asserted, however, is that many schooling systems do little for these areas of growth in relation to certain ethnic groups and may often produce curricula offerings that oppose, ignore or denigrate those crucial aspects of the child's background.

The causes of education systems' failure to meet the needs of many such groups of children adequately are varied. Among the most significant are inadequate policies and funding, discussed earlier in this chapter, and poor or inadequate curricula and teacher education. These latter two points are the concerns of the next two sections of the chapter.

CURRICULUM ISSUES

Discussions about the curriculum are obviously related to resolution of the access issues discussed earlier in the chapter. The nature of the learning that takes place is again based on individual state views of the knowledge, skills and information that students should possess. The issues raised by the curriculum in relation to ethnic diversity makes an already complex area doubly so. Most states provide broad guidelines within which education systems operationalize provision in relation to diversity. Interestingly, the educational issues are not, in the first instance, resource-driven. In other words, much more could be done to meet more adequately such groups' needs and aspirations within the school curriculum, without demanding an input of expensive extra resources.

What is needed initially is an answer to a seeming contradictory set of propositions. The first is that the educational system has a responsibility to help produce a loyal and unified citizenry. To do this the curriculum should avoid the accentuation of difference. The dissatisfaction that this may give rise to may well endanger the unity of the state. The second is that the education system, by supporting and encouraging linguistic, religious, historical and other differences, may well endanger the unity of the state. In other words, whatever decisions that are made may well cause difficulties.

There are at least two ways of resolving this seeming paradox. The first is that each state education system has to make contingent decisions based on the current inclination of the state. The second is that state education systems must recognize the essentially contested nature of their enterprise and neither seek nor expect consensus on the most appropriate stance that is to be taken in relation to curricula issues within an intercultural education system. Both these positions consciously reject relativism, but do assert that there is an increasing perception of the contingency and complexity of the late modern agenda and that simplistic and deterministic solutions are unlikely to work.

Most states provide differentiated curricula just as they provide or accept differentiated institutional arrangements. So a state may provide a curriculum for an academic elite which is different from that offered the majority of students. Some states will offer different curricula for males and females: more commonly, gender differentiation in the wider society is unconsciously reflected in the curriculum, particularly where choices are offered to students. The classic example of this is the way in which girls are less likely to be involved in science, particularly at the second and higher levels of education systems.

As systems all tend to be differentiated in terms of the curriculum involved, it is not surprising that education systems attempts to deal with ethnic diversity raise complex issues that few systems have successfully resolved.

Three basic issues can be identified in this respect that deserve further attention. They are:

1. Language and literacy issues
2. Religious issues
3. Issues relating to the history curriculum

Language and Literacy Issues

What language or languages should be used as the medium of instruction appears a straightforward question. The official language or languages of the state clearly have to be those used in the schooling system. But most states have many other languages spoken within their boundaries. More, there is a worrying loss of languages across the globe that schooling could and should do more about. All over the globe, small language groups are disappearing, particularly if they are used by economically or politically powerless groups. Of the 6000 or so languages in the world, a mere 100 account for some 95 per cent of the world's population: in other words, 5 per cent of the world's population speak the remaining 5900. It is within this latter group that language loss occurs. At the same time, other languages are rapidly growing in terms of numbers of speakers, particularly Chinese and English, the latter mainly as a second language (Moseley and Asher, 1994).

The figures are so vague because linguists argue interminably about the differences between a language and a dialect. Professor Harold Rosen once said that the main difference was that a language had an army and an air force, a dialect did not. In other words, the distinction is often made on non-linguistic grounds and has more to do with the politics of language than with academic linguistics. The issue becomes even more complicated when language becomes part of political disputation. For example, there is currently considerable discussion as to the name of the major language spoken in Bosnia, with many Bosnians denying that the language that they speak is called Serbo-Croat. The 6000 estimate given here comes from Moseley and Asher (1994) and is probably the most widely accepted figure.

This language loss is, of course, not new. Languages have been disappearing for as long as records of them have been kept. Even the linguistic landscape of Europe, which to an extent escaped the colonizing linguistic power of European colonialism, is strewn with the memories of dead languages. Perhaps the most famous of these is Latin, but even countries so seemingly linguistically homogeneous as England have Cornish and Manx as dead or nearly dead languages. State educational policies in regard to such variety ranges from support, through benign neglect to denial. Yet denial or neglect creates linguistic and subsequent educational disadvantage for many linguistic groups. Also, denial of an educational place for a language often denies literacy to its speakers, further demonstrating its status. Educational system response to multilingualism is therefore a key element in broader minority/majority relations in many states (Skutnabb-Kangas and Cummins, 1988; Skutnabb-Kangas, 1990). Yet despite the importance of languages in education, few states have provided an adequate intercultural instructional programme to satisfactorily address the issue.

Religious Issues

Religion and state education have always been interconnected. In some cases resolution has been sought through secularization, in others through the provision of state schools with an overt religious ethos. And even those states with an explicit secular stance in relation to education, such as France and the United States, have found it difficult to maintain that stance in the face of determined religious opposition. Frequently, the educational response to secularity has been the parallel provision of schools by the religions concerned. In religious-dominated systems, on the other hand, it is often more difficult to establish similar structures that are secular.

A further complication is that, particularly in urban areas, a great variety of religious practice is present, much of it demanding some form of educational recognition. The issues such complexity raises are complicated and difficult to resolve. Until the 1970s it was thought that modern states were generally moving towards a decoupling of religion from state practice in general and educational practice in particular. The rise of religious fundamentalism, particularly in relation to Christianity and Islam, has meant that the relations between religion and the state have become more contested in many states around the world (Kepel, 1993). It is a contest that has clearly impacted upon education, in particular, in relation to the place of religion within the curriculum. Whether schools should teach religion or teach *about* religion remain issues that are not subject to easy resolution. The specific religious inclination of the state is critical to this discussion of course, but what does seem more general is that whatever decision is made, certain religious groups in most states feel that the education service does not meet their justly demanded spiritual needs.

The History Curriculum

How, or rather what and whose, history is taught is often predicated on the individual resolutions that states have made to the issues of languages and religions that have just been discussed. In most state educational systems, history is the view of the past that is held by the dominant group or groups within that state. Given that most states have a colonial past, either as colonizers, colonized or both, the scope for differing interpretations of the state's past in just that one area is vast. Most states are fictions in that they present a view of the past that both leads to and justifies the present. A brief example would be the military events in India in 1857. In British history books, if it is mentioned, the event is called the Indian Mutiny, the heroes the British soldiers. In Indian history books, it is the First War of Independence, the villains being the same British soldiers.

The presentation of past religious wars, the history of the formation of the state's current boundaries, the movement of peoples into and within the state are just some of the examples of critical historical events to be found (or not found) within the history curriculum. To take a broad European example, it is within the history curriculum that the hidden hatreds of Europe linger on most insidiously as some of the statements that have come from participants in the breakup of the former Yugoslavia indicate. Similarly, in Northern Ireland, where the hatreds of history are seldom hidden, Catholic and Protestant children learn alternative histories and oppositional perspectives from within their own particular families and communities, such perspectives being increasingly supported by residential segregation. In many ways, this segregation has been a less violent form of 'ethnic cleansing'. On a more positive note, the work of educational institutions, like Lagen College in Belfast, that make a real effort to bridge the gap between the two communities should also be mentioned. However, suppressing such partial and xenophobic histories within a school history curriculum is not enough. Indeed, suppression is seldom an effective pedagogical or didactic strategy: such narrow, communalistic histories have to be constantly challenged. For example, the current rise of anti-Semitism, fascism and racism across Europe may show how unsuccessful the education service has been in teaching about Europe's past. On the other hand, this may be unfair as comparisons cannot readily be made. It could equally be argued that things could be a good deal worse if it had not been for the efforts made in schools, colleges and other educational institutions. However, and perhaps more to the point, it would seem that the Holocaust, perhaps the key to an understanding of contemporary Europe, is still not given the curricula space and treatment that it deserves. Clearly, the teaching of history in the former states of Yugoslavia failed to give many people the skills with which to deal with the rise of ethnic particularism. Indeed, in respect of this, the response of many within Europe (and elsewhere) to the Muslim/Christian violence has been one of puzzlement about the presence and long-standing survival of Islam within Europe. It is useful to point out that the current disgust in relation to 'ethnic cleansing' (hopefully now ended) within the states of the former Yugoslavia seldom mentions that this Christian/Moslem antagonism has deep historical roots and also that ethnic cleansing has contemporary precedents, as in Cyprus following its UN supervised partition in the mid-1970s and the Northern Ireland example given earlier in the chapter. Similar examples could, sadly, be readily drawn from all around the world.

Although school may appear to be insignificant in relation to these powerful xenophobic forces, it is surely correct that schools should constantly, in the history curriculum and elsewhere, give children alternative histories that challenge narrow nationalism and xenophobia. In other words, the curriculum can include, exclude or ignore ethnic groups consisting of citizens of the state and whose children attend school within it. But it does this at a cost. An intercultural curriculum, on the other hand, that is including of groups rather than excluding of them, is potentially a source of a much more effective, appropriate and successful education for all students. To bring this about, however, requires a well-prepared teaching force. The issues that such an idea raised are the concern of the next section of the chapter.

TEACHER EDUCATION

Greater teacher competence and a higher order of knowledge and skills are needed to make the profession more competent to deal with issues of social diversity within an intercultural education pro-gramme. Professionally and rigorously educated teachers are essential to raise the profile of the teaching profession working in complex societies. As a part of this accreditation, there is a need for the intercultural dimension of education to be built into the teacher education process. However, a highly rigorous and professional teacher education programme presents a dilemma. Students from smaller nationalities and minorities who have done well at university tend to join other professions and not teaching. Yet, to make inter-cultural teacher education effective, both teacher education institu-tions and schools need to reflect the diversities of the wider society. This dilemma needs to be resolved. Not only should teaching be made an attractive profession, but the education of minority and smaller nationalities should be improved and measures instituted to ensure that a number of them do join the teaching profession.

An accredited teacher competence which is validated and includes an integral intercultural dimension is essential to ensure that a crucial educational issue is not marginalized. In this sense, intercultural education for teachers should not be seen as an issue for urban culturally diverse schools, but for all schools including rural ones, in both rich states and poor ones. Teachers from minority communities have a function in educating children in all parts of the state to help try and bring about a genuine cross-cultural understanding.

The issues for teacher education in general and the intercultural dimensions of it are twofold: What do teachers need to know in terms of knowledge and secondly, what are teachers able to do? If teacher education is of high quality, then the expectations of their under-standing of knowledge, issues and skills would be of a higher order. The role of teacher education institutions should be to ensure that this is the case, particularly given the nature of the complexities presented by the presence of minorities.

Those who join the teaching profession ought to bring to this field a learning experience from their earlier education that ensures that there is a systematic study of teaching and learning, as well as planned teaching experience in schools, which is closely supervised and mon-itored. Teachers not only need a command of the subjects they teach, a sound grasp of the techniques of teaching, but they also need information on educational research a grasp of children's growth and development and a knowledge of differing intercultural needs and learning styles.

The status of teacher education institutions and their structure is critical for the role and position of teacher education itself. If teacher educators are seen as consisting of previous school teachers only, whose knowledge of subject and knowledge areas or of the educational sciences, interculturalism and research is of a low order, then teacher education and its intercultural dimensions will not be rigorous enough. Particularly well-educated teachers are needed to work in minority areas, where the standards of teacher competence in many cases is very low.

Another question is how intercultural teacher education is conceptualized in schools and in higher education. For instance, in Britain, the lead came from a Department of Education and Science (DES) circular, which suggested that British society had 'become multicultural' (DES, 1965). The question to have asked the DES would have been, what was it before? To initiate intercultural teacher education, a taxonomy of societies along the lines mentioned earlier in this chapter becomes essential. Such an historical and contemporary map of a multicultural society in descriptive terms is a useful starting point. It would, for instance, inform teachers of the similarities or differences between national minorities and so called 'ethnic' minorities. It also ought to help in the analysis of the way in which nation-states obfuscate the underlying features of social diversity. Hence, how historians and other social scientists analyse this issue is important, in order to enable teacher education programmes to include intercultural issues, including those dealing with the problems of racism, narrow nationalism and growing xenophobia.

Thus in most national contexts an intercultural curriculum is essential at teacher education level, to ensure that teachers not only have non-ethnocentric knowledge, but also the skills to teach an intercultural curriculum. The development, therefore, of an intercultural curriculum in schools and more importantly in teacher education institutions, requires pedagogues to work closely with academic historians, social scientists and other researchers in the cultural fields in an attempt to construct such a non-ethnocentric curriculum.

The problem that the implementation of intercultural teacher education faces is that the languages, histories and cultures of subordinated groups are not seen as having equal value as dominant ones. Such an entitlement to an intercultural curriculum is perhaps one of the greatest challenges facing the development of such an intercultural teacher education. However, such a structuring of intercultural dimensions would be marginalized if teacher education institutions themselves have lower status as a university institution or, more likely, a non-university training institution.

A further issue is how intercultural issues are located within teacher education institution themselves. If intercultural dimensions are left to a few interested staff without any structural arrangements to allow for a more integrated approach within teacher education institution, then such issues would be marginalized.

Few states have managed to provide for an effective and efficient intercultural teacher education programme. Without it, and supporting professional development and in-service education and training, much of the intercultural educational needs identified in this chapter are unlikely to take place or be sustained.

CONCLUSIONS

This chapter has argued for a systematic and sustained approach to the issue of providing an effective intercultural education within the modern, multicultural state. The chapter is not putting forward a postmodern relativistic agenda for combatting racism and xenophobia within schools and the wider society. It is arguing that the modern agenda is not discredited but should be seen as more complex than has hitherto been the case (Coulby and Jones, 1995). As Giroux puts it:

> Modernism is far from dead – its central categories are simply being written within a plurality of narratives that are attempting to address the new set of social, political, technical and scientific configurations that constitute the current age.   (Giroux, 1991: 63)

Such plurality of narratives make it difficult for policy makers in general, and educational policy makers in particular, to plan. In education, the need for an intercultural education policy and practice remains contested in most state education systems. It is the argument of this chapter that this is inevitable, but that such contestation better reflects the fragmented nature of much of the modern state. Planning an effective intercultural education system is thus a remarkably difficult challenge. However, it is a challenge that can no longer be safely ignored. In other words, plurality and complexity have been constant but unrecognized features of states for a long period of time; it has now become an urgent task for education to recognize this state of affairs.

REFERENCES

Aronowitz, S. and H. Giroux, 1991. *Postmodern Education*. Oxford: University of Minnesota Press.

Batelaan, P., 1983. *The Practice of Intercultural Education*. London: CRE.

Bauman, Z., 1992. *Intimations of Postmodernity*. London: Routledge.

Brownlie, I. (ed.), 1992. *Basic Documents in Human Rights*. Oxford: Clarendon Press.

Burger, J., 1987. *Report from the Frontier*. Cambridge, MA: Survival International.

Child-to-Child Trust, 1993. *Directory of Child-to-Child Activities Worldwide*. London: Institute of Education.

Convention on the Rights of the Child, 1990. Stockholm: Swedish Government.

Coulby, D. and C. Jones, 1995. *Postmodernity and European Education Systems*. Stoke-on-Trent: Trentham Books.

Department of Education and Science, 1965. *Circular 9/65*. London: DES.

Ginsburg, N., 1992. *Divisions of Welfare*. London: Sage.

Giroux, H., 1991. 'Postmodernism and the Discourse of Educational Criticism'. In S. Aronowitz and H. Giroux (eds.), *Postmodern Education*. Oxford: University of Minnesota Press.

Glyn, A. and D. Miliband (eds.), 1994. *Paying for Inequality: The Economic Cost of Social Injustice*. London: IPPR/Riverdram Press.

Gordon, M., 1964. *Assimilation in American Life*. Oxford: Oxford University Press.

Gordon, M., 1978. *Human Nature, Class and Ethnicity*. Oxford: Oxford University Press.

Hawes, H. and C. Scotchmer, 1993. *Children For Health*. London: UNICEF and Child-to-Child Trust.

Jones, C. and K. Kimberley (eds.), 1986. *Intercultural Education: Concept, Context, Curriculum Practice*. Strasbourg: Council of Europe.

Kepel, G., 1993. *The Revenge of God: the Resurgence of Islam, Christianity and Judaism in the Modern World*. London: Polity Press.

Minority Rights Group, 1993. *The Orang Asli of Peninsular Malaysia*. London: Minority Rights Group.

Moseley, C. and R. Asher (eds.), 1994. *Atlas of the World's Languages*. London: Routledge.

Sen, A., 1992. *Inequality Examined*. Oxford: Clarendon Press.

Sills, D. (ed.), 1972. *International Encyclopedia of Social Sciences*. New York: Macmillan.

Skutnabb-Kangas, T., 1990. *Language, Literacy and Minorities*. London: Minority Rights Group.

Skutnabb-Kangas, T. and J. Cummins, 1988. *Minority Education: From Shame to Struggle*. Clevedon: Multilingual Matters.

Street-Porter, R., 1976. *Race, Children and Cities*. Milton Keynes; Open University Press.

UNESCO, 1993. *DOC 27c/38, Annex 1, 17.8.1993*. Paris: UNESCO.

5 Indigenous Peoples: Emerging International Actors

Rodolfo Stavenhagen

INTRODUCTION

The struggles of indigenous and tribal peoples for survival in a rapidly changing global environment are one of the many instances of ethnic conflict in which the needs and demands of a specific ethnic population are pitted against the overriding interests of the state.

Public opinion has become aware over the years of the plight of tropical forest tribes in the Amazon as well as in South East Asia, and more recently in Central Africa.[1] At the World Conference on the Environment, Rio de Janeiro, 1992, numerous indigenous as well as other non-governmental organizations made the point that environmental devastation in tropical areas also signifies the destruction of myriad indigenous and tribal peoples. After lengthy debates in the UN on how to commemorate the misnamed 'Discovery of America' (now called, more poetically, the 'Encounter of Two Worlds'), 1993 was proclaimed the Year of Indigenous Peoples and 1995 saw the beginning of an International Decade of Indigenous Peoples. Public opinion has focused on endangered tropical forest tribes; but many other indigenous groups have signalled their distress at being ignored, relegated, neglected, marginalized and discriminated against, when they are not actually being physically or culturally destroyed by more powerful groups and by the national state itself.[2]

WHO ARE THE INDIGENOUS?

Public policies regarding indigenous peoples will vary considerably according to the way these are defined. Also referred to as Natives or Aborigines, and in the Americas as Indians, the indigenous are considered to be the descendants of the original inhabitants of a

territory which at some date that is still alive in the historical memory
of the populations concerned, were conquered or otherwise subjug-
ated by a more powerful outside group and incorporated, usually
against their will and without their consent, into a larger polity that
might have been either a colonial empire or an independent national
state. The special rapporteur of the UN study on discrimination
against indigenous peoples, defines them as follows:

> Indigenous communities, peoples and nations are those which,
> having a historical continuity with pre-invasion and pre-colonial
> societies that developed on their territories, considered themselves
> distinct from other sectors of the societies now prevailing in these
> territories, or parts of them. They form at present non-dominant
> sectors of society and are determined to preserve, develop and
> transmit to future generations their ancestral territories, and their
> ethnic identity, as the basis of their continued existence as peoples,
> in accordance with their own cultural patterns, social institutions
> and legal systems.   (Martínez Cobo, 1987)

However, no general consensus exists about an exact definition of
indigenous peoples. Some states, such as Canada and the United
States, have adopted legal criteria.[3] In a number of Latin American
countries cultural or linguistic definitions are widely used (Stavenhagen, 1992); in India and South East Asia governments deny that tribal
peoples ('scheduled tribes' or *adivasis* in India) are any more 'indigenous' than the rest of the population, but numerous governments have
adopted legal measures and policies regarding tribal populations
which are similar to those concerning aboriginal and indigenous
peoples elsewhere.[4] Some tribal organizations do indeed identify
themselves with indigenous peoples elsewhere, and attend international meetings and indigenous fora in the United Nations. Nowadays, indigenous organizations demand the right to define themselves
as a basic human right which they have been denied.

Just as a clear-cut, agreed upon definition is difficult to achieve, so
is an exact count of the number of indigenous and tribal peoples
around the world. Depending on who does the counting and what
criteria for classification are used, estimates of indigenous populations
vary between 100 and over 200 million, most of whom are found in
Asia (mainly in India, China and the Philippines) as well as in Latin
America (CELADE, 1994). However, industrialized countries have no
lack of indigenous populations: Norway (Sami), Canada and the
United States (Native-Americans, Inuit and Hawaians), New Zealand

(Maori), Australia (Aborigines), Japan (Ainu) and Russia ('small' peoples of the North) (IWGIA, 1990).

SOCIAL AND ECONOMIC CONDITIONS

The social and economic situation of indigenous peoples is usually characterized as less than satisfactory by contemporary standards of well-being. The International Labour Organization produced a study on the subject in the 1950s, which served as background material for the adoption of ILO Convention 107 on the protection of indigenous and tribal peoples (ILO, 1957). The United Nations issued a report on discrimination against indigenous populations in the mid-1980s (Martínez Cobo, 1987). Both reports were based mainly on information provided by governments. The Independent Commission on International Humanitarian Issues published a brief report on the situation of indigenous peoples in 1987; and a number of global as well as local and national studies have been produced by several non-governmental organizations (Burger, 1987; ICIHI, 1987). On the occasion of activities surrounding the 1992 commemoration of 'The Encounter of Two Worlds', a spate of publications focusing on the Indians of the Americas fuelled debate on the continuing plight of indigenous groups (Jaimes, 1992; Wright, 1992). A recent World Bank study on indigenous populations in Latin America characterizes their condition as 'abysmal' (Psacharopoulos and Patrinos, 1994).

Land and Territory

Perhaps the fundamental problem facing indigenous peoples is the issue of land and territorial rights. Many tribal and indigenous communities are hunter-gatherers, others are nomadic pastoralists, requiring expanses of forests or pastures for the maintenance of their traditional ways of life and for economic survival. Hundreds of millions of indigenous peoples are subsistence farmers, who live in compact peasant communities and depend on agricultural land for their livelihoods (Burger, 1990). Since colonial times, these groups have suffered the loss of their lands and ancestral territories at the hands of the colonial state, immigrant colonists, religious missions, state-sponsored settlers, large plantations, livestock ranchers, transnational corporations, miners, lumber companies and other agents of civilization, progress and social change (Bodley, 1990; Escobar, 1989).

During the nineteenth and twentieth centuries, countless indigenous and tribal peoples were uprooted from their homelands or simply exterminated, to make way for incoming farmers, ranchers or settlers. From the Argentinian Pampas to the North American Frontier, indigenous populations in the Americas suffered the brunt of the expanding capitalist economy, and what the earlier colonial administration had not achieved was to be accomplished by the modern state in the period of nation-building.

As a result of this history of pillage and destruction, many groups disappeared; others retreated into some isolated 'last frontier' in the mountains, deserts and jungles, which may not have been of immediate interest to 'economic developers'; and still others resisted as best they could with their diminishing resources. Population pressures on limited and dwindling land resources has generated vast ecological destruction in many indigenous areas, accompanied by the outmigration of labour in search of income and employment. The defence of their land, and the demand for more acreage to satisfy their basic needs for economic survival, has become one of the principal mobilizing issues of indigenous peoples in various parts of the world (Burger, 1987; Clay, 1988).

The struggle over land has many facets. In remote areas occupied by hunter-gatherer groups or by nomadic pastoralists (tropical jungles, steppes, deserts, tundras and arctic domains) economic activities require ample spatial mobility and therefore access by the indigenous and tribal populations to areas that can provide them with the needed resources. When modern economic activities upset this necessary balance between a population and its 'perimeter of deambulation' (logging of tropical areas, damming of rivers, laying of pipelines, mining), then the survival of the group is threatened. This has occurred again and again in recent decades, in different parts of the world. Still, just as their very survival is at stake, many indigenous and tribal peoples in threatened areas have been able organize their resistance and some of them succeeded in obtaining a reprieve, at least temporarily. The struggle of the Amazonian Indian tribes against encroachment is widely reported in the world media and led the Brazilian and other Amazon Rim governments to adopt protective legislation of various kinds. How effective these policies will be in the long run is still a matter of debate (Cherif *et al.*, 1991; Price, 1989).

Similarly, tribal forest groups in Borneo have organized to resist logging activities by foreign companies in their traditional habitat. *Adivasi* groups in India have found support in the World Bank to resist the negative effects of hydroelectric development projects in their tribal areas. Likewise, the Sami in northern Norway were able to stop a similar project that imperilled their reindeer grazing areas. Success stories abound, but in the long run observers consider that such highly vulnerable groups have little chance of making it past the twenty-first century.[5]

A different kind of land question besets indigenous peasant farmers in the densely settled areas of Mesoamerica and the South American Andes, as well as the tribal regions of South East Asia and the Philippines. Here communal land tenure has sustained traditional agricultural activity, often subsistence farming or small market-oriented production. Village life centres on the communal use of agricultural resources (including, as the case may be, water rights and access to grazing areas and forest produce). The introduction of individual land-titling has long been a major policy objective of national governments, and while it may have led in some cases to the consolidation of private landholdings among indigenous farmers, it has more often than not generated the transfer of formerly communally held land to outside, that is non-indigenous, proprietors and contributed to the breakdown of community structures. This is indeed what many governments have fostered with their drive towards nation-building and economic development. When the local agrarian structure is acutely bipolar, as was traditionally the case in Latin America, then large privately owned estates exert endless pressure on the subsidiary and dependent Indian peasant communities, underpinning a rigid and stratified social system that lasted for several centuries, well into the late twentieth century. The struggle over communal land has inspired countless indigenous uprisings from colonial times onward. Indigenous peasantries have been known to resist passively but they have also been the protagonists of violent rebellions and revolutions, as well as drawn-out guerrilla warfare. While Indian peasant revolutionaries rarely strive for state power (except when in alliance with more 'national'-oriented political groups), they do struggle for local and regional autonomy, for land reform and redress of ancient grievances (principally loss of land). There is an old saying among Native-Americans that 'an Indian without land is a dead Indian'. This holds true for indigenous peoples everywhere, in that indigenous identity is closely linked to the land, though this has changed in recent decades.

The need for land as a productive resource is not unrelated to the requirements of territory, as the geographical space necessary for the survival and reproduction of a distinct ethnic group. Indigenous and tribal peoples are rooted historically in specific areas; they know from experience that the loss of these areas leads to the loss of cultural identity and the eventual disappearance of the group. Consequently, many of them demand the formal protection of their territories by law, or legal deeds to specific areas to which they are traditionally attached. Governments have responded to these demands in various ways. As a consequence of political mobilization and international support, some indigenous peoples in Brazil and other Latin American countries have been granted territorial rights; others are still negotiating, or in some cases, struggling over such rights. In Panama, for example, the San Blas Indians have long enjoyed territorial autonomy (achieved after an armed uprising in the 1920s), and after years of violent internal conflict (linked to external aggression), the Sandinista government in Nicaragua established a regime of regional autonomy for the indigenous and other communities in the Atlantic Coast region in the mid-1980s. The new political constitution in Colombia, adopted in 1991, recognizes territorial rights to indigenous peoples in the former Indian reservations to which they were formally restricted since early independent times. One of the demands of the current Indian peasant uprising in south-eastern Mexico is local and regional autonomy, though its details have not yet been worked out. Designated tribal areas are the backbone of tribal survival in a number of Asian countries as well as in Australia. In Canada, some native tribes have been granted designated areas with a certain degree of regional self-government (Boldt, 1993).

Indigenous peoples usually resent the idea that governments can 'grant' them title or formal control over the territories they inhabit, because they argue that in fact such territories have belonged to them all along and that national states have simply usurped them. Rather than asking for territorial grants or cessions, indigenous organizations claim restitution of historical territorial rights. In centralized state systems these claims are often seen by governing elites as threatening the territorial integrity of the state, and in a number of cases they are forcefully rejected. Governments generally pursue policies of 'territorial integration' whereby indigenous and tribal areas become the object of colonization and settlement schemes by elements of the 'national' population. Sometimes these processes lead to major demographic shifts, and they may generate local inter-ethnic conflict between the aboriginal population and the settlers. In a number of Asian countries (Bangladesh, India, Indonesia, China, Thailand), indigenous and tribal populations may find themselves becoming a demographic minority in their traditional homelands, a situation which has led in numerous instances to political and social, and at times, violent conflict. A number of these areas, particularly when they are close to international borders, are placed under military control and considered as questions of national security. Indigenous and tribal peoples have complained about exactions and repressive measures committed against them by insensitive and unscrupulous national military elements who treat them as potential subversives or traitors, foreigners in their own land (Amnesty International, 1992).

Cultural Identity

Whereas indigenous identities are usually rooted in a common collective history, the emergence of 'identity politics' among indigenous peoples is a relatively recent phenomenon. Cultural distinctiveness is not only a descriptive label that insiders and outsiders use to distinguish the indigenous from other populations, but it has also increasingly become a controversial issue in the ideological and political battlefields of the day. Indigenous and tribal peoples have long been attached to their cultural heritage, as have other nations, peoples and ethnic minorities all over the world, but perhaps they have been more vulnerable in terms of cultural survival than others. Indeed, resistance against rapid loss of cultural identity has become one of the main issues in the area of indigenous peoples' rights.

The destruction of indigenous cultures is of course related to the processes of economic development and modernization, and to the extent that such processes are global there is not a single human group anywhere any more that can escape their consequences. Whether the cultural destruction of an indigenous population is unavoidable as a result of 'modernization', or whether it is able to change and adapt without losing its core identity, is a matter for debate. In recent decades it was widely believed that such groups would inevitably have to 'modernize', therefore disappear as such, and this was generally referred to as 'progress'. Indeed, to the extent that economic development was – and still is – posited as a global objective, linked to so-called modern or Western values (consumption of material goods, accumulation of wealth, individual entrepreneurship and achievement, private ownership, profit motive), it is held that the cultural values of

non-Western populations, particularly indigenous peoples, constitute
an obstacle to progress, development and modernization. Their progressive disappearance is then considered to be inherent in the natural
evolution of humanity in contemporary times. Moreover, it would
seem that this is the case, because numerous indigenous peoples and
their cultures have in fact disappeared from the face of the earth in the
500 years since the famous 'Encounter of Two Worlds'.

All too often, these 'natural' tendencies are helped along actively by
state policies specifically designed to hasten the disappearance of
indigenous and tribal cultures. One of the major concerns of many
governments, engaged in 'nation-building' since the nineteenth century, has been to create a single national culture, based on the idea
that only a culturally homogeneous national population could become
a modern nation. This national ideology, which came in many guises
and variants, usually led to policies intended to 'assimilate', 'incorpor-
ate' or 'integrate' the indigenous populations into the so-called
national mainstream, that is, the dominant culture, sometimes but
not always that of the demographic majority (in Guatemala, for
instance, it is the subordinate Maya indigenous population which
constitutes a demographic majority) (Smith, 1990).

These objectives pursued by national governments may be achieved
through various means, but undoubtedly the most widely used and
most effective instrument has been the school system. While schools
have been vital in transmitting new skills, values and knowledge to
indigenous populations, they have also contributed to demeaning and
destroying local cultures. At one time, indigenous and tribal schooling
was mainly in the hands of missionary institutions, whose main objective was religious conversion and the destruction of native religions.
But government schools did not remain far behind: the inculcation of
'national' values through the school curriculum specifically meant the
eradication of native cultures. This begins at an early age, when
schoolchildren are taught to feel ashamed of their 'primitive' ways
and to reject the traditions and values of their elders. Soon the elder
generation itself learns that for their children to 'make it' in the
outside world, it is necessary to shed their traditional cultures and to
assimilate to the dominant society. Numerous accounts by people who
have gone through this process testify to the psychological damage
that they have suffered. By the time native youngsters are able to enter
secondary or higher education (if they get that far) they have learned
to deny their cultural identity and to assume the masks that the
dominant society has taught them to put on (Hodgson, 1992).

A major means whereby national states achieve their objective of assimilation is language policy. Native tongues are demoted to the status of 'dialects', and are thus deemed not to be worth retaining, and all citizens are expected – when not actually compelled – to use the 'national' language, which is sometimes legally established as the only official language in public administration and the school system. As most indigenous languages do not possess their own script, native tongues and with them, their oral literatures, histories, philosophies and cosmologies, tend to disappear, unless counteracting policies are put into effect. In numerous countries, indigenous peoples become unable to use their own maternal languages in daily life (except in the private sphere of the home), and are called upon to engage in the business of survival in an imposed language which is not their own.

This process of ethnocide through the natural tendency of modernization and the operation of specifically designed state policies has led to the effective disappearance and decline of indigenous populations in numerous countries. In others, it leads to tensions and conflicts, and quite often to various forms of resistance by indigenous peoples. In fact, the right to their own culture is currently claimed by indigenous peoples' organizations as a fundamental human right. While assimilation and national integration are still claimed as important objectives by most states, in recent years the respect for cultural pluralism and the preservation of cultural diversity has been presented as an alternative not only by indigenous peoples, but also by advocacy groups of all kinds, as well as international organizations, and governments are slowly taking up this new discourse themselves (Cassidy, 1991; Assies and Hoekema, 1994).

Educational and cultural policies for multilingual and multi-ethnic states are now being developed and experimented with in different areas. Indigenous languages are beginning to be recognized in some parts as legitimate vehicles of social and commercial communication as well as in public administration and in the schools. Bilingual educational programmes have been introduced in school systems designed for indigenous populations. Curricula and textbooks are being modified to include local cultures and history. The challenge for educators and policy-makers is how to balance the nation-state's objective of instilling national values and a shared culture in all its citizens with the legitimate desires of indigenous peoples (or other ethnic minorities for that matter) to preserve and develop their own cultures. Still, for many indigenous peoples the multicultural approach in public policy, to which much attention has been given in recent years in international meetings and organizations as well as at the national level in some countries, is more of an ideal than a reality.[6]

The right to cultural development is included in international human rights instruments, and it is generally understood as pertaining to all the citizens of a given state. In multi-ethnic countries it has become a matter of debate whether this right should be exercised by different cultural communities to develop their own cultures, or by the overarching state to promote the concept of a 'national culture', even when this might imply the ethnocide (i.e. cultural destruction) of non-dominant ethnic groups. Indigenous peoples are caught squarely in the middle of this controversy. Being generally few in number and marginalized from the national society, indigenous and tribal groups rarely have the political clout to press systematically for their views at the centres of political power (state ministries, legislatures, political parties). They often rely on sympathy and support from teachers' associations, academics, religious organizations or advocacy groups of various kinds, as well as international non-governmental organizations to press their case at the seats of power and before the general public (which is usually quite poorly informed about the situation of indigenous populations and tends to romanticize and patronize them) (Dyck, 1985; Falk, 1988).

Indigenous cultures are not merely a collection of picturesque artifacts and customs that delight international tourists. They are rooted in forms of social organization, local government, customary law and networks of interpersonal relationships that make up the framework for the set of reciprocal rights and duties which assign membership in the group and provide the sense of belonging and identity that distinguish individual members of the community as well as the group as a whole from other such groups and from the population at large. Being indigenous is not usually a matter of individual choice, nor merely a question of personal identity or consciousness. It often relates to community structure and to the community as a way of life. Thus, even when indigenous people migrate to other settings in search of work or better opportunities (the big city or even to foreign countries), the link with the original community is maintained as far as possible through the establishment of ethnic associations, seasonal (back and forth) migrations, participation in communal festivities, monetary remittances, tribal or ethnic endogamy, and perhaps even an increased awareness of ethnic identity in the alien environment. Observers of the African scene have noted the strengthening (indeed, the emergence) of 'ethnicity' in the urban setting, and others have signalled the growth of 'transnational communities' of migrant indigenous peoples (for example, linking Mixtec Indian villages in southern Mexico with migrant communities in the agricultural fields of California and Oregon) (Epstein, 1978; Kearney, 1992).

In the turmoil of 'nation-building' and economic globalization it would seem that the maintenance of community is not likely, and there are many indications that indigenous communities are in fact breaking down rather rapidly, depending on the particular circumstances. On the other hand, it is precisely because of such external pressures, which are often perceived as threatening by their members, that indigenous and tribal communities are showing renewed vitality. This often means attempts to maintain and eventually strengthen local traditional government including tribal legal customs that may, at times, enter into contradiction with national law (the civil and penal codes, land tenure and land use regulations, family law). Traditional authority structures (village government) are not always recognized or respected by national or provincial administrations, and life in indigenous communities is often regulated by district or village-level administrators who are accountable only to their bureaucratic superiors, a state of affairs which further weakens community structures. Indigenous organizations often demand recognition of traditional customary law and their local authorities as part of the claim for cultural identity.

All of these issues boil down fundamentally to questions of control over resources and political power, which indigenous peoples have generally been in short supply of. The emergence in recent years of new kinds of assertive indigenous and tribal organizations, often set up and managed by a younger generation of modern, educated, politically astute militants, as well as by 'natural' leaders who have risen through the ranks in popular struggles such as those of the grass-roots indigenous ecological movements in tropical forest areas, provides the link between local level demands, national politics and the global agenda.

INDIGENOUS RIGHTS

Indigenous claims are increasingly being framed in the language of human rights. Given their subordinate and marginalized status in most countries, indigenous and tribal peoples are particularly vulnerable to human rights abuses, and the protection of their human rights as well as the effective implementation of human rights legislation and protective mechanisms figures high on their political agenda. This refers particularly to equal protection under the law, equal opportunity in education and employment, the combatting of racism and discrimination, and in general the package of international economic, social and cultural rights that most states have now ratified and adopted in their internal legislation (Boldt and Long, 1985).

While the struggle for universal individual human rights is given high priority, the debate concerning group rights also appears as a fundamental issue. Indeed, indigenous organizations argue that unless their collective rights as indigenous peoples are recognized and protected, their individual human rights will continue to be threatened. Collective human rights here mean the right of the group to survival as such with an alien environment, implying language, education, religious practices, the exercise of traditional customs and social organizations, and most particularly, self-government and autonomy (Assies and Hoekema, 1994; Stavenhagen, 1988).

International human rights law includes two different approaches to the protection of the collective rights of ethnically distinct populations. One is the system designed for the protection of ethnic and national minorities within existing states, an issue that appeared prominently in the League of Nations, and has again been taken up by the United Nations. Article 27 of the International Covenant of Civil and Political Rights (adopted by the General Assembly in 1966) deals with the rights of members of minorities and their protection. This was followed many years later by the adoption in 1992 of the Minority Rights Declaration (Phillips and Rosas, 1993). While in none of these texts do minorities as groups appear as the subjects of the right in question, but only their individual members, it is clear that minority rights can only be exercised collectively and that the protection of minority rights implies a certain recognition of the minority as a collective entity. Observers note that the minority protection regime in international law may be regarded as a stepping stone towards the recognition of group rights (though there are numerous scholars who resist this interpretation) (Brölmann *et al.*, 1993).

While there are valid arguments for including indigenous populations in the minority protection schemes developed within the framework of the United Nations, indigenous organizations have steadfastly resisted this approach. They have made it clear that they consider their specific demands and rights as qualitatively distinct from those of national, ethnic, religious, linguistic or racial minorities.

First, they argue that in some cases indigenous populations are not a minority, but actually constitute a demographic majority in a given state. Secondly, and more importantly, they argue that being the descendants of the original populations of a given territory at the time of conquest, invasion or foreign settlement, they have legitimate 'original' historical rights which different kinds of ethnic minorities do not share, particularly when the latter claim links with a foreign nation or when they relate to recent immigrant groups. Thirdly, in numerous cases indigenous peoples were actually considered sovereign nations in earlier times by the expanding colonial states, and often entered into formal treaties with such states. Their descendants now claim that such treaties should be considered as valid in international law (though most of them were abrogated unilaterally by the dominant state) and that consequently their group rights are quite different in legal terms from those of national or ethnic minorities (Deloria, 1985). The United Nations has embarked on a study of treaties concerning indigenous peoples as part of its activites concerning indigenous rights.

The indigenous critique of the 'minority protection' approach in international human rights law points to the alternative strategy that indigenous organizations have pursued assiduously for some years. This is the claim to the right of peoples to self-determination as stated in the most important UN human rights instruments. Indigenous organizations argue that they represent 'peoples' not only in the sociological and cultural meaning of the concept, but also in the sense that this term has gained in international law: that is, as a subject of international law imbued with distinct rights that states are expected to respect. Ever since it was adopted by the United Nations as a principle of international law, the right of peoples to self-determination has been limited to that of colonial territories seeking their political emancipation; the UN explicitly denies such a right to minorities or to any group attempting to use it to break up an existing state. Government representatives are usually quite adamant in that the right of self-determination does not apply to indigenous populations. The latter in turn have argued that it does, and that in the exercise of this right they claim self-government and local and regional autonomy, though they do not usually claim the right to secession. As a part of this controversy, indigenous representatives at numerous international meetings insist on the use of the term 'indigenous peoples' and not 'populations' (which does not have any implications in international law), an issue that has been discussed in the UN Working Group on Indigenous Populations as it prepares a Draft Declaration on Indigenous Rights to be adopted by the General Assembly, in the International Labour Organization during the debates leading up to the adoption of Convention 169 in 1989, at the 1993 World Congress of Human Rights in Vienna, and in other fora (Alfredsson, 1993).

The issue of local and regional autonomy, whether phrased in the language of the right of self-determination or in the more administrative language of decentralization and devolution, is rapidly becoming a subject of negotiations between indigenous peoples and the state in more than one country. But more than a question of working out the complex details of autonomy arrangements, the struggle over these issues relates to the wider problems of democracy in pluri-ethnic societies and of democratic participation of formerly excluded and neglected peoples in the building of new kinds of polity and society.

In 1982 a Working Group on Indigenous Populations, established a year earlier as a subsidiary organ of the United Nations Sub-Commission on the Prevention of Discrimination and the Protection of Minorities (which reports to the Human Rights Commission), began its yearly week-long sessions in the Palais des Nations in Geneva. The Working Group was set up as one of many activities in the United Nations in the field of combatting racism (which had mainly centred on the problem of apartheid in South Africa). It was mandated to examine the situation of indigenous populations in the world and to help develop standards for the protection of the human rights of these populations. While the formal membership of the Working Group was limited to five individual members of the UN Sub-Commission, its annual sessions were soon attended by an increasing number of indigenous representatives from all parts of the world (several hundred in 1994), who came to expound their grievances, claim their rights, exchange information with fellow-indigenous and tribals from other countries and continents, and to help with critiques, ideas and suggestions in the task of drafting a UN Declaration on Indigenous Rights, which the Working Group had been entrusted to prepare. In 1994 the Working Group presented a final draft of the Declaration to the Sub-Commission, which in turn passed it on to the UN Human Rights Commission. Before it will eventually reach the floor of the General Assembly, the draft Declaration may suffer some transformations. While indigenous input was strong at the Working Group level (the Sub-Commission is composed of 'individual experts'), it is unlikely that the government representatives who sit on the Human Rights Commission and who will have to approve the draft, will be equally sympathetic to all of the claims put forward by indigenous peoples (beginning with their claim to be treated as 'peoples') (Wilmer, 1993).

As the Working Group continued with its labours during the 1980s, the International Labour Organization (likewise located in Geneva) began its own preliminary activities designed to revise ILO's Convention 157 on the Protection of Indigenous and Tribal Populations, which had been adopted in 1957. This Convention had been criticized as being too paternalistic and 'assimilationist' in its orientation (true to the prevailing thinking in those years), and by the early 1980s indigenous representatives at international meetings (in Geneva and elsewhere) were openly voicing their dissatisfaction. After a few years involving the preparation of technical reports, the organization of expert meetings, and the tabling of preliminary resolutions by the ILO's governing bodies, the General Conference in 1989 adopted a new Convention 169, which is open to signature and ratification by member states. Convention 169 addresses a number of the issues mentioned in this chapter and is generally considered as being more in line with current thinking than the earlier instrument. The Convention does not shun the use of the term indigenous 'peoples' but the ILO clearly admonishes that this should not be interpreted as having any effect in international law. (Indigenous organizations, on the contrary, consider the use of the term 'peoples' in this Convention as already constituting an act of international law. Some observers feel that the scant number of ratifications of the Convention to date reflects some governments' disapproval of the wording of the text.)

The UN Working Group and the ILO currently constitute the only truly international multilateral organizations in which indigenous issues are dealt with. At the regional level, the Organization of American States, through the Inter-American Commission of Human Rights, has initiated consultations that may lead eventually to the drafting of a regional legal instrument on indigenous rights. While indigenous organizations have been consulted about this, nothing like the massively attended hearings organized by the UN Working Group has taken place at the inter-American level so far. The Ibero-American heads of state, meeting at a summit session in Madrid in 1992, decided to establish a Fund for the Development of Indigenous Peoples of Latin America and the Caribbean, in whose governing bodies (general assembly, executive board) indigenous representatives have an equal say with government representatives. This is to date the only inter-governmental organization in which indigenous peoples have such a high level of representation. The Fund receives support from the World Bank, the Inter-American Development Bank and other multilateral agencies to channel resources to indigenous communities and organizations for projects that will be managed directly by the beneficiaries.

International indigenous non-governmental organizations have flourished in recent years, as a by-product, and in a way as one of the causes, of the emerging international awareness of indigenous rights. Some of these associations are well endowed, are extremely active and have obtained consultative status at the United Nations and its specialized agencies. Others have been less successful. Like all NGOs and social movements, indigenous organizations are subject to varying fortunes, to internal factionalism and external pressures, to ideological and political dissension, and to the vagaries of having to compete for limited resources in a highly competitive international environment. Some of the major donor agencies involved in international indigenous issues are European governments, transnational religious organizations of various denominations, as well as private foundations (Van de Fliert, 1994).

Some observers feel that in a crowded market with dwindling resources, external support for indigenous NGOs will surely diminish and that as a consequence their presence on the international scene will also decrease, particularly now that the excitement generated by the 1992 celebrations of the Encounter of Two Worlds and the 1993 International Year of Indigenous Peoples has waned. However that may be, there is no doubt that indigenous peoples have already made their mark on the international system. Only a few decades ago, observers held that indigenous peoples had little chance of survival in the modern world. Later, efforts were made to accelerate the individual adaptation of their members to the national societies in which they lived. Nowadays there is a good chance that indigenous and tribal peoples, strengthened by a new awareness of their collective worth and identities will not only survive, but may actually blossom in a more humane, human-rights oriented and democratic world, in which respect for cultural and ethnic diversity will be more the rule than the exception.

NOTES

1.   'The extent to which the plight of the world's rapidly diminishing tribal peoples is addressed in national, regional and global agendas is a litmus test of the willingness of the dominant cultures and civilizations of the world to defend the socio-cultural rights of minority cultures that is an essential ingredient of global and local socio-cultural diversity' (Ghee and Gomes, 1990: 1). On the Amazon, see Davis (1977) and Hecht and Cockburn (1990). For an assessment of the situation of indigenous peoples in Africa, see IWGIA (1993).
2.   On the peoples of the Arctic, see Hall (1987).
3.   For legal purposes in the United States, Indian is defined 'as a person meeting two qualifications: (a) that some of the individual's ancestors lived in what is now the United States before its discovery by Europeans, and (b) that the individual is recognized as an Indian by his or her tribe or community' (Cohen, 1982: 9). In Canada, 'Indian' refers to a person who, pursuant to the Indian Act, is registered as an Indian or is entitled to be registered as an Indian (Frideres, 1983: 7). Indians, together with Inuit and Metis, are considered 'Aboriginal peoples' in Canadian law (Asch, 1993: 2–5).
4.   In Malaysia, for example, an aborigine is defined as a person who speaks an aboriginal language, follows an aboriginal way of life and aboriginal customs, and includes a descendant through males of such a person. This relates mainly to the Orang Asli people, but the Malaysian constitution also refers to the majority Malays and the natives of Sabah and Sarawak as indigenous people of the country (Rachagan, 1990: 101, 106).
5.   These events have been reported in various publications of the International Work Group for Indigenous Affairs (Copenhagen), Cultural Survival (Cambridge, MA) and Survival International (London). See, for example, Moser (1972) and Paine (1982).
6.   The United Nations General Assembly adopted the Declaration on the Rights of Persons Belonging to National or Ethnic, Religious and Linguistic Minorities in 1992. It is still examining the possibility of adopting a Declaration on the Rights Indigenous Peoples, that would include the right to cultural identity and the use of native languages.

150   *Indigenous Peoples*

REFERENCES

Alfredsson, Gudmundur, 1993. 'The Right of Self-Determination and Indigenous Peoples'. In Christian Tomuschat (ed.), *Modern Law of Self-Determination*. Dordrecht: Martinus Nijhoff Publishers.

Amnesty International, 1992. *Human Rights Violations against Indigenous Peoples in The Americas*. New York: Amnesty International.

Asch, Michael, 1993. *Home and Native Land. Aboriginal Rights and the Canadian Constitution*. Vancouver: University of British Columbia.

Assies, W.J. and A.J. Hoekema (eds.), 1994. *Indigenous Peoples Experiences with Self-Government*. Copenhagen: IWGIA.

Bodley, John H., 1990. *Victims of Progress*. Palo Alto: Mayfield Publishing Company.

Boldt, Menno, 1993. *Surviving as Indians. The Challenge of Self-Government*. Toronto: University of Toronto Press.

Boldt, Menno and J. Anthony Long (eds.), 1985. *The Quest for Justice. Aboriginal Peoples and Aboriginal Rights*. Toronto: University of Toronto Press.

Brölmann, Catherine, René Lefeber and Marjoleine Zieck (eds.), 1993. *Peoples and Minorities in International Law*. Dordrecht: Martinus Nijhoff Publishers.

Burger, Julian, 1987. *Report from the Frontier. The State of the World's Indigenous Peoples*. Cambridge, MA: Cultural Survival.

Burger, Julian, 1990. *The Gaia Atlas of First Peoples*. London: Robertson McCarta.

Cassidy, Frank (ed.), 1991. *Aboriginal Self-Determination*. Montreal: Institute for Research on Public Policy.

Centro Latinoamericano de Demografía (CELADE), 1994. *Estudios Sociodemográficos de Pueblos Indígenas*. Santiago de Chile: CELADE.

Cherif, Alberto, Pedro García and Richard Chase Smith, 1991. *El indígena y su territorio*. Lima: Coordinadora de las Organizaciones Indígenas de la Cuenca Amazónica.

Clay, J.W., 1988. *Indigenous Peoples and Tropical Forests: Models of Land Use and Management from Latin America*. Cambridge, MA: Cultural Survival.

Cohen, Felix, 1982. *Handbook of Federal Indian Law*. Charlottesville: Michie Company.

Davis, Shelton, 1977. *Victims of the Miracle: Development and the Indians of Brazil*. Cambridge: Cambridge University Press.

Deloria Jr, Vine, 1985. *Behind the Trail of Broken Treaties. An Indian Declaration of Independence*. Austin: University of Texas Press.

Dyck, Noel (ed.), 1985. *Indigenous Peoples and the Nation-State: Fourth World Politics in Canada, Australia and Norway*. St. John's: Memorial University of Newfoundland.

Epstein, A.L., 1978. *Ethos and Identity. Three Studies in Ethnicity*. London: Tavistock Publications.

Escobar, Ticio, 1989. *Ethnocide: Mission Accomplished?* Copenhagen: IWGIA.

Falk, Richard, 1988. 'The Rights of Peoples (in Particular Indigenous Peoples)'. In James Crawford (ed.), *The Rights of Peoples*. Oxford: Clarendon Press.

Frideres, James S., 1983. *Native Peoples in Canada. Contemporary Conflicts.* Ontario: Prentice-Hall, 2nd edition.

Ghee, Lim Teck and Alberto G. Gomes (eds.), 1990. *Tribal Peoples and Development in Southeast Asia.* Kuala Lumpur: University of Malaya (Special Issue of the Journal *Manusia & Masyarakat*).

Hall, Sam, 1987. *The Fourth World. The Heritage of the Arctic and its Destruction.* New York: Random House.

Hecht, Susana and Alexander Cockburn, 1990. *The Fate of the Forest. Developers, Destroyers and Defenders of the Amazon.* New York: Harper Perennial.

Hodgson, M., 1992. 'Rebuilding Community after the Residential School Experience'. In D. Engelstad and J. Bird (eds.), *Nation to Nation. Aboriginal Sovereignty and the Future of Canada.* Ontario: House of Anansi Press.

Independent Commission on International Humanitarian Issues (ICIHI), 1987. *Indigenous Peoples: A Global Quest for Justice.* London: Zed Books.

International Labour Office, 1957. *Indigenous Populations.* Geneva: ILO.

International Work Group for Indigenous Affairs (IWGIA), 1990. *Indigenous Peoples of the Soviet North.* Copenhagen: IWGIA.

—— 1993. '... *Never Drink from the Same Cup': Proceedings of the Conference on Indigenous Peoples in Africa. Tune, Denmark 1993.* Copenhagen, IWGIA.

Jaimes, M. Annette (ed.), 1992. *The State of Native America: Genocide, Colonization and Resistance.* Boston: South End Press.

Kearney, Michael, 1992. 'Beyond the Limits of the Nation-State: Popular Organizations of Transnational Mixtec and Zapotec Migrants'. Unpublished manuscript.

Martínez Cobo, José R., 1987. *Study of the Problem of Discrimination Against Indigenous Populations.* New York: United Nations.

Moser, Rupert R., 1972. *The Situation of the Adivasis of Chotanagpur and Santal Parganas, Bihar, India.* Copenhagen: IWGIA.

Paine, Robert, 1982. *Dam a River, Damn a People?* Copenhagen: IWGIA.

Phillips, Alan and Allan Rosas, 1993. *The UN Minority Rights Declaration.* Turku/Åbo-London: Åbo Akademi University Institute for Human Rights/Minority Rights Group (International).

Price, David, 1989. *Before the Bulldozer. The Nambiquara Indians and the World Bank.* Washington: Seven Lock Press.

Psacharopoulos, George and Harry Anthony Patrinos (eds.), 1994. *Indigenous People and Poverty in Latin America. An Empirical Analysis.* Washington: World Bank.

Rachagan, S. Sothi, 1990. 'Constitutional and Statutory Provisions Governing the Orang Asli'. In Lim Teck Ghee and Alberto G. Gomes (eds.), *Tribal Peoples and Development in Southeast Asia.* Kuala Lumpur: University of Malaya (Special Issue of the Journal *Manusia & Masyarakat*).

Smith, Carol A. (ed.), 1990. *Guatemalan Indians and the State: 1540–1988,* Austin: University of Texas Press.

Stavenhagen, Rodolfo, 1992. 'La situación y los derechos de los pueblos indígenas de América'. *America Indigena,* 12, 1–2 (January–June).

—— 1998. *Derecho indígena y derechos humanos en América Latina.* Mexico: El Colegio de México and Instituto Interamericano de Derechos Humanos.

Van de Fliert, Lydia (ed.), 1994. *Indigenous Peoples and International Organisations*. Nottingham: Spokesman.

Wilmer, Franke, 1993. *The Indigenous Voice in World Politics*. Newbury Park: Sage Publications.

Wright, Ronald, 1992. *Stolen Continents. The 'New World' Through Indian Eyes*. Boston: Houghton Mifflin.

6 Public Policies towards Immigrant Minorities in Western Europe

Sarah Collinson

International migration emerged as an important component in the process of economic expansion and liberalization which took place in Western Europe after the Second World War. Whether as migrant-receivers (north Western Europe) or as migrant-senders (southern Europe), all states became linked into an expanding migration 'system', which soon extended beyond the region, incorporating former colonies and other states to the south and to the east.

This migration system did not come about spontaneously. It was encouraged, or at least sanctioned, by the receiving states of north Western Europe, hungry as they were for cheap labour. Economic interest overshadowed almost all other considerations. Thus, it was not until after nearly a decade of large-scale immigration that governments began to show an open concern with its social and political implications. Largely because of these concerns, the receiving states halted foreign labour recruitment after the oil crisis in 1973. Immigration continued, of course, dominated during the 1970s and early 1980s by family reunion and, after the mid-1980s, undocumented 'economic' immigration and asylum inflows.[1] But by the time of the recessions of the late 1960s and early 1970s, it was clear that most of the new immigrant populations were here for good (Castles *et al.*, 1984).

Migration is not a new phenomenon for Western Europe. Indeed, the history of Europe over the centuries has been one of more or less continuous migration. As Jorgen Nielsen observes, European culture would not be what it is had it not been for the constant intellectual, artistic, spiritual and technological cross-fertilization mediated by the movement of people (Nielsen, 1992: 151). However, what set postwar immigration apart from earlier flows was that it involved not only European populations, but also large numbers of migrants from more distant countries and more distant cultures. Europe was soon host to significant immigrant populations of a kind which, in terms of the social and political challenges they posed, seemed to have no precedent.

As argued by Antonio Perotti, the national, ethnic and cultural pluralism introduced by postwar immigration differs markedly from that resulting from indigenous regional or ethnic minorities within the state. Immigrant minorities do not claim any territory. Thus the diversity introduced by the migrants cannot be managed by the state through decentralization and the granting of administrative autonomy. In contrast, their integration affects and involves society as a whole. They tend not to be perceived as having contributed to the social, economic and cultural development of the states concerned. Furthermore, they tend to be linked to a specific socioeconomic status, to a particular juridical and political status (as foreign or non-citizen), and to a cultural or racial identity which has its roots outside the national or European context (Perotti, 1993b). The fact that immigrant minority integration still figures high on the political agenda in Western Europe testifies to the difficulties that governments, the public and immigrants themselves have had in coming to terms with these challenges.

Despite a common concern over the integration of immigrants, diverse approaches to the problems have been adopted by the various host countries (and by different institutions within those countries). These reflect the different sociopolitical structures of the receiving states, contrasting immigration experiences and differing interpretations or expectations of processes of integration. 'Integration' is a rather vague term, which can be used to denote a varying range of processes across the spectrum from social and cultural assimilation of minorities to the preservation of distinct minority identities. Some countries have leant towards 'assimilate or return' policies (such as France and the Federal Republic of Germany), while others (the Netherlands, Sweden and Britain) have opted for policies promoting 'multiculturalism' or supporting recognition of a 'multiracial society'.

Attitudes and policies adopted towards immigrant minorities have also differed according to identities of the groups concerned (e.g. European versus African, Christian versus Muslim), and have varied over time and according to the 'maturity' of different immigration flows and the particular aspects of the immigration history (e.g. permanent 'colonial' immigration versus 'temporary' recruited labour). The picture is complicated further by the fact that integration – to the extent that it is accomplished – is never a straightforward, one-way process, but one based on the dynamic interactive relationships which develop between immigrants and the state, and between immigrant and receiving communities. Not only have receiving states and communities responded to immigrant populations in different ways, but immigrant groups themselves have adopted a great variety of strategies and demonstrated widely contrasting responses to their situation as minorities, in turn influencing the reactions and responses of the majority population. For this reasons, generalizations on the subject should be treated with caution.

Considerable variation is also apparent in the terminology used to describe minorities of immigrant origin. This is indicative of the specific sociopolitical, historical and legal background to the immigration phenomenon in each receiving country. The terminology is significant in that it reflects much about attitudes which have shaped the reception and integration of immigrant groups and the bases of immigrant minority status in receiving countries. For example, in Britain and the Netherlands it is usual to talk of 'ethnic minorities', in Germany of 'foreigners', 'aliens' or 'foreign co-citizens' (Tranhardt, 1993: 49), and in France it is common to refer to 'immigrants' or 'populations of foreign origin'. To some extent these terms reflect objective differences in citizenship laws, but they are also indicative of the degree to which immigrant minorities are identified as a 'class apart' (Wilpert, 1988a: 3). It should be noted that these terms are generally used to denote immigrant groups whose integration is seen as a problem, and are therefore not usually applied to immigrant minority communities of West European and/or pre-Second World War origins (e.g. Irish residents in Britain or Italians in France).

For the purposes of this discussion, the term 'immigrant minorities' or 'immigrant groups' is used to denote minorities of immigrant origin. However, the term is used loosely as it is becoming increasingly misleading to use the label 'immigrant', given that these communities now include a growing contingent of second- and third-generation members who have been born and brought up in their country of residence.

Although much of the ensuing discussion is relevant to Western Europe as a whole, reference to national policies is restricted to France, the Federal Republic of Germany, the United Kingdom, the Netherlands and – as one of southern Europe's 'new' immigration countries – Italy. These five countries not only figure significantly in Western Europe's postwar immigration history, but comparisons between them illustrate important points of divergence in the development of their integration policies.

INTEGRATION AS A POLICY ISSUE

By the mid-1970s, all the major migrant-receiving states in Western Europe had introduced policies geared towards the integration of immigrant minorities. Until then there had been virtually nothing in the way of long term planning for the integration of immigrants. Yet, even once the importance of integration had gained explicit recognition, the tendency was for policies to be adopted in a piecemeal and reactive way, in response to specific problems, rather than through the formulation of comprehensive programmes.

This was particularly apparent in the 'guestworker' countries (West Germany, Switzerland and, to a lesser extent, the Netherlands), where the emphasis on return of workers and *de facto* institutionalized segregation of foreign workers during the 1950s and 1960s delayed recognition of a need for full immigrant integration. Those countries that were more open to accepting the fact of immigrant settlement (including the United Kingdom and France) demonstrated a concern for integration or responded to integration-related issues rather earlier. Nevertheless, even in Britain, the issue took some time to reach the national political agenda. Because most immigrants entered the United Kingdom independently with full civic and political rights, special measures on their behalf were not initially considered particularly necessary or appropriate. The first race relations legislation passed in Britain (the 1965 Race Relations Act) was limited in scope (outlawing discrimination in public places) and could not have been expected to have a substantial impact on the position of immigrants in British society (Layton-Henry, 1984: 134). Similarly, in France it was for a long time assumed that immigrants' welfare could be protected sufficiently through the formal guarantee of legal rights deriving from the Constitution and the operation of state institutions applicable to French society as a whole. State action on behalf of immigrants was initially restricted to attempts to tackle the problem of immigrant housing, and then only in connection with efforts to eliminate the infamous immigrant *bidonvilles* (slum shanty towns) that had grown up around Paris and other large French cities during the 1950s.

The United Kingdom

The British experience of postwar immigration differed significantly from that of other states in Western Europe because the majority of those migrating to Britain were 'colonial' immigrants entering the country as British subjects with full citizenship rights.[2] As in France, the imperial legacy profoundly influenced the reception of immigrants in British society and their subsequent integration.

Ever since it has been a subject of national debate in Britain, the immigration issue has been dominated by the race question. Zig Layton-Henry observes that an 'immigrant' in popular discourse came to mean a non-white person: 'Such descriptions, setting non-whites apart from the rest of the population, were never applied to... Irish, Italians or Poles, and showed the depth of racial prejudice and the political potential of the issue' (Layton-Henry, 1992: 73). Although the British political elite has never been entirely free of racial prejudice, all the main political parties have consistently expressed a commitment to the elimination of racial disadvantage in a multiracial society. However, fearing a backlash from the majority population (particularly the white working class), policy-makers have been wary of instituting any programmes aimed explicitly at improving the social and economic status of immigrants. The emphasis at national level has therefore been on the promotion of equal opportunities through enforceable anti-discrimination legislation rather than on the creation of positive programmes to benefit ethnic minorities.[3] This attitude was expressed by the Home Secretary when he introduced the second reading of the 1968 Race Relations Bill:

> The Bill is concerned with equal rights, equal responsibilities and equal opportunities and it is therefore a Bill for the whole nation and not just minority groups.... Its purpose is to protect society as a whole against actions which will lead to social disruption and to prevent the emergence of a class of second-class citizens.[4]

The term 'integration', when used, has been defined 'not as a flattening process of assimilation but as equal opportunity, accompanied by cultural diversity, in an atmosphere of mutual tolerance' (Patterson, 1969: 113). More recently, British policy has been described as directed towards shaping society so that everyone 'can participate freely and fully in the economic, social and public life of the nation while having the freedom to maintain their own religious and cultural identity' (Home Office, 1990). Where housing and employment conditions and education of minorities have been the specific objects of policy, this has tended to have been at the local authority level.

By the mid-1970s it was apparent that discrimination against ethnic minorities was widespread, particularly in the fields of housing and employment, and that it could not be combatted effectively on the basis of the two existing Race Relations Acts. In 1976 a new Bill was passed which outlawed indirect as well as direct discrimination in all public life, and which established the Commission for Racial Equality (CRE) as the institution responsible for ensuring its enforcement (replacing the Race Relations Board and Community Relations Commission).

The 1976 Race Relations Act and the CRE represent the backbone of British policy aimed at promoting the integration of ethnic minorities. The CRE was granted greater powers of investigation and enforcement than its predecessors,[5] and is charged with working towards the elimination of discrimination and working to promote equality of opportunity and good relations between persons of different racial groups. Although it has had some success, in many respects the CRE has failed to live up to expectations. A survey carried out in 1984/5 revealed that over 30 per cent of employers discriminated directly against black job applicants, indicating 'a level of discrimination on racial grounds that is widespread, serious and persistent over time' (Commission for Racial Equality, 1985: paragraph 1.3).

British policy has sometimes been described as multicultural by virtue of the relative space allowed for minority cultural autonomy, and because a number of local authorities have adopted a more active multicultural line than central government, particularly in the field of education. However, Britain has never adopted an explicitly multicultural policy at national level; national government has tended to favour a more hands-off approach to cultural matters.

France

Until the late 1960s the only effective organizations set up to deal with immigration issues were those created informally on a local and voluntary basis. The state started to involve itself directly with immigrants' welfare only in the 1960s with the creation of institutional housing specifically for immigrants – *cités de transit* and *foyers-hotels* – and the resettlement of certain groups in standard social housing. However, in the years leading up to the 1974 halt on foreign labour recruitment, concern began to be expressed at state level over a whole range of immigrant issues, including employment conditions and inter-ethnic relations. With the creation of the new office of Secretary of State for Immigrant Workers in 1974, a machinery was set in motion to place all immigrant affairs – welfare, housing, employment, education, training, cultural expression – under the control of the state. Rather than relying on general measures to ensure equal opportunity, the French state embarked on a programme of direct *'insertion'* of immigrants into French society. This policy was based on the insistence on a direct and unified identification with the French state, which precluded the recognition of minorities. The French approach thus contrasted significantly with Britain's emphasis on anti-discrimination and recognition of a multiracial society. Moreover, in France it was the question of culture, rather than race, which came to dominate debates on the issue.

In the very restrictive climate of the 1970s, immigrants' *insertion* was pursued in tandem with the contradictory aim of encouraging certain immigrant groups to return to their countries of origin, an objective which could only be carried out by maintaining a sense of insecurity among immigrant populations. This policy had little impact on rates of return, but, as Philip Ogden notes, it did prove 'an effective way of souring the political atmosphere' (Ogden, 1993: 114). Those groups perceived to be least 'assimilable' – North Africans and to some extent Portuguese – suffered the brunt of a state policy that was based largely on the notion of 'assimilate or return'. This policy stance reinforced the concept of 'cultural distance' and strengthened ideas of 'desirable' versus 'undesirable' immigrants which persist to a large extent today, particularly in respect of the Algerian minority.[6] Immigration came to be perceived increasingly as a problem of the Arab presence in France (Ogden, 1993: 115).

On coming to power in 1981, the new socialist government promised to replace the discriminatory and assimilationist policies of the past with a more open recognition and acceptance of the reality of immigrant settlement and the cultural heterogeneity that it implied. A more liberal approach aiming for immigrants' *'intégration'* was adopted in an attempt to ease growing inter-ethnic tensions in French society. The new policies emphasized the right to live and work in France without having to assimilate and without discrimination in employment and housing (Verbunt, 1985): foreign nationals were granted rights of political association (though not the right to vote); most were granted a ten-year renewable residence permit which guaranteed their right to settle in France; and the status of over 150,000 undocumented immigrants was regularized. The Chirac government of 1986–8 would almost certainly have reversed this policy had it remained in power for longer, but, as it turned out, the more liberal stance dominated into the early 1990s.

Since the 1970s, French governments have seen the integration of immigrants as the direct responsibility of the state. This view is reflected in a plethora of state bodies created to deal with the immigrant issue, including bodies concerned with housing, urban development, education and religion. However, governments have been reluctant to formulate any policies betraying an institutional recognition of immigrant minorities *qua* minorities. The overarching emphasis on individuals as targets of policy was articulated in a report issued in 1991 by the *Haut Conseil à l'Intégration* which aimed to define integration policy in France. It states that:

> The *Haut Conseil* does not deny the existence of minorities in France, as elsewhere. It thinks, however, that the traditional principles of equality, recognition of individual rights and nondiscrimination better assure individual freedom and opportunity in the country as a whole than the institutional recognition of minorities, which would necessarily be discriminatory... An integration policy stresses similarities and convergences in the equality of rights and obligations... in order to bind the different ethnic and cultural elements of our society together and give each person, whatever his or her origin, the opportunity to live in this society, whose rules he or she has accepted, and become a constituent element of that society.[7]

The liberal approach of the 1980s has come under attack from the French Centre-Right, now in government. In response to growing anxieties in French society about continuing immigration, and under pressure from Le Pen's *Front National*, the new government has picked up where the 1986–8 Chirac government left off by introducing new laws to strengthen immigration controls, to reduce security of residence for certain categories, and to restrict naturalization for 'second generation' immigrants. The politicization of the migration issue has encouraged the development of increasingly defensive and restrictive policies, with the social aspects of integration increasingly overshadowed by, or conflated with, broader immigration concerns – concerns which are in turn discussed increasingly in terms of national security and which are associated with all manner of social and political ills, including 'delinquents, drugs... and violence' (Farine, 1993: 12; Perotti, 1993a).

Although the principle of non-discrimination is written into the French Constitution, no anti-discrimination machinery has been introduced comparable to that operating in Britain.[8]

The Federal Republic of Germany

The French authorities had been forced to consider the issue of immigrants' welfare relatively early on because of problems that arose in connection with housing shortages. West Germany was also faced with a considerable housing shortage in the decades following the Second World War, but this did not initially affect immigrants because employers in Germany were bound to provide accommodation for all foreign workers. Immigrants were housed in workers' hostels or barracks, often on site, and were effectively segregated from the general population and from the German housing market. This, coupled with the notion that foreign workers would eventually return, meant that for the first two decades of postwar immigration there was no pressure or incentive for the state to consider questions of integration. It was only with the increase in family immigration towards the end of the 1960s that German policy-makers began to concern themselves with the social aspects of immigration.

The first official attempts to develop a policy framework geared towards integration appeared in the form of the 1973 Action Programme for the Employment of Immigrant Labour, aimed primarily at housing and education for immigrants, and in the creation in 1975 of a committee responsible for formulating guidelines for an immigration policy (Esser and Korte, 1985; Castles, 1985). The emphasis at this time was less one of 'assimilate or return' than one of 'temporary integration and return', reflecting a reluctance to accept that a large proportion of immigrants were here for good (Castles *et al.*, 1984). As in France, the interest to maintain a 'preparedness to return' among immigrant groups was translated into policies which kept immigrants in 'a state of dependence and insecurity' (Castles, 1985: 522). The 1965 Aliens Act linked residence permits to work permits and did not include a right of residence, even for those who had been in the Federal Republic for over ten years. The Act also excluded foreigners from the basic rights of freedom of assembly and association, freedom of movement, free choice of occupation, place of work and place of education, and protection from extradition abroad.

The first official report representing an attempt to come to terms fully with the presence of immigrant minorities in the Federal Republic was that published in 1979 by Heinz Kuhn, the federal ombudsman for foreign workers and their families. Kuhn stated that 'future policy towards foreign employees and their families living in the FRG must be based on the assumption that a development has taken place which can no longer be reversed and that the majority of those concerned are no longer guestworkers but immigrants. He recommended a series of measures designed to ensure a more secure legal status and greater opportunities for foreigners (Esser and Korte, 1985). In the same year, a list of guidelines was drawn up by the Coordination Committee on Foreign Workers, which stressed in particular the need to concentrate on the social integration of the second and third generations.

However, the progressive tone of these two reports was not reproduced in government policy for over a decade. As in France, attitudes towards immigrants became more restrictive in the lead-up to the 1982 national elections, with politicians talking more and more in terms of 'assimilate or return' (Wilpert and Gitmez, 1987: 107). These sentiments were reaffirmed in 1983 with the Act to Promote the Preparedness of Foreign Workers to Return (Federal Minister of the Interior, 1991: 6–7). While, in Britain, the immigrant issue had come to be seen primarily as a problem of black immigration, and in France as an 'Arab problem', the 'foreigners' issue in Germany had come to be seen predominantly as a 'Turkish problem'.

The 1980s witnessed a growing recognition of immigrants as a permanent and structural feature of German society and an increasing concern for the integration of immigrant minorities. A new Foreigners Act was passed in January 1991 whose primary objective was the improvement of conditions for the integration of immigrants, and which included for the first time a 'right to reside' for foreigners holding a residence permit for eight years or more. However this right is dependent on the applicants' ability to prove that they can finance their living costs.

There is little reference to the notion of 'multiculturalism' in official circles in Germany; the emphasis is placed firmly on improving immigrant minorities' social and economic status rather than on cultural matters. Indeed, the broadly assimilationist stance most prevalent at the beginning of the 1980s was echoed in the 1991 Act, which states that 'integration as a process of adaptation to German conditions... requires some participation of the aliens who have to accustom themselves above all to the values, norms and ways of living prevailing here' (Federal Minister of the Interior, 1991). Notwithstanding this orientation, immigrants have generally enjoyed considerable cultural autonomy in Germany by virtue of policies which have stressed the maintenance of a return-orientation among immigrant groups. The support of immigrants' links with their countries of origin and the socialization of children into the culture of the country of origin was seen as a way to facilitate and encourage return migration. However, because federal control over integration policies is limited to that assumed by the regional (*Länder*) and local authorities, the degree to which policy has promoted segregation, assimilation or more liberal approaches has varied from one region or city to another, particularly in relation to housing and education.

Netherlands

The Netherlands is the only West European country apart from Sweden in which central government has attempted to translate an explicit endorsement of multicultural values into a coherent policy framework. Such an approach reflects the country's pluralist tradition, discussion even turning at times to the possibility of encouraging the formation of a Muslim 'pillar' to match those of the Christian Churches and established secular or humanist bodies. The government has thus accepted some responsibility for helping minorities preserve, develop and express their cultural identity on the basis that strong group identities would help them overcome social and economic disadvantage (Netherlands Scientific Council for Government Policy, 1990).

This so-called 'minorities policy' did not appear until the 1980s, however. As in Germany, the prevailing view during the first two decades of postwar immigration was that the Netherlands 'was not and should not be an immigration country' (Penninx *et al.*, 1993: 160). Reception facilities were 'meagre in general' (Penninx *et al.*, 1993: 160) and developed as short-term responses to immediate problems as they arose. What cultural policies were pursued – such as the 1974 Mother-tongue and Culture Programme for Children from Mediterranean Countries – were geared to facilitating immigrants' reintegration in the country of origin.

Policy changed radically after the late 1970s. Forced to some extent by a series of hijackings and occupations by groups of young Moluccans in the mid-1970s, the idea of temporary stay was declared outdated and unrealistic for Moluccans, and, in 1979, the Scientific Council for Government Policy issued a report on 'ethnic minorities' which stated that the presence of immigrants should in principle be regarded as permanent (Netherlands Scientific Council for Government Policy, 1990: 1957). The conclusions of this report led to the announcement of a new 'overall ethnic minorities policy' in 1980, the Draft Minorities Bill in 1981 and the final Minorities Bill in

1983. The policy approach was two-pronged: first, a tolerant multi-cultural society should be promoted in which cultural and ethnic differences would be accepted and supported; and second, policy should be geared to overcoming immigrant minorities' social and economic disadvantage. In stark contrast to the French approach, their minority status was given explicit recognition in the Netherlands, facilitating group-specific measures in both the cultural and social and economic fields.

However, worried by the continuing and, in some cases, worsening social and economic marginalization of many immigrant groups, the government began shifting the balance of its minorities policy at the end of the 1980s to give the 'anti-deprivation' element more weight. As argued in the Scientific Council's second report on 'immigrant policy', issued in 1990:

> the government's present policy... [has] placed excessive emphasis on the creation and maintenance of facilities designed to promote a multi-cultural society. One result is that too little has been achieved in reducing inequalities in the fields of education and employment... Immigrants who so wish should be able to maintain and develop their own cultural identity ... however, this forms part of the responsibility of the individual groups themselves. The government's task is confined to helping eliminate the barriers experienced by ethnic groups as a result of their non-indigenous origins.

(Netherlands Scientific Council for Government Policy, 1990: 61)

Italy

Like Europe's traditional receiving states, Italy has adopted the dual policy of restricting immigration while at the same time promoting the integration of those who have already settled within its borders. Italian immigration policy has developed only recently, however, as a response to the new escalation in immigrant inflows and in an effort to bring its immigration control and treatment of immigrants more in line with that of other European Union member states. Italy's first major policy response to immigration came in the form of Law no. 943, passed in December 1986. This was followed in February 1990 by Law no. 39, commonly referred to as the 'Martelli Law'. Perhaps the most significant integration measures to arise out of these laws were the amnesties providing for large-scale regularization of 'irregular' or undocumented immigrants. According to one estimate, roughly 80 per cent of North African immigrants were in Italy on an irregular basis before 1986 (Blackstone, 1989: 58; Melotti, 1988). Law 943 came into effect in January 1987 with an amnesty extended by successive amendments to September 1988. Law 39 introduced the second amnesty, which provided for the registration of illegal immigrants who were present in Italy on the 31 December 1989 and who came forward to register before 29 June 1990. However, neither amnesty proved particularly successful: only about 10 per cent of irregular immigrants came forward under the first amnesty (Blackstone, 1989), and in 1991 it was estimated that up to 50 per cent of immigrants in Italy were present and/or working on an irregular basis (OECD, *SOPEMI* 1990, 1991: 53).

A comprehensive framework of integration policies which could substantially affect the living and working conditions of immigrants is only at an early stage of development in Italy. Law 39 is concerned primarily with immigration control; thus, apart from the 1981 law ratifying the 1975 ILO Migrant Workers Convention[9] (ratified in the context of Italian emigration), Law 943 still stands as the primary piece of Italian legislation dealing with integration. This law appears relatively far-reaching in its intention to guarantee 'all non-Community workers...and...their families equality of treatment and full equality of rights to the use of social and health services...to the maintenance of cultural identity, to schooling and to the availability of housing.' Yet the legislation has not been backed up by an effective enforcement machinery, nor does it provide clear guidelines on what policies should be implemented. In practice, it places considerable responsibility on the shoulders of local authorities and the voluntary sector. According to a survey published in 1991, the 'variegated world of voluntary associations performs a vital task in helping immigrants with social, bureaucratic and work-related problems', but 'analysis of local policies...shows the fragmentary and incoherent nature of most interventions...[which] range from a total abandoning of responsibility and buck-passing to (rarely) full integration' (CENSIS, 1991b: 333).

In connection with a National Conference on Immigration held in Rome in 1990, the Bocconi University was commissioned to carry out an analysis of the immigration and integration polices of France, the FRG, the Netherlands and Great Britain so as to provide information on the main types and forms of immigration policies that could potentially be applied in Italy (CENSIS, 1991a). The conclusion presented at the conference included 'the necessity of...an integration which neither produces ghettos nor is complete assimilation... of structures which ... would monitor the various aspects of integration ... [and] a promotion of greater understanding and respect between ethnic groups' (CENSIS, 1991c: 462–3).

IMMIGRANT SETTLEMENT AND INTEGRATION: SOCIAL AND ECONOMIC RIGHTS AND OPPORTUNITIES

Despite the variation in approaches to integration, an element common to the policies of every country is a concern with communities which are both economically disadvantaged and which display a distinct ethnicity based on a culture, race, religion, language and/or national identity with roots elsewhere. It is not the immigrant status of these groups which seems to matter so much as their cultural, racial or religious 'difference' from the receiving society, reinforced by social and economic marginalization. Thus integration policies have focused on immigrant communities which are at once visible and disadvantaged.

If integration is understood as a process which prevents or counteracts the social, economic and political marginalization of immigrant groups, then – regardless of the particular policies pursued – all of Western Europe's immigrant-receiving states have failed in this regard. Since the early to mid-1980s, there has been a growing recognition, at least in principle, that efforts are needed to strengthen and improve immigrant minorities' social and economic rights and opportunities. This is reflected in a report on integration published by the European Commission in 1991 which stresses the need for greater security of stay for immigrants and their offspring and the need for action in areas of employment, business, education and housing (Commission of the European Communities, 1990: 14).

Of course, the status of different immigrant groups *vis-à-vis* the dominant society is determined by a range of factors, including discrimination, the timing of immigration, the sectors of housing and employment into which particular groups originally entered, and levels of unemployment in areas where immigrants have tended to settle. This is illustrated by the well-documented process of geographical concentration of immigrant groups in the inner-city areas of Britain's largest conurbations,[10] a process which is in many respects common to the main cities of all the postwar receiving countries. To what extent this concentration has been as a result of 'exclusion, attraction or retention'[11] is debatable, and would anyway have varied from group to group. In the case of Britain, the process may be very generally – if somewhat crudely – explained in terms of immigrants' original location in the housing and labour markets. The majority of immigrants initially filled unskilled or manual jobs in industries that were located in the cities. However, British society was at that time undergoing a major process of economic and social decentralization. Economic and technological developments were already underway which were favouring shifts in the industrial sector to cheaper out-of-city locations, from heavy to light industry, and from a reliance on cheap unskilled labour to a demand for skilled workers. This process was accompanied by a growth in real incomes among the white population and a significant population movement out of the inner cities to more preferable housing in the suburbs or smaller towns. Unable to compete equally in the housing markets (owing to discrimination and low income), and initially excluded from local authority housing, immigrants were generally forced into the cheapest and most marginal privately rented [12] or owner-occupied accommodation[13] in the declining inner cities. The disadvantaged position of immigrants in the labour market can therefore be explained not only in terms of discrimination, but also in terms of a combination of sectoral and spatial segregation: from the very beginning, immigrants became concentrated in sectors of the economy and in geographical areas that have been marked by a progressive decline in demand for labour and eventually, by high levels of unemployment.

Various approaches to countering immigrant minorities' social and economic marginalization have been developed over the past decade. Although too numerous to summarize here, these have tended to be based on one of two general approaches: (i) policies aimed at equipping immigrants to compete better with the majority population (particularly education and training policies); and (ii) policies aimed at opening up the major institutions of society to greater immigrant participation (particularly in the areas of housing and employment). In both cases, there has been a constant tension between the institution of policies which directly target minorities (and therefore risk resentment from sections of the majority population) and those of more general application (which may benefit the majority population more than minorities). Whatever the approach adopted, in all areas of policy concerned with minorities' social and economic integration, the challenges and problems have become greater with the onset of economic recession, the rise in overall unemployment levels and the increasing financial squeeze on the welfare state.

The most prominent measures aimed at improving immigrant minorities' access to institutions are those taken in the field of employment, where policies have been introduced to overcome structural discrimination in the labour market. In a 1990 report on immigrant policy, for example, the Netherlands Scientific Council for Government Policy advocated the introduction of a non-punishable obligation on the part of employers to implement employment equity and prepare a plan setting out the goals that the employer intends to achieve in this respect; and advocated the introduction of a punishable obligation for employers to file an annual report concerning the extent to which members of 'visible' and other minorities are represented in the various positions of employment (Netherlands Scientific Council for Government Policy, 1990: 75). This policy – defined as 'positive action' – should not be confused with 'positive' or 'reverse' discrimination, which has not been pursued by any government in Western Europe.

As regards policies to counter direct discrimination against individual members of minority groups, only the United Kingdom has a comprehensive legal enforcement machinery of longstanding. Recent moves to amend legislation in other countries have tended to be limited to the consideration of laws to combat overt racist behaviour. The Council of Europe's Committee of Experts on Community Relations recommended in its final report in 1991 that member states strengthen their anti-discrimination laws and promote the use of the legal remedies available to minority members (Council of Europe, 1991: 66). This is a view shared by the European Commission and European Parliament, but there are no signs as yet that this will lead to an enforceable European instrument to combat racial discrimination.

An issue that has attracted particular attention is the integration of the so-called 'second' and 'third' generations, since it has become increasingly apparent that the marginal position of immigrants in housing, employment and public life has tended to be perpetuated among their children and their children's offspring. Indeed, unemployment levels among descendants of immigrants are frequently higher than among their parents. Anxious to prevent the formation of a permanent 'minority underclass', governments have developed policies aimed at improving opportunities for the younger age-groups through education and training. However, in all the postwar receiving countries, ethnic minority children continue to be over-represented in the slowest tracks of the education system and under-represented at the higher levels of secondary and tertiary education (although the extent of underachievement varies considerably from group to group).[14] In all countries, certain groups have been targeted for special language classes,[15] since language has been seen as one of the most important factors contributing to their problems at school.[16] Other efforts to improve employment opportunities for ethnic minority labour-market entrants have included programmes of vocational training (e.g. Youth Opportunities and Youth Training Programmes in Britain). However, these have failed to have a significant impact because, among other things, training cannot guarantee jobs, particularly in areas of high unemployment. Furthermore, ethnic minorities are frequently over-represented in programmes that offer little or no opportunity for skilled or more qualified occupations (Wilpert, 1988b: 127).

Aware that disadvantage among minority groups as a whole is often connected with economic stagnation in areas with high immigrant populations, governments have also instituted programmes of urban renewal and rejuvenation. A common pattern, however, is the displacement of immigrant groups from areas that have undergone redevelopment,[17] a trend frequently associated with inner-city 'gentrification'.

INTEGRATION AND 'ETHNICITY': IDENTITY, CITIZENSHIP AND POLITICAL RIGHTS

Despite the *de facto* marginalization of many immigrants and immigrant groups in the social and economic spheres of society, most immigrants and their descendants in Western Europe now enjoy a relatively secure legal status that allows for permanent settlement and *de jure* equal treatment in areas such as housing, employment, education and welfare benefits. Thus most enjoy, at least formally, full economic and social rights, and – as indicated in the previous section – much of the effort made by governments and other authorities in respect of integration is devoted to promoting and protecting immigrants' and minorities' access to and enjoyment of these rights.

Yet if integration is simply a question of improving immigrant minorities' social and economic status, one is led to question what it is that sets immigrants apart from other disadvantaged groups in society. To a large extent, immigrant disadvantage is synonymous with class disadvantage: as indicated above, most immigrant workers originally entered positions in the labour market which placed them firmly within the working class, and thus their present socio-economic position may be largely explained in terms of their class position.[18] Why, therefore, should integration policies differ from wider policies designed to counter all forms of class-based disadvantage? It is interesting to note that in the Netherlands and the United Kingdom, 'urban regeneration' and other policies designed to improve the social and economic status of immigrant minorities have exploited this linkage at times so as to prevent any resentment that might arise within other sectors of the population if policies were seen to favour minorities. Indeed, as Van Praag notes, in the Netherlands it is unclear whether foreign origin or deprivation is the primary criterion in selecting the groups to which 'minority policy' applies (Van Praag, 1986: 40; Netherlands Scientific Council for Government Policy, 1990: 40).

However, while class status is undoubtedly a central factor explaining the position of many immigrant minorities in Western Europe, it is clearly not the only factor to be considered. It should be noted that immigrant and ethnic minorities' socio-economic or class status does, in fact, vary considerably: many individuals and certain immigrant groups have been very successful as entrepreneurs or have competed successfully in the education and labour markets, and yet continue to experience problems in their relations with the majority population or sections of it. And even those policies aimed at improving immigrants' social and economic mobility have run up against a number of problems behind which lie important questions relating to immigrants' juridical or perceived status as foreign. This becomes clear once one ventures into the realms of identity, political rights and citizenship. As noted by G.S. Cross in the context of France, foreign labour became a 'radically distinctive class in France. Not merely were immigrants predominantly propertyless and unskilled, but they were non-citizens' (Cross, 1983: 16).[19]

The importance of identity and ethnicity in the shaping of integration policy has been marked in Western Europe since the early 1970s. As indicated above, European receiving states have demonstrated varying ways of working around the issue, ranging from direct efforts to minimize cultural difference ('assimilation' policies, as in France during the 1970s and early 1980s), to avoidance[20] (Germany, and France during the 1950s and 1960s), acceptance[21] (United Kingdom), through to direct and explicit encouragment[22] ('multicultural' policies, as in the Netherlands).

The variations and shifts in approaches to the cultural dimension of immigrant status in themselves indicate the difficulties that European receiving states have had in coming to terms with the presence of culturally, ethnically or religiously distinct immigrant minority communities. In the Netherlands, as noted above, there has been a retreat from the multicultural stance of the past in favour of anti-deprivation and anti-discrimination policies. This shift has taken place not only because the earlier stance seemed to be failing in its aim to improve the socio-economic position of immigrant minorities, but also because the explicitly multiculturalist line became more difficult to uphold in an environment of growing anti-immigrant sentiment among the wider public (Netherlands Scientific Council for Government Policy, 1990). In Britain, equivocal attitudes towards the status of immigrant culture, and particularly non-Christian religions, were forced into the open by the 'Rushdie affair' of 1989/90 which raised fundamental question about the role of Islam (and religion in general) in public life and revealed a comprehension gap between sections of the Muslim community and the wider society. Equally difficult questions have been brought to the fore by the 'headscarves' issue in France. This question has taken on great symbolic importance there, not least because its emergence coincided with the Republic's 1989 bicentenary celebrations. Girls' insistence on covering their heads at school for religious reasons has been seen as a direct challenge to the republican and lay identity of the French state (Nielsen, 1992: 163). Two years after the government passed a law prohibiting the display of distinctive religious, political or ideological symbols in school, the *Conseil d'Etat* ruled that freedom of expression should not be jeopardized by the secular principles of education (Gaeremynck, 1993).[23] The issue has yet to be resolved, however.[24]

Today's problems may be seen to stem less from continuing immigration (with the exception of the new immigration countries of southern Europe) than from a failure throughout the past four decades to reach a clear vision of what immigration means for the future of West European societies, particularly for the basis of communal or national identity. A number of basic questions still need to be addressed, including those formulated by Peter Schuck in the context of the United States: 'Who are we? What do we wish to become? Which individuals can help us reach that goal? Which individuals constitute the "we" who shall decide these questions?' (Schuck, 1985: 286).

'Multiculturalism' as a Model

As European governments have come to acknowledge the reality of cultural, ethnic and religious diversity, it has become increasingly common to refer to these societies as 'multicultural'. A recent report on the Council of Europe's Community Relations Project, for example, states that 'The presence of immigrant communities and their growth have undoubtedly reinforced the multicultural character of European society.' The report goes on to observe that 'Most immigration countries in Western Europe have discovered the strength of ethnicity' and that 'It has been acknowledged that immigration had indeed led to the development of multi-ethnic societies' (Council of Europe, 1991).

The concept of multiculturalism remains very vague, however, at least in the European context. As Isajiw has argued, 'one must distinguish between multiculturalism as an ideology, a social policy, and as a feature of the structure of society' (Isajiw, 1975: 1); As is already clear, multiculturalism as a coherent social policy has a long way to go in Western Europe. As a feature of social structure, Western Europe is certainly multicultural in the sense that a number of different cultures are present in society. However, if used in this sense, the term is devoid of any meaning other than an indication of cultural diversity. It says nothing about how this diversity is structured in society. Indeed, even as an ideology, the concept requires clarification, for, as John Rex has argued, a look at the various forms of plural 'multicultural' and 'multiracial' societies in the world reveals that 'such societies are far from providing us with an ideal and it must therefore be in some very special sense that we speak of such an ideal in contemporary conditions' (Rex, 1985: 3).

Jorgen Nielsen writes of the 'liberal myth of multicultural' Europe, and argues that those who lay too much stress on the multicultural nature of European society fail to acknowledge the significance of the nation as a central ideological and political construct in Western Europe. Indeed, he argues that to talk of Europe's 'new' multicultural identity implicitly legitimates the ideal of the culturally bounded nation by affirming the common European myth of a pre-existent monocultural society. In his eyes, the social reality of multicultural Europe is one in which immigrant culture becomes a subculture beneath the dominant national culture; in which these subcultures are tolerated only as long as they do not impinge on the life of the majority; and in which any adaptation necessary must be effected by the minorities rather than the majority as it is the bearers of European native culture who also hold the instruments of political, economic and social control (Nielsen, 1992: 150–3).

Yet, according to Ernest Gellner, advanced industrial societies such as those of Western Europe depend on a shared unitary culture at national or state level. The essential characteristics of industrial society, including universal literacy, mobility and individualism, political centralization and a costly state-supervised educational infrastructure, 'impel it into a situation in which political and cultural boundaries are on the whole congruent' (Gellner, 1983: 110). What is essential about this shared culture is that it is a 'high' culture, i.e. that it is based on standardized, literacy- and education-based systems of communication (Gellner, 1983: 54), for its primary importance is in the 'public' domain of politics and economics. In other respects, it may vary considerably. In the modern world, it is generally incorporated into forms of national culture or identification. However, as Anthony Smith argues, the concept of national identity itself takes many forms. This is illustrated by what have been termed the 'Western' and 'Eastern' models of national identity: the 'Western' model based on 'historic territory, legal-political community, legal-political equality of members, and common civic culture and ideology'; and the 'Eastern' model based on 'genealogy and presumed descent ties, popular mobilization, vernacular languages, customs and traditions' (Smith, 1991: 11and12). These may be taken as ideal types, for in the real world, every national identity incorporates both civic ('Western') and ethnic ('Eastern') elements in varying forms and to varying extents (Smith, 1991: 13).

Gellner's conception of the unified national culture does not preclude cultural difference within a state, but precludes cultural difference which is political and/or economically significant in the public domain. Drawing on the twin concepts of the unified 'high' national culture and the 'Western' model of national identity, John Rex puts forward a model for multiculturalism which does not conflict with the concept of political and cultural unity at the national level (Rex, 1985). The model is based on the liberal principle of equality of individual rights, and is therefore distinguished very clearly from what he terms a 'plural' model, in which ethnic or cultural distinctions coincide with a differentiated structure of social, economic, civil and political rights. The public domain, including the world of law, politics, economics and education,[25] is governed by a common civic culture based upon the notion of the political and legal equality of individuals. Cultural diversity of 'folk' culture is restricted to, but allowed to flourish in, the private domain, this being responsible for 'moral education, primary socialization, and the inculcation of religious belief'.

This model bears comparison to Ronald Dworkin's Kantian view of a liberal society as one that is united around a strong procedural commitment to treat people with equal respect without adopting any particular substantive view about the ends of life.[26] Rex's distinction between a 'multicultural' and a 'plural' model of society is also echoed in the distinction drawn by Charles Taylor between, on the one hand, a liberal society based on the universalist ideal of the equal dignity of all citizens – associated with the equalization of rights and culturally or ethnically 'blind' forms of nondiscrimination – and, on the other hand, a society founded on the 'politics of difference' – associated, in its liberal form, with calls for the equal recognition of the unique and distinctive identities of different groups in society and, by extension, possible calls for a redefinition of non-discrimination such that groups are treated differentially, whether temporarily in order to eradicate group-based disadvantage (e.g. through reverse discrimination), or more permanently to ensure the long-term survival of one or more different cultures in society (e.g. through forms of local groups-based autonomy) (Taylor, 1992).

A concept of society similar to Rex's multicultural model is endorsed in the Council of Europe's 1991 report on community relations. It states that:

> It has been acknowledged that immigration has ... led to the development of multi-ethnic societies and that such societies should offer possibilities for peaceful coexistence to all communities, thus enabling people to arrange their private lives in line with their own traditions, within the limits set by the existing legal order (which in itself is not unchangeable). Such ... views are based on the idea that, in the private sphere at least, cultures can be compatible and that different cultures and ethnic communities can live together peacefully in one and the same society.
>
> (Council of Europe, 1991: 22)

Rex emphasizes the potential for conflict in such a model. He argues that 'civic culture includes the notion of conflict. The social order which we have is the resultant of conflict ... minority communities at any one time may conflict with and challenge the existing order as have communities based upon social class in the past' (Rex, 1985: 15–

16). Indeed, despite the emphasis on 'peaceful coexistence' in the passage quoted above, it is precisely because of the constant potential for conflict that the Council of Europe report argues the 'determined action in the community relations field needs to be a permanent feature of a multiethnic society' (Council of Europe, 1991: 13).

'Multicultural Society' in Western Europe

Collective identities have never been fixed, but are constantly re-invented and reconstructed. The extent to which a more pluralist conception of the nation has developed in Western Europe during the second half of this century (albeit unevenly) would seem to bode well for the development of multicultural society as envisaged by Rex. It would seem to be linked to a weakening of exclusivist nationalist sentiment in the public sphere and its gradual replacement by a more inclusive and rational civic culture governing relations between individuals and sub-groups in society. However, Western Europe clearly has a long way to go before it can be said that its societies fit such a multicultural model. Perhaps most importantly, one is led to question the extent to which the public domain is structured purely on the basis of a civic culture. To what extent are national communities held together in the public sphere by rational ties based on organized political and economic association and the 'praxis of citizens who actively exercise their civil rights' (Habermas, 1991), and to what extent by affective 'bonds of solidarity among members ... united by shared memories, myths and traditions' (Smith, 1991: 15) and ethnic and wider cultural and/or religious ties?

The balance between these cohesive forces differs from country to country, but in no country in Western Europe has affective culture entirely given way to neutral 'civic' values in the public domain. In Germany, for example, there is still a strong attachment to the concept of the German *Volk*. Thus, German ethnicity tends to play a dominant role in both the private and public spheres, as reflected in Germany's restrictive citizenship policies.[27] In Britain, there is no constitutional separation between Church and state. Therefore, despite the fact that British society today may be described as predominantly secular or post-Christian, at the institutional level, the Christian (Protestant) religion is still accorded an important role in the public sphere and it is held on to as an important symbol of (English) national identity. In France, one might expect to find the clearest representation of a nation united on the basis of a universalist

civic culture deriving from the post-Revolutionary emphasis on a
unitary 'high' political culture to replace local regional or ethnic
identities. However, this unitary political culture was never devoid
of ethnic content, and, as noted above, foreign immigrants have been
expected to 'assimilate' culturally to more than basis civic values in
France, at least in the past. As argued by Michael Walzer, in the real
world most governments of liberal nation-states take an interest in the
cultural survival of the majority nation, and therefore 'don't claim to
be neutral with reference to the language, history, literature, calendar,
or even the minor mores of the majority'. At the same time, 'they
vindicate their liberalism by tolerating and respecting ethnic and
religious differences and allowing all minorities an equal freedom to
organize their members, express their cultural values, and reproduce
their way of life in civil society and in the family' (Walzer, 1992: 100).

Charles Taylor goes further in examining the limitations of the
universalist model of a liberal 'multicultural' society by challenging
the claim that 'difference-blind' liberalism, even in its ideal form, can
offer a neutral ground for the coexistence of different cultures. Taylor
argues that the very concept of liberal society, based on equality of
individual rights, derives from a Western Christian cultural context
and thus cannot be seen as culturally neutral, even in its most rigorous
or most accommodating and 'hospitable' forms. Liberalism, he
argues, 'is not a possible meeting ground for all cultures, but is the
political expression of one range of cultures, and quite incompatible
with other ranges'. This is illustrated by the Salman Rushdie controversy, in which the basic 'civic' separation of politics and religions, of
the public and private spheres and of the right to freedom of speech
confronted an alternative Islamic view of the world. Thus, 'liberalism
can't and shouldn't claim complete cultural neutrality' because liberalism 'is also a fighting creed' (Taylor, 1992: 62). Taylor therefore
argues that, in the context of a multicultural society, 'The challenge
is to deal with [minorities'] ... sense of marginalization without
compromising our basic political principles' (Taylor, 1992: 63).

A further, more concrete, deviation from the multicultural model is
evident in the extent to which immigrant minorities *as groups* are
differentially incorporated socially, economically and politically in
de facto and *de jure* terms in Western Europe. In this respect, West
European society might be seen to come closer to representing Rex's
'plural' model, in which ethnic or cultural cleavages coincide with a
differentiated structure of social, economic, civil and political rights
and opportunities.

An important factor militating against the full integration of immigrant minority groups is the legal definition and wider perceptions of immigrants and their offspring as 'outsiders' in many countries. This is a particular problem for the 'second generation' immigrants born and brought up in Western Europe. As observed by Czarina Wilpert in a study of Turkish immigrant groups in Berlin, 'there exists, for all second-generation Turks, a tension between their lack of a legitimate future and membership of German society (institutional marginality) and the *de facto* experience of a legitimate claim to belongingness through a life lived [in the Federal Republic] ... [This] conflict is enhanced by the ascriptive experiences of discrimination, denigration and youths' concomitant identification with their family and culture of origin' (Wilpert, 1988b).

The multicultural model envisaged by Rex depends on no individual having more or fewer rights than any other or a greater or lesser capacity to operate in society because of his or her ethnic category. Yet access to, and exercise of, rights has always depended on the individual's citizenship status, defined not only in formal, but also in substantive terms. This should pose no problems when it is clear who are and who are not members or citizens. However, the very same process which has made multiculturalism a salient issue in Western Europe has also brought about an erosion of the distinction between members and non-members, and between citizens and foreigners. As observed by Tomas Hammar:

> Many foreign citizens have ... gained a secure residence status [in Western Europe] ... They may have lived such a long period in the host country ... [or] their family ties may be so strong ... that they in fact constitute a new category of foreign citizens whose residence status is fully guaranteed or almost so. Those who belong to this category have also in several countries been entitled to equal treatment in all spheres of life, with full access to the labour market, business, education, social welfare, even to employment in branches of the public service, etc. A new status groups has emerged, and members of this groups are not regular and plain foreign citizens any more, but also not naturalized citizens of the receiving country.   (Hammar, 1990: 12–13)

What is particularly salient to the multicultural model is the fact that, where immigrant minorities are present in society, the boundaries separating one citizenship or membership status from another tend to coincide with ethnic or cultural boundaries. This is because the different frontiers of citizenship affect immigrants and their offspring rather than native-born members of the majority population (as opposed, for example, to a situation in which rights are differentiated according to social class or gender). As argued by Gellner, modern industrial society will have to respect cultural differences where they persist, 'provided that they are superficial and do not engender genuine barriers between people, in which case the barriers, not the cultures, constitute a grave problem' (Gellner, 1983: 121).

Rainer Baubock argues that the inequalities inherent in this structure can be minimized either by equalizing the rights attached to each status or by modifying the boundaries between categories such that upward mobility from one position to another is made easier (Baubock, 1992: 73–114). Moves have been made to ease immigrants' transition from one status to another, for instance, through amnesty programmes for illegal immigrants, a shortening of the time period necessary to achieve permanent residence status, and a relaxation of naturalization laws and procedures. Efforts have also been made to equalize immigrant minorities' social and economic rights, as already discussed. However, these have not been matched in the political sphere. Although foreign nationals are generally allowed to express themselves politically in Western Europe (to form associations, to take part in union activities, to demonstrate and strike, and to join political parities), they are excluded from participation in national elections in all Western European countries apart from the United Kingdom, and it is only in recent years that a number of states have introduced the right to vote for certain categories of foreign nationals in municipal or regional elections.[28] As a result, a substantial proportion of immigrants and immigrant minorities are not represented politically and have no formal political voice.

This not only raises questions as to the health of representative democracy in Western Europe, but can also be argued to constitute a significant obstacle to the substantive integration of many immigrant minority groups (Hammar, 1990; Layton-Henry, 1990). Because, in such a situation, the promotion of immigrants' interests through formal political channels has to take place on the basis of a potentially weak and distorting filter-through process (or outside such channels altogether), the opportunity for immigrants to have a meaningful say in the policies which affect their status is likely to be limited, as is the incentive or potential for such groups to develop any sense of political citizenship (Garcia, 1992). This carries a danger of alienation, disaffection and a persistent orientation towards the country of origin among minority communities which is prone to work against the processes of social and economic integration which the host governments are so keen to promote. Czarina Wilpert observed in Berlin, for example, the persistence of a return-orientation (or 'myth of return') not only among first generation migrants, but also among their children, a situation which she ascribed in part to their imposed status as 'outsiders' or 'denizens' (Wilpert, 1988b).

In this context, however, generalization is extremely problematic. Just as approaches to the social and economic integration of immigrants differ from country to country and group to group, so do policies affecting the substantive and juridical citizenship status of immigrant minority communities. Immigration policy in the United Kingdom represents the most obvious exception: the majority of immigrants who arrived in the UK during the postwar period did so as British subjects with full citizenship (and thus full political) rights; naturalization and dual citizenship are comparatively easy to attain; most offspring of immigrants born in the country are accorded British citizenship; and all Commonwealth citizens migrating today gain the right to vote in national elections after one year's residence in the UK. In France, the situation differs in that most immigrants did not enter with citizenship rights. Nevertheless, naturalization has been relatively easy for settled immigrants, and all offspring of immigrants born in France are entitled to French citizenship. However, foreign nationals cannot vote in either local or national elections in France. In Germany, on the other hand, the majority of second- and third-generation descendants of immigrants remain unnaturalized. Meanwhile, long-settled foreign nationals can vote in the regional elections of some *Länder* but not of others.

These differences can be explained largely in terms of the varying concepts of citizenship which apply in the different countries of Western Europe; these concepts in turn derive from the specific historical development of the nation-states concerned. Thus, in Britain and France, residence, allegiance to the state and submission to its jurisdiction represent the traditional hallmarks of citizenship. Consequently, territorial concepts – i.e. place of birth (*jus soli*) and place of residence – came to determine nationality in these countries (Ra'anan, 1991: 3–32). Such concepts lent themselves to conceiving of the populations of these states' colonies as attached juridically to the centre as subjects or citizens. Meanwhile, the Netherlands' relatively liberal stance on foreigners' voting rights can be explained in terms of the country's pluralist history and political structure. In

Germany, by contrast, the centralized nation-state developed much later, and in such a way that encouraged the definition of citizenship in terms *jus sanguinis* as opposed to *jus soli*. As Ra'anan describes, 'it is not where an individual resides and which state has jurisdiction over him that determines his nationality, but rather who he is – his cultural, religious and historic identity, i.e. his ethnicity, a heritage received from his ancestors and carried with him, in mind and body, irrespective of his current place of domicile' (Ra'anan, 1991: 13). German citizenship is thus traditionally defined in terms of membership of the German *Volk*, encompassing 'ethnic Germans' or '*Aussiedler*' residents outside Germany, but not foreign immigrants' descendants who might have been born in Germany.

In substantive terms, however, the significance of these differences should probably not be overemphasized. The problems that France has experienced since the 1950s in accepting immigrants of different cultures and the United Kingdom's difficulties in coming to terms with the new multiracial nature of its society demonstrate the limits to the territorial of 'civic' basis of membership and citizenship of these states. Indeed, in Britain, the experience of black and Asian immigration during the postwar period led directly to an erosion of the territorial foundations of British citizenship. The distinction between 'patrial' and 'non-patrial' citizens introduced in the 1970s – criticized so much at the time because it was seen to discriminate against potential migrants from the so-called 'New Commonwealth' (non-white) countries – demonstrated a growing emphasis on the principle of *jus sanguinis* in the operation of British citizenship laws, and hence a retreat from policies which had allowed the entry and settlement of substantial numbers of black and Asian immigrants. Similarly, the French nationality law was revised in July 1993 so that children born in France of foreign parents would no longer become French nationals automatically at the age of 18.[29]

The citizenship question is still a very thorny issue in most countries, particularly in the context of political rights, naturalization and dual citizenship. This indicates not only that traditional concepts of citizenship or membership have become more difficult to apply, but also that no clear alternative structure has yet been found to take their place.

Thus, to the extent that particular immigrant minority populations can be singled out as groups which are excluded from certain rights because of their legal status as outsiders or as groups that are deprived of equal access to those and other rights (economic, social and political) because of their perceived status as outsiders, many remain a 'class apart', whether it be in their own eyes or in the eyes of majority populations. In the development of all of Western Europe's 'nation-states', ideas of 'belongingness' became tied to those of cultural, linguistic, ethnic and/or religious identity. Those who have least easily conformed to this identity have often been those who have remained the most marginalized. Despite efforts to speed immigrant and ethnic minorities' integration by strengthening or improving their social, economic and (to a lesser extent) political rights and opportunities, it is not at all clear that Western European society is reconciled to the cultural and ethnic diversity which the last few decades of immigration have brought about. Indeed, at a time of considerable economic and political uncertainty, and at a time when the traditional frontiers of the state are being eroded by a range of transnational and global economic, political and social forces (including migration), there is a potential for society in Western Europe to turn increasingly to negative symbols of identity, i.e. to base their identity on opposition to the identities of others. Nothing demonstrates this more clearly than the upsurge in extreme anti-immigrant opinions in Western Europe and the increase in incidents of racial violence and harassment in recent years.

Extreme Anti-Immigrant Opinion and Racial Violence and Harassment

As noted by Robin Oakley in a 1991 report on racial violence and harassment, racism is not a new phenomenon in European history: anti-Semitism, for example, has been present in Europe for over a millennium. Yet postwar immigration has introduced 'a new chapter' into the history of racism in Europe. According to Oakley, whether it has emerged as a question of 'racial' difference, as in Britain, or as a question of cultural difference, Europe's 'new racism':

> confronts many of the Mediterranean and Third World immigrants who form its new 'internal colonies' with a form of xenophobia which ... articulates a deep-rooted though previously latent Eurocentrism which appeals to the superiority and inherent proprietorship of certain lifestyles and 'civilised' values. This strong and assertive form of xenophobia has displace earlier intra-European rivalries, and has become manifest in the ideologies of right-wing movements across Europe, some of which have achieved considerable electoral success. (Oakley, 1991: 9–10)

While the growing strength of extreme right-wing anti-immigrant political movements in Western Europe has attracted considerable attention over recent years, less attention has been paid to the linked (but not necessarily causally related) increase in racial violence and harassment. Thus, with the partial exception of the United Kingdom, institutional recognition of the issues of racial violence and harassment has been slow to develop. In official circles, both forms of racist expression have tended to be treated in isolation, as a failing on the part of a particular minority within the population.

There is clearly a strong link between, on the one hand, overt racism and racial violence, and on the other, poverty, insecurity and competition for jobs and housing among the more vulnerable sectors of society. Thus it is not altogether surprising that extreme anti-immigrant attitudes and incidents of racial violence and harassment tend to increase during periods of economic recession and high unemployment and tend to be found among 'persons who feel threatened and who do not have access to other forms of personal and institutional power' (Oakley, 1991: 41). Nevertheless, these forms of racist expression and behaviour cannot be properly understood in isolation from the broader and deeper tendencies towards racial or cultural exclusion and domination in contemporary European societies. As argued by Liz Fekete, it is not enough to see the growth of right-wing organizations 'as confined to the extremities of society ... like a gangrenous limb that needs amputation'. It can only be properly examined 'within the framework of the body politic as a whole, [involving] the health of the whole organism, so to speak' (Fekete, 1991: 148). It is because the most overt forms of racist behaviour have wider resonance in community relations – or are seen to have such resonance by members of the victim communities – that their impact is so significant. Racial violence and harassment do not only affect the individuals directly involved, for it is not the violent acts themselves which have so much impact on the wider community as the racist message which they convey; indeed, everyday 'low-level' forms of harassment may carry as much force as more isolated incidents of extreme violence. As Oakley notes, 'Such harassment is an effective means of maintaining racial boundaries at the local level ... [and] of keeping victim communities subordinated.' Moreover, 'few individuals need to be actively involved in the use of force to establish or maintain the pattern of inter-group relations; provided others condone or at least do not oppose the action, the racial order at the collective or group level will still have been successfully imposed' (Oakley, 1991: 13).

CONCLUSION

It is because of what isolated or localized forms of racism and inter-group tension say about relations in the wider society that the recent Council of Europe report on community relations lays great stress on the need for integration policies and other forms of action which start from the basis that integration is a process involving society as a whole: 'It is no longer appropriate to think of the migrant population and the host population as separate, possibly even antagonist groups; rather we should think of society as a single whole in all its ethnic and cultural diversity' (Council of Europe, 1991: 24).

It should not be forgotten that European societies have powerful anti-racist impulses which have deep roots in European liberal tradi-tions, as illustrated by the strength of such movements as the Anti-Nazi League in the United Kingdom and *SOS Racisme* in France. This impulse is in constant tension with nationalistic, xenophobic and exclusionist tendencies, and it is for this reason that political leaders have a central role to play in influencing community relations by virtue of the messages they convey through their policies and in political statements. The immigration issue has always been a subject easily manipulated for political advantage. Whether explicitly or implicitly, politicians have tended to find more immediate advantage in playing on people's fears and insecurities by drawing on xenopho-bic and exclusionist tendencies. While this may have proved an effect-ive way of winning votes, its more significant or long-term effect is likely to have been to sour community relations and increase inter-group tensions at the local and national levels.

Immigrant minority integration and the promotion of good com-munity relations is a complex and difficult process for all European countries, particularly at a time of increasing economic and social insecurity. The substantive obstacles are considerable and the chal-lenges enormously varied. There are no 'quick fixes' available to governments and no single mix of policies which would be appropriate to all countries and all localities in all situations. But if there is one goal which could be seen as applicable to Europe as a whole, it is the aim of reconciling majority populations to the ethnic and cultural diversity that the last few decades of immigration have brought about. Only when acceptance of the multicultural and multi-ethnic nature of European societies takes as strong a hold as exclusionist tendencies have had up until now will immigrant and ethnic communities see themselves – and be seen – as an integral and valued part of society.

The messages currently being conveyed by Western European leaders are at best confused in this regard. Governments have expressed a positive commitment to securing the successful integration of immigrant minority populations at both the national and European Union or Council of Europe levels. This is reflected in the conclusions reached by the Council of Europe's Committee of Experts on Community Relations in 1991 which stress the need for governments and the public to understand that most immigrants have come to stay and that they have much to contribute to the countries in which they live. It emphasizes the need for legislation to combat discrimination and ensure equality of opportunity; the need to consider immigrant and ethnic communities as key partners in promoting good community relations and to encourage immigrants to develop a sense of belonging to their new society; and the need to accept that integration and the development of good community relations are long term processes that require long term policy views (Council of Europe, 1991: 26). Yet governments have shown a tendency to respond more readily to negative than to positive public attitudes towards immigrant minorities; and at the EU level, they have done little to ensure that immigrant minorities feel or are seen to be an integral part of the 'European project'.[30]

Importantly, governments seem not to have paid serious attention to how their stance on continuing immigration might interact with processes of immigrant minority integration. In a climate of growing public anxiety over immigration, policies have been presented increasingly in terms that label immigration – both past as present – as a problem, even a security threat. The widespread negative perception of immigration which is bolstered by this approach can only reinforce hostile tendencies in society towards immigrant minorities. The need for vigilance to prevent such perceptions taking root is all the greater at a time of economic downturn and rising unemployment, when immigrant minorities are already a vulnerable target for public discontent. Immigration policy conveys important messages relating to public perceptions of society and its future. The perception of Western society as founded on concepts of openness, tolerance, respect for human rights and commitment to democracy and civic values – arguably essential for the future stability of Westernn European societies – is difficult to reconcile with immigration policies which convey messages of closure, isolation and intolerance of the outsider, and which erode basic civic or human rights principles such as family unity and protection for victims of persecution. The Council of Europe's Committee of Experts on Community Relations concluded that 'Open, welcoming and tolerant attitudes are the only sound basis for good community relations' (Council of Europe, 1991: 25). It is to be hoped that this conclusion finds concrete expression in the policies adopted by Westernn European governments in their future efforts to promote immigrants' integration and good community relations.

Foreign population by nationality: major recruitment countries and major immigrant groups in the early 1980s and 1990s (in thousands)

Nationality	'Host' Country											
	Belgium		France		Germany		Neth-erlands		UK		Switzerland	
	1981	1990	1982	1990	1980	1990	1980	1990	1984	1990	1980	1990
Italy	277	241	340	254	618	548	21	17	83	75	421	379
Ireland	1	2	-	-	-	-	-	-	491	638	-	-
Spain	58	52	327	216	180	135	23	17	25	24	97	116
Portugal	11	17	767	646	112	85	9	8	10[a]	21	11	86
Greece	21	21	-	-	298	315	4	5	-	-	9	8
Turkey	66	85	122	202	1462	1675	139	204	-	-	38	64
Yugosl.	6	6	63	52	632	653	14	14	-	-	44	141
Algeria	11	11	805	620	5[b]	7	-	-	-	-	-	-
Morocco		110	142	441	585	36	66	83	157	-	-	-
Tunisia	7	6	191	208	23	26	2	3	-	-	-	-
Poland	-	-	65	46	88[c]	241	-	-	-	-	-	5
New C'wealth & E/W Africa	-	-	-	-	-	-	-	-	442	394	-	-
Other countries	318	322	593	781	1000	1491	225	267	698	761	273	301
Total	886	905	3714	3608	4453	5242	521	692	1601	1875	893	1100
of which EC	594	550	1595	1309	1494[d]	1325[e]	171	168	701[f]	889	701	760

(a) Less than 10,000; (b) Figure for 1982; (c) Figure for 1983; (d) Figure for 1982; (e) Figure for 1989; (f) Figure for 1983.

Source: SOPEMI (OECD Continuous Reporting System on Migration), *Trends in International Migration*, OECD, Paris, 1992.

NOTES

1. Not only into the longer-standing 'receiving' states of north-western Europe, but also into what had been the 'sending' states of southern Europe.

2. Under the 1948 Nationality Act, all colonial and Commonwealth citizens were British subjects, and as such were free to hold a UK passport, to enter Britain to find work, to settle and to bring families without being subject to immigration controls. Once in the UK, all UK passport holders had the same rights and duties, including the right to vote in local and national elections. (Note that European migration to Britain continued to be dominated by that of Irish nationals, who continue to enjoy full citizenship rights in the UK.)

3. Cf. the Netherlands, discussed below.

4. See Layton-Henry (1984: 134).

5. The Commission for Racial Equality (CRE) is empowered to investigate complaints (individual or collective) of racial discrimination (direct or indirect) in all areas of housing, employment, education, provision of services, etc., and to take cases to court where appropriate (except in employment, where cases are dealt with by an industrial tribunal). The CRE received 1381 applications for legal assistance in 1990. See Commission for Racial Equality (1991: Appendix 6).

6. Perceptions of whom are coloured by the French colonial experience in Algeria, particularly the war of independence, and by the current political upheaval in Algeria.

7. *Le Premier Rapport du Haut Conseil à l'Intégration*, 18 February 1991. Quoted in Philippe Farine (1992: 7, translated by the author).

8. Britain stands out in Europe in respect of its comprehensive framework of anti-discrimination legislation. See UN Centre for Human Rights (1991).

9. ILO Migrant Workers (Supplementary Provisions) Convention of June 1975.

10. See, for example, Phizacklea and Miles (1980); Cross (1983); Massey (1984).

11. See, for example, Rex and Tomlinson (1979).

12. West Indian immigrants particularly, followed later by movement into council housing. Immigrants were initially excluded from local authority housing because eligibility depended on a certain period of residence in the area, and housing was generally allocated to those who had been waiting the longest.

13. Particularly Asian immigrants.

14. Note, for example, that, in the United Kingdom, children of Indian ethnic origin tend to perform above the level of their white peers, whereas children of West Indian descent are more likely to underachieve; children of Turkish descent tend to underachieve to a greater extent than those of Yugoslav, Greek, Italian, or Spanish descent.

15. Women have also been targeted for language training. Note also 'mother-tongue' language teaching, which has sometimes been supported by the state, either (in the past) to promote the preparedness of immigrants and their children to return to their country of origin (especially in the FRG), or to promote cultural identity within immigrant groups (particularly in the Netherlands).

16. Note that Dutch language lessons will be mandatory for foreigners in the Netherlands after 1996 (at present they are voluntary). This reflects

the shift away from 'minorities policy' towards 'anti-deprivation' policies in the Netherlands.

17. There is no consistent pattern as to whether the outcome is a *de facto* displacement of entire communities or whether the result is a break-up of immigrant communities. Immigrant/minority settlement patterns should not be seen as a static or finished process; communities are in a constant state of flux, and one area of concentration may all but disappear only to be replaced by another elsewhere.

18. For a discussion of how initial entry into the labour market affects immigrants position in society, see Piore, 1979. For a discussion of immigrants class status in Britain, see Phizacklea and Miles (1977); and in the European context, Castles and Kosack (1973).

19. Quoted in Ogden (1993: 111).

20. Meaning that no national policy was developed which dealt either directly or indirectly with the cultural question.

21. Meaning that considerable room was allowed for cultural difference, but that no consistent and explicit policy was developed to support or encourage cultural difference at the national level.

22. That is, policies which lent explicit support to cultural difference.

23. See also *Libération*, 3 November 1992.

24. See Migration News Sheet no. 129/93–12 (December 1993), p. 8; and subsequent issues. See also *Libération*, 16 November 1993.

25. Education restricted to a public role, i.e. the transmission of skills and public values.

26. See, for example, Dworkin (1978); and Charles Taylor's discussion of Dworkin's treatment of liberal society in Taylor (1992: 44 and 56–7).

27. Note that German citizenship has traditionally been based on the principle of *jus sanguinis*, i.e. ethnic ties. For this reason, ethnic Germans from Eastern and Central Europe have had comparatively little difficulty in acquiring German citizenship. However, as regards other groups, not only first-generation immigrants, but also the majority of their offspring born in Germany, remain unnaturalized owing to the juridical and administrative barriers to naturalization. Some of the administrative barriers to naturalization were removed in 1990, while a possible change in the German nationality law (including the possible acceptance of dual nationality) is now a subject of national debate. See, for example, Migration News Sheet, July 1993, and December 1993.

28. Including limited rights in Hamburg and Schleswig-Holstein in Germany; Spain (on the basis of reciprocal agreements); Ireland; the Netherlands; Portugal (nationals of Portuguese-speaking countries only); all five Scandinavian states; and Switzerland (certain cantons only).

29. *Journal Officiel* (Paris), 23 July 1993.

30. For example, the majority of immigrant minority residents are excluded from free movement and establishment rights associated with European Union citizenship.

REFERENCES

Baubock, R., 1992. 'Immigration and the Boundaries of Citizenship', Monographs in Ethnic Relations 4, Warwick, Centre for Research in Ethnic Relations.

Blackstone, R., 1989. *The Salt of Another's Bread, Report of a Western European Union Study Visit*, London: Home Office.

Castles, S., 1985, 'The Guests Who Stayed – The Debate on "Foreigners Policy" in the German Federal Republic', *International Migration Review*, 19, 3.

Castles, S., H. Booth, and T. Wallace, 1984. *Here for Good: Western Europe's New Ethnic Minorities*. London: Pluto Press.

Castles, S. and G. Kosack, 1973. *Immigrant Workers and Class Structure in Western Europe*. Oxford: Oxford University Press.

CENSIS (Centro Studi Investimenti Sociali), 1991a. *Atti Della Conferenza Nazionale dell'Immigrazione*. Rome: Editalia-Edizione d'Italia.

CENSIS, 1991b. *Immigrati e Società Italiana. Rome: Editalia-Edizione d'Italia.*

CENSIS, 1991c. *Immigrazione e Diritti di Cittadinanza*. Rome: Editalia-Edizione d'Italia.

Collinson, S., 1993. *Beyond Borders. West European Migration Policy towards the 21st Century*. London: Wyndham Place Trust and the Royal Institute of International Affairs.

Collinson, S., 1994. *Europe and International Migration*. London: Pinter Publishers for the Royal Institute of International Affairs, 2nd revised edition.

Commission for Racial Equality, 1985. *Review of the Race Relations Act 1976: Proposals for Change*. London: CRE.

Commission for Racial Equality, 1991. *Annual Report 1990*. London: CRE.

Commission of the European Communities, 1990. 'Policies on Immigration and the Social Integration of Migrants in the European Community'. Experts Report drawn up on behalf of the Commission of the European Communities. Brussels: Commission of the European Communities.

Council of Europe, 1991. 'Community and Ethnic Relations in Europe'. Final report of the Community Relations Project of the Council of Europe, (MG-CR (91) 1 final E). Strasbourg: Council of Europe.

Cross, G.S., 1983. *Immigrant Workers in Industrial France: The Making of a New Laboring Class*. Philadelphia: Temple University Press.

Cross, M., 1983. 'Migrant Workers in European Cities: Concentration, Conflict and Social Policy'. Working Papers on Ethnic Relations, no. 19. Birmingham: SSRC Research Unit on Ethnic Relations.

Esser, H. and H. Korte, 1985. 'Federal Republic of Germany'. In Tomas Hammar (ed.), *European Immigration Policy: A Comparative Study*. Cambridge: Cambridge University Press.

Farine, P., 1992. 'Les Conditions Juridiques et Culturelles de l'Intégration: le troisième rapport du Haut Conseil à l'Intégration', *Migrations Société*, 4, 20.

Farine, P., 1993. 'Immigration, Intégration et Alternance', *Migrations Société*, 5, 27.

*Sarah Collinson*189

Federal Minister of the Interior, 1991. 'Survey of the Policy and Law Regarding Aliens in the Federal Republic of Germany'. The Federal Minister of the Interior (V II 1-937 020/15 [Translation]). Bonn: Federal Ministry of the Interior.

Fekete, L., 1991. 'Report of the European Committee on Racism and Xenophobia: A Critique. Race and Class' (Special Issue: 'Europe: Variations on a Theme of Racism'), 32, 3.

Gaeremynck, J., 1993. 'Les Croyances Réligieuses à l'école: à propos de la décision récente du Conseil d'Etat sur le port du foulard', *Migrations Société*, 5, 25.

Garcia, S., 1992. 'Europe's Fragmented Identities and the Frontiers of Citizenship'. RIIA Discussion Paper No. 45. London: Royal Institute of International Affairs.

Gellner, E., 1964. *Thought and Change*. London: Weidenfeld & Nicolson.

Gellner, E., 1983. *Nations and Nationalism*. Oxford: Blackwell.

Gieseck, A., U. Heilemann, and H. Dietrich von Loeffelholz, 1993. 'Economic and Social Implications of Migration into the Federal Republic of Germany', RWI-Papière No. 35. Essen: Rheinisch-Westfulisches Institut für Wirtschaftsforschung.

Grillo, R.D., 1985. *Ideologies and Institutions in Urban France: The Representation of Immigrants*. Cambridge: Cambridge University Press.

Habermas, J., 1991. 'Citizenship and National Identity: Some Reflections on the Future of Europe'. Paper presented at the conference 'Identité et Différences dans l'Europe Démocratique'. Lovain-La-Neuve.

Hammar, T., 1990. *Democracy and the Nation-State: Aliens, Denizens, and Citizens in a World of International Migration*. Aldershot: Avebury (Gower Publishing).

Home Office, 1990. Policy Statement on the Criteria for Ethnic Minority Grants. London: Home Office.

Isajiw, W., 1975. 'Immigration and Multiculturalism – Old and New Approaches'. Paper prepared for the Conference on Multiculturalism and Third World Immigrants in Canada. University of Alberta.

Kubat, Daniel, ed., 1993. *The Politics of Migration Policies. Settlement and Integration: The First World into the 1990s*. New York: Center for Migration Studies, 2nd edition.

Layton-Henry, Z., 1984. *The Politics of Race in Britain*. London: Allen and Unwin.

Layton-Henry, Z., 1990. *The Political Rights of Migrant Workers in Western Europe*. Sage Modern Politics Series 25. London: Sage Publications.

Layton-Henry, Z., 1992. *The Politics of Immigration. Immigration, 'Race' and 'Race' Relations in Post-War Britain*. Making of Contemporary Britain Series (Institute of Contemporary History). Oxford and Cambridge, MA: Blackwell.

Lebon, A., 1990. *Regard sur l'Immigration et la Présence Etrangère en France, 1989/90*. Paris: Ministère des Affaires Sociales et de la Solidarité, Direction de la Population et des Migrations.

Leitner, H., 1987. 'Regulating Migrants' Lives'. In Gunther Glebe and John O'Loughlin (eds.), *Foreign Minorities in Continental European Cities* (Erdkundliches Wissen, Heft 84). Stuttgart: Steiner Verlag.

190   *Immigrant Minorities in W. Europe*

Massey, D., 1984. *Spatial Divisions of Labour: Social Structures and the Geography of Production.* London: Macmillan.
Melotti, V., 1988. 'Gli Immigrati Stranieri in Italia: Considerazione dopo la Sanatoria', *Up and Down.* ISPES (February).
Migration News Sheet, various issues. Brussels: European Information Network.
Netherlands Scientific Council for Government Policy, 1990. 'Immigrant Policy: Summary of the 36th Report'. Reports to the Government 36. The Hague.
Nielsen, J.S., 1992. *Muslims in Western Europe.* Islamic Surveys 20. Edinburgh: Edinburgh University Press.
Oakley, R., 1991. *Racial Violence and Harassment in Europe.* Report for the Council of Europe. Strasbourg: Council of Europe document MG-CR (91) 3 rev. 2.
OECD, various dates. *Continuous Reporting System on Migration* (SOPEMI). Paris: OECD.
Ogden, P., 1993. 'The Legacy of Migration: Some Evidence from France'. In Russell King (ed.), *Mass Migration in Europe. The Legacy and the Future.* London: Belhaven Press.
Patterson, S., 1969. *Immigration and Race Relations in Britain, 1960–67.* Oxford: Oxford University Press.
Penninx R., J. Schoorl and C. Van Praag, 1993. *The Impact of International Migration on Receiving Countries: the Case of the Netherlands.* Amsterdam: Swets and Zeitlinger – NIDI CBGS Publications.
Perotti, A., 1993a. 'Revue de Presse', *Migrations Société,* 5, 28–29.
Perotti, A., 1993b. 'La Pluriculturalité des Sociétés Européennes,' *Migrations Société,* 5, 30.
Phizacklea, A. and R. Miles, 1977. 'Class, Race, Ethnicity and Political Action', *Political Studies,* 25, 4.
Phizacklea, A. and R. Miles, 1980. *Labour and Racism.* London: Routledge and Kegan Paul.
Piore, M., 1979. *Birds of Passage: Migrant Labour and Industrial Societies.* Cambridge: Cambridge University Press.
Ra'anan, U., 1991. 'Nation and State: Order out of Chaos'. In Uri Ra'anan, Maria Mesner, Keith Armes and Kate Martin (eds.), *State and Nation in Multi-Ethnic Societies: The Breakup of Multinational States* (Institute for the Study of Conflict, Ideology and Policy, Boston). Manchester: Manchester University Press.
Race and Class (Special Issue: 'European Variations on a Theme of Racism'), 1991. 32, 3.
Rex, J. 1985. 'The Concept of a Multi-Cultural Society'. Occasional Papers in Ethnic Relations 3. Warwick: Centre for Research in Ethnic Relations.
Rex, J., D. Joly and C. Wilpert, eds., 1987. *Immigrant Associations in Europe.* Aldershot and Vermont: Gower Publishing for the European Science Foundations.
Rex, J. and S. Tomlinson, 1979. *Colonial Immigrants in a British City.* London: Routledge and Kegan Paul.
Rosoli, G., 1993. 'Italy: Emergent Immigration Policy'. In D. Kubat (ed.), *The Politics of Migration Policies. Settlement and Integration: The First World into the 1990s.* New York: Center for Migration Studies, 2nd edition.

Schuck, P., 1985. 'Immigration Law and the Problem of Community'. In N. Glazer (ed.), *Clamor at the Gates*. San Francisco: ICS Press.

Smith, A., 1991. *National Identity*. London: Penguin Books.

Smith, A., 1992. 'National Identity and the Idea of European Unity', *International Affairs*, 28, 1.

Taylor, C., 1992. *Multiculturalism and 'The Politics of Recognition'. An Essay by Charles Taylor*. Princeton: Princeton University Press.

Tranhardt, D., 1993. 'Les Relations Ethniques et l'Immigration en Allemagne après la Réunification'. In M. Martiniello and M. Poncelet (eds.), *Migrations et Minorités Ethniques dans l'Espace Européen*. Brussels: De Boeck-Wesmael.

United Nations Centre for Human Rights, 1991. 'Second Decade to Combat Racism and Racial Discrimination'. Global Compilation of National Legislation Against Racial Discrimination. New York: UNCHR.

Van Praag, C.S., 1986. 'Minderheden voor en na de nota' (Minorities before and after the Policy Document). *Migrantenstudies*, 2, 4.

Verbunt, Gilles, 1985. 'France'. In Tomas Hammar (ed.), *European Immigration Policy: A Comparative Study*. Cambridge: Cambridge University Press.

Walzer, M., 1992. 'Comment'. In Charles Taylor. *Multiculturalism and 'The Politics of Recognition'. An Essay by Charles Taylor*. Princeton: Princeton University Press.

White, P., 1987. 'The Migrant Experience in Paris'. In Gunther Glebe and John O'Loughlin (eds.), *Foreign Minorities in Continental European Cities* (Erdkundliches Wissen, Heft 84). Stuttgart: Steiner Verlag.

Wilpert, C., 1988a. 'From One Generation to Another: Occupational Position and Social Reproduction – Immigrant and Ethnic Minorities in Europe'. In C. Wilpert, (ed.), *Entering the Working World. Following the Descendants of Europe's Immigrant Labour Force*. Aldershot: Avebury (Gower Publishing).

Wilpert, C., 1988b. 'Work and the Second Generation: The Descendants of Migrant Workers in the Federal Republic of Germany'. In C. Wilpert (ed.), *Entering the Working World. Following the Descendants of Europe's Immigrant Labour Force*. Aldershot: Avebury (Gower Publishing).

Wilpert, C. and Gitmez, A., 1987. 'A Micro-Society or an Ethnic Community? Social Organization and Ethnicity amongst Turkish Migrants in Berlin'. In John Rex, Daniele Joly, and Czarina Wilpert (eds.), *Immigrant Associations in Europe*. Aldershot and Vermont: Gower Publishing for the European Science Foundation.

ACKNOWLEDGEMENT

This paper is based on material in two books by Sarah Collinson: *Europe and International Migration*, second revised edition, Pinter Publishers for the Royal Institute of International Affairs, London, 1994; and *Beyond Borders. West European Migration Policy Towards the 21st Century*, Royal Institute of International Affairs and the Wyndham Place Trust, London, 1993.

7 Preferential Policies for Disadvantaged Ethnic Groups: Employment and Education

Laura D. Jenkins

In addition to political representation and freedoms, access to education and employment are crucial components of ethnic accommodation. Concerns about the relative standing of groups and the distribution of resources in society can lead to conflicts along ethnic lines (Horowitz, 1985: ch. 4). Remedial policies of preferential access to higher education and employment in various countries may quell such tensions, although at times they may spark these tensions anew. In addition to having the practical goal of preventing conflicts, such policies may embody moral commitments to equity and distributional justice for all groups in society.

Charles Taylor, in his essay on identity and recognition, notes the trend towards demanding recognition of one's group, or the 'politics of difference', which has resulted in preferential policies such as affirmative action.

> Where the politics of universal dignity fought for forms of non-discrimination that were quite 'blind' to the ways in which citizens differ, the politics of difference often redefines nondiscrimination as requiring that we make these distinctions the basis of differential treatment. (Taylor, 1992: 39)

Seemingly neutral principles and policies may actually reflect a hegemonic culture. 'Consequently, the supposedly fair and difference-blind society is not only inhuman (because suppressing identities) but also, in a subtle and unconscious way, itself highly discriminatory' (Taylor, 1992: 43). Preferential policies based on social categories such as race, caste or ethnicity may 'misrecognize' some people, such as multiracial people, but the alternative, non-recognition of any particular groups, may be even more damaging.

Preferential policies in the arenas of education and employment can uplift groups that have been disadvantaged owing to histories of slavery or colonization, as well as owing to continuing discrimination. Such policies may include special access to scholarships and admissions in higher education as well as to government contracts and jobs.[1] This chapter presents some of the many current cases of preferential policies, addressing common themes that cut across each in spite of their variety.

In the following case studies, policy-makers have defined beneficiary groups in a variety of ways, by caste in India, by region in Pakistan, by 'indigenousness' in Malaysia, by race in the United States and by religion in Northern Ireland.[2] These cases include preferential policies originating in colonial times, as well as policies implemented quite recently. While most policies are for the benefit of minorities, Malaysia's policies protect a majority group that has been economically subordinate. The nature of the preferences used also vary from policies that assign explicit quotas to policies that prohibit such quotas.

Long-standing official and unofficial preferences for dominant groups have contributed to conditions of inequality, prompting the countervailing preferential policies discussed here.[3] These countervailing policies disadvantage to various degrees dominant groups in their competition for employment and educational opportunities as the dominated become the recipients of new advantages. The shifting of resources and opportunities and the use of ethnic categories make these policies quite controversial. They may have the contradictory effect of sparking ethnic tensions. Yet in ethnically stratified societies, policies that can effectively overcome such disparities may need to be written in explicitly ethnic terms. Case studies can illuminate the problems and possibilities of preferential policies for disadvantaged groups. To aid comparison, four topics will be explored in each case: the *origins* of the preferential policies, their *effectiveness*, their *longevity* and likely future, and the societal *reception* of the policies.

First, brief historical sketches of the origins and types of preferential policies in each case will set the context. Second, how effective are such programmes in advancing the targeted groups? A major question is whether preferential policies alone effectively help the neediest members of the disadvantaged groups. Although some segments of disadvantaged groups gain, uneducated, lower-class or female members of the targeted groups may fail to reap advantages owing to other forms of discrimination or to lack of qualifications (Dunn, 1993;

Jones, 1993: 354; Sokoloff, 1992). Another limit on preferential policies is temporal. Donald L. Horowitz notes that, although ethnic tensions surrounding these policies may be quite visible in the short term, the wider effectiveness of preferential policies may be apparent only over the long term, through the cumulative effect of subsequent generations building on the advances made by original beneficiaries (Horowitz, 1985: 660). Such critiques suggest the need to revise preferential policies or supplement them with more substantive policies for the immediate needs of the neediest people.

Third, the issue of the longevity of preferential policies stems from their goal of creating a more equitable society. Since the ultimate aim of these programmes is to be no longer be necessary, governments should have long-term plans for such programmes. Yet stopping such programmes may become politically difficult in some cases:

> The logic of the system makes these policies very easy to initiate but extremely difficult to dismantle. As more and more people get a stake in the preference system, it will be easier to expand the system than to take privileges away.   (Means, 1986: 115)

There may be pressure to consider adding more or different groups. On the other hand, policies that disadvantage majority groups may be difficult to sustain in a majoritarian democracy. In some cases, pressures to cut back such programmes may occur when inequality is still rampant. How can governments successfully adapt preferential programmes to changes in society?

Fourth, the nature of a society's reception of preferential policies is critical to the outcome of ethnic accommodation. Spreading opportunities more widely through society may diffuse ethnic tensions. On the other hand, preferential policies can contribute to ethnic mobilization in the form of a backlash against the beneficiary groups. By codifying ethnic categories, do such policies perpetuate the group-based discrimination and prejudices they are trying to eradicate?

MALAYSIA

Origins

Malaysia's preferential policies are offshoots of colonial precedents: 'a system of ethnic preferences and privileges has been steadily expanded from the time of independence to the present day' (Means, 1986: 96).

The Malaysian case is an example of preferential policies for a politically dominant majority community, the Malays, in order to improve their position *vis-à-vis* the economically dominant minorities, the Indians and Chinese. Malay Special Rights, originating in 1874 under British colonial rule, distinguished Malays from 'alien' communities. Under these 'protective' policies, Malays received special treatment in land tenure laws, were recruited into a special 'Malay Administrative Service', and, had free, public, primary education. Although some children of Malay aristocrats reaped the benefits of higher education and the Administrative Service, these laws more generally had the effect of insulating the majority of Malays from the modern economy and giving them a poor education (Lim, 1985: 251–4). The British goal was not the economic uplift of the Malays, but rather the 'protection' of their traditions and the symbolic preservation of their aristocracy. Although preferential policies persist, the original goals of the colonial policies have been transformed:

> It was only later, after independence, that Malay special rights were viewed as an appropriate public policy mechanism to effect the economic uplift of the Malays and the transformation of the ethnic compartmentalization of society as a whole.   (Means, 1986: 98)

In 1957, the Federal Constitution encoded these new goals, requiring preferential access for Malays to public sector employment, business permits, and scholarships.

Effectiveness

Malaysia's New Economic Plan (NEP) embodied in the Second Malaysian Plan (1971–5), had, in addition to the goal of eradicating poverty in general, the renewed goal of advancement for the Malays, who continued to fall behind economically. The NEP's target was that by 1990 Malays and a smaller number of other indigenous peoples, now lumped together as Bumiputras, would own and manage a higher percentage of firms and would be employed in the various sectors of the economy in proportion to their percentage of the population. This resulted in new employment quotas in the public sector and pressure in the private sector to hire Malays, as well as government assistance programmes and higher quotas for education (Means, 1986: 102–11; Wyzan, 1990: 54–67).

The 'Malayanization' of the public services has been quite successful, although non-Malays have tended to be predominant in technical divisions (Lim, 1985: 256–7). In education, the over-representation of non-Malays prior to racial riots in 1969 has been shifted in favour of the Malays through quotas, not only for admission to universities but to specific fields in which Malays are under-represented. Government scholarships for advanced study at home and abroad are also targeted to Malay students. Ethnic preferences in Malaysian education seem to go beyond the usual targeting of certain groups for admission. For example, 'all grades must be submitted to an evaluation review committee having heavily Malay representation' and may be adjusted to achieve 'ethnic balance' (Means, 1986: 108). In industry, the government has invested in Bumiputra trust agencies, quasi-public corporations run by Malays.

The NEP made great strides toward evening out economic disparities between ethnic groups but not within them. Many Malays are still stuck in the relatively low-income agricultural sector (Brown, 1994: 218). As in many preferential policy programmes, most of the poorest people in the targeted groups have been left in the dust, but the Malaysian government has made an effort to alleviate this disparity within ethnic groups by targeting programmes to the poor Malay peasants. In general, the system has 'helped to break down ethnic compartmentalization, and schools, the workplace, and the neighborhood have been made much more ethnically balanced' (Means, 1986: 113). Notably, the NEP's success owes much to Malaysia's economic growth during its implementation. This growth reduced domestic friction over the preferential policies. By the early 1980s, the Malays had made enough advances that the government felt that they could benefit from privatization. Thus this 'twist' on the NEP also helped Malays, as they were in a position to take over the management of enterprises formerly run by the government (Milne, 1986).

Longevity

A constitutional commission led by Lord Reid recommended in 1957 that Malay special rights should not be permanently included in the constitution, but rather that existing laws should remain on the books, to be reviewed after 15 years. The Reid Commission said that preferential policies for Malays should continue 'for a substantial period, but that in due course the present preferences should be reduced and ultimately cease' (Sinnadurai, 1989: 337). These recommendations were rejected, and Malay rights were given constitutional status in

Article 153 'to safeguard the special position of the Malays'. This Article supplements Article 8, which notes that 'Except as expressly authorized by this constitution, there shall be no discrimination against citizens on the ground only of religion, race, descent or place of birth' (Sinnadurai, 1989: 331). Since amendments to Article 153 require the consent of the Conference of Rulers, the Malay's special status is more difficult to amend than the rest of the constitution. Thus the temporary laws envisaged by the Reid Commission became quite permanent.

In 1966 Prime Minister Mahathir Mohamad suggested that Malay special rights were temporary (Means, 1986: 114). However, only a few years later the special status of Malays was further entrenched in the NEP. With the expiration of the NEP in 1990, there was an opportunity to reconsider the pro-Malay policies. Yet they continue intact, although with a lower profile, in the New Development Plan launched in 1990 (Brown, 1994: 256–7). Preferential policies in Malaysia seem to be so durable not only due to constitutional assurances, but also because governments in Malaysia rely on the numerically dominant Malays for political support. The increasing demographic, cultural[4] and political dominance of Malays, as well as their growing economic power, erode the justification for preferential policies, yet make it politically difficult for the government to phase them out. The government fears the consequences of a policy change: 'The government assumes that the paramount power and vital interests of the Malay community must not be threatened or compromised if the country is to avoid fratricidal civil conflict' (Means, 1986: 113).

Yet recently, perhaps due to the peaking business cycle, the topic of enforcing the Malay's special privileges seems to be waning in current political debate (Case, 1994: 928). There is a growing perception that general economic growth is more important to Malay mobility than preferential policies, and some top leaders have even suggested that that the Malay's special status may end in 20–30 years if they have enough economic strength (Jesudason, 1995: 351).

Reception

The expanding policies of preference for Malays have led to non-Malay alienation. Preferences for Malays in education 'made it possible for Malays with distinctly poorer scores to secure admission to upper secondary school' (Horowitz, 1985: 662). Morale is particularly low at universities, where non-Malay faculty are frequently given limited contracts and little opportunity for advancement (Means, 1986: 102, 108, 114). Chinese resentment of the Malay's special status has been exacerbated by the increasing Malay migration to urban areas, where they compete for jobs against the long-time urban dwelling Chinese (Brown, 1994). Young Chinese professionals, having endured limited scholarship opportunities for higher education, resent the additional burden of their disadvantage in competition for jobs. Tensions over preferential policies have contributed to various problems in Malaysia, ranging from the racial riots in 1969, which resulted in nearly two years of emergency rule, to the 'brain drain' of non-Malay professionals. Due in part to state management of ethnicity, 'Ethnic and religious consciousness has hurt the development of civil society because it is difficult for larger groupings which cross-cut ethnicity to emerge' (Jesudason, 1995: 350).

On the other hand, as Donald Horowitz points out,

> In at least one way, the effort to foster Malay entrepreneurship has assuaged Malay-Chinese tensions. With the expansion of opportunities targeted specifically for Malays, Malay politics has grown more complex, and Malay intraethnic competition has increased considerably.   (Horowitz, 1985: 668)

This may reduce the bipolarity of Malay/non-Malay competition. Non-Malay resentments are softened by 'ethnic forbearance that has seeped out of the country's rapid economic growth' (Case, 1994: 929). According to interviews with non-Malays and Malays, the continuing possibility of making money is a major reason for the lack of ethnic violence; thus Malaysia's economic growth has been characterized as 'the most important variable' in explaining this lack of overt conflict (Mauzy, 1993).

In Malaysia, as in many other cases, disputes over ethnic categories accompany preferential policies. Under colonial rule special 'Malay' rights were first accorded on the basis of religion to Muslims and, later, to subjects of Malay rulers. The constitution at independence defined 'Malay' as a Muslim, Malay speaker who keeps Malay customs and whose parents (or self) were born in the country before independence. The NEP included non-Muslims with Malays in the broader 'indigenous' category of Bumiputra, the focus of NEP preferential policies. Other non-Malay indigenous peoples known as Orang Asli, who are mostly animists and may be the original inhabitants of the peninsula, are the poorest group in Malaysia but do not benefit from preferential policies. Although they are included in the

Bumiputra census category, their advancement is left to the Department of Aborigines rather than Bumiputra preferences (Means, 1986: 112). These contested and overlapping ethnic categories have caused some of the social tension associated with preferential policies in Malaysia.

INDIA

Origins

In India, in contrast to Malaysia, most preferential policies are aimed at helping minorities that are socially, politically and economically disadvantaged, although in some states eligibility has been extended to a vast majority of the population, including some politically influential groups. The extent of India's policies, both historically and today, to help the lowest castes and communities is remarkable; 'probably nowhere else in the world was so large a lower-class minority granted so much favorable treatment by a government as were the depressed classes of India' (Jalali, 1993: 97). As in the other Asian cases, precedents for India's contemporary preferential policies extend back to group-based policies prior to independence, such as British policies of separate electorates for certain protected minorities, as well as policies in the princely state of Mysore that granted non-Brahmins preferential access to public service employment, special scholarships and schools (Parikh, 1990).

Several categories of citizens in India are beneficiaries of preferential policies, including Scheduled Castes (SC), Scheduled Tribes (ST) and Other Backward Classes (OBC).[5] The 'Scheduled Castes' category encompasses various 'untouchable' groups. The category was originally created by the British in 1936 in order to implement the 1935 Government of India Act, which gave special electoral representation to certain minority groups, including untouchables. After Independence, the Scheduled Caste list was re-enacted with the Scheduled Caste Order of 1950. The Scheduled Tribes are 'those groups distinguished by "tribal characteristics" and by their spatial and cultural isolation from the bulk of the population' (Galanter, 1984: 147). They were also included as a protected minority in the 1935 Act. Both of these groups are given special protection in the Indian Constitution, which leaves the contents of these lists up to the President, in consultation with the governors.

No method is specified in the Constitution to define another constitutionally protected group, the Other Backward Classes, except that the President should appoint a Backward Classes Commission (Article 340). The term Backward Classes 'was used as far back as 1880 to describe a list of groups, also called illiterate or indigent classes, entitled to allowances for study in elementary schools' (Galanter, 1984: 154, footnote 1). The term has had a variety of local usages, but notably, in spite of the use of the word 'classes', the group was not designated by applying solely economic criteria to individuals. The constitutional debate makes it clear that Backward 'Classes' were to be a list of castes or communities, rather than the lower classes in general (Kumar, 1994: 1), but the Supreme Court has ruled that both caste and poverty should be considered when determining the backwardness of groups (Faundez, 1994: 23–4).

The special policies for STs and SCs include what are commonly called 'reservations' of posts in government service and public sector undertakings and of admissions into schools, particularly in government-funded technical and professional schools, as well as special scholarships. Other special policies affect the distribution of resources such as land, housing, grants, loans and health and legal aid, or offer special protections from debt bondage, land transfers and 'social disabilities', or caste-based discrimination and persecution (Galanter, 1986: 131). Preferential policies for OBCs in educational institutions and in state services have a long history in parts of the south, but OBC reservations in central government services are a more recent development and are not yet fully operational in some states.

Effectiveness

According to one leading scholar of these policies, India's 'policy of compensatory discrimination has been pursued with remarkable persistence and generosity (if not always with vigor and effectiveness)' (Galanter, 1986: 129). Generalizations about effectiveness are nearly impossible when considering policies for the OBCs, due to the disparate policies and eligible groups in the different states. In terms of the Scheduled Castes and Tribes, however, the policies have 'undeniably succeeded in accelerating the growth of a middle class within these groups – urban, educated, largely in government service'; moreover, '[T]here is a sizable section of these groups who can utilize these opportunities and confer advantages on their children; their concerns are firmly placed on the political agenda and cannot readily be dis-lodged' (Galanter, 1986: 139).

Recent statistical studies show that Scheduled Castes and Tribes have made gains in education and employment, but not enough to close the gap between them and the general population, which in some cases has increased (Sudarsen, 1994).

The most striking limit on the effectiveness of these policies is the vast number of potential beneficiaries and the limited number of reserved jobs. Since reservations are limited to the public sector in a liberalizing economy, they cannot replace broader policies to combat poverty and exploitation, especially for rural landless labourers and women. A danger of group-based policies is that status differences within the group may not be addressed. Government-sponsored schol-arships and hostels for the poor and for women have helped some of the most disadvantaged people within the scheduled groups. Yet gender inequality among scheduled groups continues, as many SC and ST women are still 'doubly disadvantaged' (Dunn, 1993: 53).

On a more optimistic note, the masses may benefit vicariously by the successes of the few that are helped by the preferential policies. Beyond the material benefits to an individual working for the civil service, for example, the prestige associated with this position may provide a 'psychological spin-off' that affects the person's entire com-munity (Backward Classes Commission, 1980: 57). The effectiveness of such a psychological boost, however, pales in the face of abject poverty. Beneficiaries of preferential policies sometimes offer material or organizational help to others in their communities (Jalali, 1993), but sometimes 'the prosperity of the few... stops there' (Raman, 1994: 17).

Longevity

It is difficult to foresee an end to preferential policies in India, although they were intended to be 'self-liquidating': 'The notion that permanent protection is needed mirrors the original hierarchic ideo-logy that caste forever measures inherent human ability' (Galanter, 1991: 11). Preferential policies, however, will probably persist in India not only due to continuing disadvantages, but because they have both specific constitutional protection and political momentum.

The Indian Constitution of 1950 prohibits discrimination in admis-sions to state-aided schools on the basis of 'religion, race, caste, or language' (Article 29–2) and discrimination in state employment on the basis of 'religion, race, caste, sex, descent, place of birth, or residence' (Article 16); however, clause 4 of article 16 permits reservations of state employment 'in favor of any backward class of citizens which, in the opinion of the State, is not adequately represented in the Services under the State' (Tripathi, 1989: 44). The year after the Constitution was adopted, two Supreme Court decisions limited eligible groups and barred preferential policies in arenas other than government employment (*State of Madras* v. *Champakam Dorairajan* (1951) 1 S.C.R 226, and *Venkataramana* v. *State of Madras* (1951) 1 S.C.R 229). In response, the Constitution was amended by adding a clause to protect educational reservations for Backward Classes.[6]

Political momentum also perpetuates preferential policies. Frankel cites reservations as an example of Tamil Nadu's 'populist policies':

> Tamil Nadu, which pioneered in providing reservations to Backward classes in education and the government services, had by the 1980s pushed up the proportion of reserved seats in college admissions and government employment to almost 70 percent.... eligibility itself was subject to political bargaining. (Frankel, 1988: 246)

Politicians have generally expanded reservations rather than running the political risk of taking away benefits from potential voters.

There are two brakes on the runaway use of preferences. The first is court oversight. For example, the Supreme Court has ruled that the percentage of total reservations should be limited to 50 per cent (*M. R. Balaji* v. *State of Mysore*, AIR 1963 SC 649). Many policy variations complicate this ruling, such as having temporarily higher reservations to allow an under-represented group to 'catch up', or adding one year's unfilled slots to the next year's total reservations (Faundez, 1994: 24–5; Galanter, 1984: 399–420). Former Prime Minister V.P. Singh's 1990 order that 27 per cent of government jobs would be reserved for other backward classes, in addition to the 22.5 per cent reserved for scheduled castes and tribes, narrowly met the 50 per cent cut-off. In the aftermath of the national debate sparked by this policy, the Supreme Court set out other limitations, ruling that the 'creamy layer', or economically advanced, must be disqualified from benefits for other backward classes, but that backwardness is not just economically determined, thus excluding poor forward castes from the 'backward' lists (*Indra Sawhney* v. *Union of India* (1992) Supp (3) 217).

A second brake on preferences is regular national debate over preferences. Another type of preferential policy, the constitutional provisions of reserved legislative seats for Scheduled Castes and Scheduled Tribes, expires and must be reviewed every decade. Although reservations in employment and education do not have such a renewal process, the mandated national debate on some preferential policies puts some scrutiny on such policies in general.

Reception

In Indian society there is general acceptance of the need to uplift the lowest, untouchable groups, particularly when the policies' 'costs' are widely diffused among the non-beneficiaries, as in the building of special schools and the reservation of legislative seats. Sharper criticism of preferential policies occurs when preferences are extended above the neediest groups and when the 'cost' is more focused. 'Resentment has been focused on settings where the life-chances of specific others are diminished in a palpable way, as in reservations of jobs and medical college places' (Galanter, 1986: 147). In 1985, for example, there were violent riots in Gujarat against government reservations of civil service and university positions for lower castes (Mitra, 1987). In other states, however, preferences have been more readily accepted, as in Karnataka, which had a history of such policies in the Princely State of Mysore. In addition to historical and demographic differences between states, preferential policies themselves vary considerably, particularly those directed at the Other Backward Classes. Consequently, the social reception of these policies is not homogeneous.

The categories used in India's preferential policies are perhaps the most contested and complicated of all the cases examined here. Galanter, for example, lists ten types of definition for 'Other Backward Castes' (Galanter, 1984: 155). The OBC lists are set at the state level and include groups with scheduled caste-like disadvantage as well as some politically powerful middle castes. Such broad reservations for OBCs undermines the legitimacy of these policies by painting a 'picture of unrestrained preference for those who are not distinctly worse off than non-beneficiaries, which attaches indiscriminantly to all preferential treatment' (Galanter, 1986: 140). Attempts by Prime Minister V.P. Singh in 1990 to enact portions of the 1980 recommendations of the Mandal Commission to extend more preferences to OBCs sparked protests and self-immolations and contributed to Singh's being ousted from office. More recent moves by the central government to extend reservations have generated some protest but had a relatively low key reaction.[7]

Societal reception of preferential policies is mediated by perceptions and misperceptions about the scope and effects of the policies. At the time of riots over reservations in Gujarat, studies show that 'the public was ignorant of facts and was acting on the basis of the false impression that the SC/ST has advanced quite far' (Chitnis, 1984: 41). There is a 'pervasive overestimation of the amount and effectiveness of preferential treatment' which 'reinforces the notion that enough (or too much) is already being done and nothing more is called for' (Galanter, 1986: 138). Aside from the resentment and violence that can erupt from such misperceptions, they also may undermine people's motivation to take individual responsibility to hire or otherwise uplift lower castes in the growing private sector.

PAKISTAN

Origins

Preferential policies in Pakistan have been organized primarily along regional lines, to allocate opportunities between ethnic groups that may be roughly defined linguistically and territorially. Since the first official preferential policies in 1949, Pakistan's preference system has proliferated to an astonishing degree. Now an ethno-regional quota system allocates most jobs in the public sector and admissions in institutions of higher education (Kennedy, 1986: 64).

Pakistani policies, as in Malaysia and India, were influenced by the precedents established under British rule prior to the formation of Pakistan, such as the establishment of special protections and separate electorates for certain groups. Consciousness of disparities between ethnic groups has a long history in Pakistan. Such consciousness was in fact a major factor in the birth of Pakistan, for Muhammed Ali Jinnah emphasized a vision of a Hindu-dominated India in order to justify the formation of Pakistan. Fear of the dominance of Hindus and under-representation of Muslims before partition was replaced by a similar disparity between West and East Pakistan after partition. The Bengalis of East Pakistan were not only politically under-represented, but were relatively scarce in public service, including the military, and business. Indicative of the disparity was the ironic situation that 'even the East Bengal administration was filled with West Pakistanis' (Horowitz, 1985: 242). To amend this situation Pakistan's first preferential policy, in 1949, reserved 40 per cent of vacancies in

Pakistan's elite civil service for East Pakistanis, allocated 20 per cent
on the basis of merit and divided the rest among the regions of West
Pakistan. Regional admissions quotas for education started in the
early 1950s, mainly 'to ensure the admission to professional schools
of candidates domiciled in provinces or regions in which no such
institutions existed' (Kennedy, 1986: 71). Nevertheless, continuing
disparities were a major factor leading to the secession of Bangladesh
in 1971.

Since the breakup of Pakistan, the regional quota system has continued – despite losing its original impetus – due to ethno-regional
disparities and tensions between the major ethnic groups in the
remainder of Pakistan, namely Punjabis, Pathans, Sindhis and
Baluch. Muhajirs, a group made up of people who immigrated from
India after Partition, and their descendants have demanded to be
considered a fifth national group (Ahmed, 1989: 46). As Donald L.
Horowitz has noted, 'Pakistan, twice the product of partition, is
testimony to the propensity for new cleavages to supplant the old'
(Horowitz, 1985: 591). Resentment of the highly developed Punjab
province and Punjabi dominance as well as of urban Sindh and its
Muhajir population has fuelled secessionist sentiment in Baluchistan,
parts of the Sindh, and some Pathan areas (Kennedy, 1986: 67; T.
Wright, 1991). Not only did the percentage of bureaucratic positions
that are allocated through regional quotas go up to 90 per cent,[8] but
also the number of positions that are subject to quotas increased due
to the nationalization of several industries in the mid-1970s. Also
since the breakup of Pakistan, quotas have proliferated at the provincial level, as provincial level government jobs are divided among
various 'zones' (Kennedy, 1986: 70).

Effectiveness

The bureaucracy and higher education in Pakistan historically have
been disproportionately dominated by Punjabis, the largest ethnic
group, and Muhajirs, who, although a minority, have dominated
urban opportunities in Sindh. In terms of reducing the inequality of
regional representation in the bureaucracy and educational institutions, the quota system has been quite effective. On the other hand,
the comprehensive quota system ensures that this inequality will not
be reduced 'too much'; the 50 per cent quota for Punjabis in bureaucratic positions ensures they will remain dominant. Another limitation
on the effectiveness of Pakistan's preferences for disadvantaged

groups is that they are not applied to the military, which is mostly Punjabis (Alavi, 1987: 18). Similarly, Punjabi-dominated police in Pakistan have been accused of persecuting the Muhajirs (T. Wright, 1991: 305). Another limit is that the apparent advances in regional representativeness do not extend down to district-level representativeness. Most candidates are selected from five relatively well-developed districts in Pakistan, while 'less developed districts have remained woefully under represented', leading to a situation in which 'inequalities of intraprovincial representation are greater than interprovincial inequalities' (Kennedy, 1986: 81). A final critique is that the quota system in Pakistan has been 'an imperfect tool to dispense compensatory justice' since the quota 'favors the relatively well-off candidate' (Kennedy, 1986: 81).

The doling out of opportunities has somewhat effectively spread opportunities among regions, but the broader goal of alleviating ethnic tension has not been achieved. Charles Kennedy notes,

> despite such policies, which are ostensibly designed to reduce ethnoregional conflict, Pakistan has remained persistently beset by ethnoregional conflict. Ironically, some of this conflict is attributable to the redistribution policies themselves. (Kennedy, 1986: 64)

Longevity

The scope and robustness of Pakistan's comprehensive quota system make it an extreme case. In spite of the fact that the policy-makers who originated the quotas felt they would end in five or ten years (Kennedy, 1986: 86), systems to divide up education and employment opportunities among regions have proliferated to cover a higher percentage of more positions at more levels of government. The rapid proliferation of Pakistan's quotas bodes ill for any hopes of phasing out such policies in the future. The preferences have grown beyond their original justification towards an uncertain, even unlikely, endpoint (Sowell, 1990: 121, 181). They have ballooned into a 'program of entitlement for virtually every governmental vacancy and training slot' (Kennedy, 1986: 73).

Quotas, particularly for educational admissions, have been set for various 'special interests' in addition to ethnoregions.[9] The association of preferential policies with patronage in Pakistan gives them further momentum (Kennedy, 1986: 68). Bureaucracies, a focal point for ethnic quotas, are holders and distributors of significant resources –

and may not be neutral: 'What is problematic is the extent to which the bureaucracy can be simultaneously an effective instrument of integration and an arena in which preference policies get full play' (Nevitte and Kennedy, 1986: 8). In addition to entrenching this type of policy further, patronage related preferences may undermine the original goals of the preferential policies as well as public support for them.

One potential 'brake' on runaway preferences is the courts; however, the courts have upheld reservations of 'special interest' seats in medical colleges in a case that has ramifications for all preferential policies. The Court ruled 'it is to be borne in mind that marks alone cannot be the sole criterion for determining the suitability of a person for admission to medical colleges' (*Nassem Mahmood* v. *Principal, King Edward Medical College*, PLD 1965 Lah 272; quoted in Kennedy, 1986: 74).

Preferential policies have permeated Pakistan to such a degree that even Muhajirs, long-time opponents of preferences and proponents of a pure merit based system, have changed their tune by demanding a larger quota for themselves rather than an end to the system (Alavi, 1987: 18–20).

Reception

The distribution of civil service jobs between groups is viewed as particularly important in Pakistan, due to the power associated with bureaucratic office there, one legacy of the British administrative state. 'It can be argued that denial of civilian bureaucratic office in Pakistan is functionally equivalent to the denial of political representation' (Kennedy, 1986: 68).

Varying from purely merit-based recruitment based on civil service test scores is, as anywhere, controversial in Pakistan. 'Indeed hardly a day passes when one of the major Pakistani dailies does not run an editorial by a disaffected individual, usually a Punjabi, calling for greater reliance on merit in some phase of federal personnel policy and implicitly claiming reverse discrimination' (Kennedy, 1986: 85). Such reactions reinforce ethno-regional tensions. In fact, the newest ethnic group in Pakistan has arisen in part due to the threat preferential policies have posed to their previous privileged position in government service and higher education. 'The entire phenomenon of Muhajir alienation, the growth of Muhajir nationalism and the rise of the MQM [Muhajir Qoumi Movement] has been premised on the notion that Muhajirs are victims of discrimination' (Ahmed, 1989: 45). Muhajir students, feeling that their opportunities were threatened, formed the core of the MQM, which emerged out of the All Pakistan Muhajir Students Organization in 1984 (T.Wright, 1991: 305).

As in the other cases, categorizing citizens in Pakistan is controversial. Pakistan's use of regional categories to distribute opportunities is becoming more problematic due to migration between provinces and the shift of populations from rural to urban areas. Determining an individual's domicile for the purposes of these policies is extremely complex, sometimes resulting in delays that make students miss entire academic years, which does little to increase the popularity of the policies. Various provinces have different policies for issuing residence certificates, tending to be more stringent in those provinces, such as Sindh and Baluchistan, that benefit most from preferential policies. Litigiousness over these remedial policies, in the form of hundreds of court cases brought by rejected candidates, is telling. Certainly the quotas have not ended ethnic tensions, and they may have created a new arena of conflict.

NORTHERN IRELAND

Origins

Northern Ireland has a history of religious discrimination, particularly against Catholics in employment.[10] In addition, the school system in Northern Ireland has historically been unofficially segregated along religious lines, with Protestants attending the state schools and Catholics attending Catholic schools. This *de facto* segregation, in turn, contributes to a divided labor market. Similar to the patterns of many of the ethnically divided societies considered here,

> In Northern Ireland, a person's community of origin greatly affects who that person will marry, the area they will live in, the schools their children will attend, often the companies they will approach when seeking employment, and the cemeteries they will be buried in.   (Cormack and Osborne, 1991: 7)

There has been a pattern of Catholic disadvantage in employment opportunities stemming from as far back as the nineteenth-century period of industrialization. These inequalities are due not only to word-of-mouth hiring, which seldom crosses community boundaries, but also to more direct acts of discrimination. In 1964 the Northern Ireland Civil Rights Association, modelled after the US civil rights movement, insisted on an end to such discrimination. In the face of increasing civil disorder, the British sent in troops and, in 1972, established Direct Rule.

A 1973 committee under the auspices of the Ministry of Health and Social Services (MHSS) recognized the degree of religious discrimination in employment in Northern Ireland but felt that quotas 'would not 'reconcile the communities' but rather would 'perpetuate the divisions between them' (quoted in Cormack and Osborne, 1991: 11). Their recommendations resulted in the birth of the Fair Employment Agency and the introduction of fair employment to the government's agenda. The FEA could direct companies who prove not to provide 'equality of opportunity' to start affirmative action programmes (1976 Fair Employment Act). The Catholic disadvantage continued, and in 1983 the Northern Ireland Civil Service (NICS) started its own continuous system monitoring civil service employment in terms of religion (as well as gender and disability) creating 'the most sophisticated monitoring system in the U.K.' (Cormack and Osborne, 1991: 14).

International influence is one of the unique aspects of the Northern Ireland case. In 1983, the Irish-American lobby forced an Irish aircraft company to revamp its discriminatory employment policies by preventing the United States. from buying planes from them. That same year, an article from the *Brooklyn Spectator* sparked the development of the MacBride Principles for US firms in Northern Ireland, modelled after the Sullivan Principles for South Africa (Bertsch, 1991). This international attention spurred on further policy debate in Northern Ireland itself (Hepple, 1990: 409).

An external model for reform was also influential among Northern Irish officials. The US model of affirmative action was not embraced because it had sparked so much political controversy in America, particularly around the issues of 'quotas' and 'reverse discrimination'. Because Canadian policy stressed 'remedies' and 'positive action' instead, 'Northern Ireland officials found the tenor and content of Canadian policy, which avoided the term "affirmative action" in favor of "employment equity", more congenial and possibly more likely to secure Prime Ministerial approval in the U.K'. (Osborne, 1992: 13). Aspects of the Canadian model were abandoned, however, due to circumstances peculiar to the Northern Irish case. For example, whereas Canada included a variety of protected groups in its policies, Northern Ireland's policies stress religion 'due to the extreme sensitivity felt by the government to the argument that if such strengthened policy could be promoted in Northern Ireland then why not in the rest of the UK?' (Cormack and Osborne, 1991: 47).

> The Fair Employment (Northern Ireland) Act of 1989, in its official summary, puts new duties on employers to ensure the active practice of fair employment. Employers must register, monitor their workforces and regularly review their recruitment, training and promotion practices. They must take affirmative action measures and set goals and timetables where necessary.
>
> (Cormack and Osborne, 1991: 32)

This Act is monitored by the new Fair Employment Commission and enforced by criminal fines and sanctions such as the loss of government grants and business. The new Fair Employment Tribunal hears individual discrimination cases. The Act moves towards the US model in that it attempts to outlaw indirect and unintentional discrimination (Hepple, 1990: 411). 'It makes it illegal to use job selection requirements or conditions which – though applied equally to both religious groups – have disparate or adverse impact on one group' (DED, 1989: 14).[11]

One promising way of implementing the 1989 Act is the introduction, in 1990, of 'equal opportunity proofing'. All legislation and government policies 'will first be considered against a guidance checklist to ensure that they do not give rise to direct or indirect discrimination' (Cormack and Osborne, 1991: 34). The 1989 Act allows employers to take steps especially to encourage under-represented groups to apply (Hepple, 1990: 414). Another policy to advance equal employment in Ireland pertains to education. Full public funding for Catholic schools was undertaken in 1992 on the grounds that the two communities would have more equal access to fair employment if they have more equal opportunities to become qualified.

Effectiveness

Findings that the Fair Employment Act 1976 had not eradicated glaring inequalities between the religious communities in Northern Ireland sparked the tougher 1989 legislation. Monitoring even in the private sector became compulsory, but the 1989 Act has been criticized owing to a 'contradiction between compulsion to ascertain the problem and a high degree of voluntarism as to its solution' (Hepple, 1990: 417). Often employers get only 'recommendations' by the Fair Employment Commission. If employers are subjected to a formal investigation, however, they may be served with an enforceable 'goals and timetables notice'.

Implementation of affirmative action in Northern Ireland is complicated by conditions of violence. For example, 'some employers justify imbalances in their work force by saying that people from one religious group do not apply for jobs because they are afraid of traveling through a hostile neighborhood' (Bertsch, 1991: 61). In spite of such obstacles, Catholic disparity has decreased in the civil service and education. Yet Catholics are still 'disadvantaged' in terms of most socioeconomic indicators. Not only are Catholics under-represented in management, but 2.5 Catholic males are unemployed for every 1 unemployed Protestant male (O'Duffy, 1993: 131).

There has been debate over the proper way to evaluate the fair employment initiative. The Standing Advisory Commission on Human Rights recommended as a yardstick the relative male unemployment rate of the religious communities, with the goal of reducing the Catholic:Protestant ratio from 2.5:1 to 1.5:1. The government, however, rejects this criteria on the grounds that the fair employment legislation cannot make new jobs but only fairly distribute those that are opened or created. One study suggests that 'even if the legislation is implemented effectively, Catholic and Protestant unemployment rates will converge rather slowly' (Armstrong, 1994: 142). Thus using the unemployment differential as a measure of success could result in the conclusion that the policy has failed, when it may have some other measures of success. Supplementing the fair employment provisions with complementary policies to reduce unemployment would make them more effective by any measure (O'Duffy, 1993).

Like the other cases examined here, the Northern Irish policies seem likely to help those of the disadvantaged group who need it least. Thus they have little effect on the lives of many of the unqualified, unemployed, residents of certain disadvantaged regions, and women.

> It is likely that considerable further improvement will take place for those Catholics with good educational qualifications entering professional, technical, and administrative posts.... Such a development could leave the substantially disadvantaged areas of West Belfast, Newry, Derry, etc. largely untouched.
>
> (Cormack and Osborne, 1991: 37)

Women have been overlooked in many studies on fair employment policy in Northern Ireland, in which women were not included as a protected group. In the public debate over the importance of male unemployment figures, the unemployment disparity between Catholic and Protestant women (10 per cent versus 7 per cent) has received less attention (Armstrong, 1994: 139). Even the Fair Employment Commission keeps incomplete data on women's employment, since it does not include employees who work under 16 hours per week in its census, and women often work part time. The intersection of gender and religious discrimination will need to be addressed in future evaluations of the Fair Employment Act's effectiveness (Heaton *et al.*, 1993).

Longevity

Since the 1989 Act is relatively recent, it is difficult to foresee its longevity. The Act is not intended to remain static, since it is to be reviewed by the Central Community Relations Unit (CCRU). The likelihood of the fair employment act's goals being met depends on a plethora of unknowns:

> the rate of new job creation, the work of the Fair Employment Commission, the operation of the Fair Employment Tribunals, and, perhaps in particular, the degree to which the government pursues the fair employment 'proofing' of its policies.
>
> (Cormack and Osborne, 1991: 48)

Such factors will shape the success and lifespan of the current Fair Employment Act. Notably, in terms of economic and social status, 'in Northern Ireland, the differences between the Protestant and Catholic communities are nothing as great as those between blacks and whites in the United States' (Cormack and Osborne, 1991: 44). Perhaps these policies will not become as entrenched as they have in other cases before achieving some notable success.

Reception

Northern Ireland's class disparities influence people's reception of these policies. Many working-class Catholics do not personally benefit from the policies and many working-class Protestants feel they are put at risk. Demands to equalize the unemployment rates in the two communities also cause Protestant anxiety, since, in a context of high unemployment, this is seen as a zero-sum proposition, involving the loss of Protestant jobs.

When the 1989 legislation required employers to monitor and report the religious composition of their employees, the problems associated with categorizing people became apparent.

> Anticipating problems from asking the direct question – 'what is your religion?' – the legislation has suggested indirect methods of assigning people to a religion, most notably on the basis of primary school attended. The latter approach points up contradictory approaches taken by government, in that the Education Reform Order of 1989 gives considerable encouragement to the expansion of integrated schools.   (Cormack and Osborne, 1991: 6)

Clearly, policies to deal with ethnic accommodation can clash, particularly those designed to play down group identity and those offering protection or advantages on the basis of group identity. In Northern Ireland, a trend on censuses is that fewer and fewer people reveal their religion. The necessity of identifying employees on the basis of religion could result in some tensions. Reluctance to reveal religious identity, on the other hand, could make it easier to phase out certain aspects of Northern Ireland's fair employment policies when or if they are successful.

Northern Ireland's policies, like Canada's, have sparked a milder reaction than in some other cases, probably because 'Employment equity in Canada and fair employment in Northern Ireland have been defined as affirmative action incorporating goals and timetables but not quotas' (Cormack and Osborne, 1991: 42). Is this only a semantic distinction? The line between 'quotas' and 'goals' is grey, as we can see from the US debate as well.[12]

UNITED STATES

Origins

The United States has a long history of anti-discrimination legislation, but actual preferential policies to increase opportunities in education and employment for racial minorities are highly circumscribed. Although the term 'quota' is often associated with affirmative action in political rhetoric, affirmative action in the United States, in stark contrast to a case like Pakistan, eschews strict quotas, which are prohibited in many cases. Nevertheless, affirmative action measure have resulted in pressures to hire or admit minorities. The historical development of preferential policies involves legislation, most notably the Civil Rights Acts, as well as executive orders and litigation.

Race-specific preferential policies extend back to Reconstruction Era legislation, most notably the 1866 Freedmen's Bureau Act, which provided benefits such as land and education on the basis of race to help ex-slaves.[13] Since then there has been a series of measures to achieve equal employment opportunities for African-Americans, originally in government employment and later in employment with government contractors. A 1940 civil service rule, as well as the 1958 Ramspeck Act, prohibited racial and religious discrimination in the civil service. During the New Deal, congressional and executive action established a policy of equal employment opportunity covering federal employment, government contractors, and jobs and training funded by grant-in-aid programmes. At this stage, however, standards by which to identify discrimination and mechanisms to enforce these policies were embryonic and ineffective. Current affirmative action primarily stems from, first, the 1964 Civil Rights Act and, second, the 1965 Executive Order 11264, as well as judicial interpretations of each.

The term 'affirmative action' first officially appeared in the equal employment opportunity provisions of Title VII of the Civil Rights Act of 1964. Title VII prohibits discrimination in employment on the basis of race, colour, religion, sex or national origin by employers with 15 or more employees. Congress included specific language to prevent Title VII from being interpreted as requiring racial or gender preferences or quotas on the basis of population percentages:

> Nothing contained in this title shall be interpreted to require any employer...to grant preferential treatment to any individual... because of the race, color, religion, sex or national origin of such individual or group. (Fuchs, 1990: 431)

Nevertheless, Title VII has resulted in preferential policies in two ways. First, it permits courts to 'order such affirmative action as may be appropriate' when employers have engaged in discrimination. Second, the threat of litigation based on Title VII has inspired many voluntary affirmative action policies.

Subsequent court decisions have set parameters on the court's ability to order affirmative action. Early judicial interpretation held that affirmative remedies under Title VII were limited to actual victims of discrimination (*Firefighters Local Union No. 1784* v. *Stotts,*

467 US 561 (1984)). Subsequent reinterpretation has authorized courts to order hiring goals where an employer has a clear history of discrimination, but the court clearly noted that Title VII cannot be used to require an employer to hire an unqualified employee (*Local 28 of the Sheet Metal Workers* v. *EEOC*, 106 S.Ct. 3019, 92 L.Ed. 2d 344 (1986)). Preferential policies as a response to demonstrated discrimination were given further approval when the court allowed an order requiring that 50 per cent of all promoted police officers be black if a qualified individual was available. Four factors were considered:

> In determining whether race conscious remedies are appropriate, we look to several factors, including the necessity for the relief and the efficacy of alternative remedies, the flexibility and duration of the numerical goals to the relevant labor market; and the impact of the relief on the rights of third parties
> (*United States* v. *Paradise*, 480 US 149, 171 (1987))

Even when no court has ordered them to take affirmative action, many employers attempt to achieve racially balanced workforces out of fear of liability under Title VII. Several court decisions interpreting Title VII make employers particularly eager to bring their workforce in line with the racial balance in the surrounding community. The 'pattern and practice' analysis allows the court to infer discrimination on the basis of a statistically significant difference between the level of minority employment and the relevant labor pool if the employer is unable to otherwise explain this disparity (*Hazelwood School District* v. *United States*, 433 US 299 (1977)). If the employer explains that the statistical disparity is due to a hiring practice, such as a test, that disproportionately disqualifies minorities, the employer must be able to show that the test is necessary to ensure qualified employees; a test having such a 'disparate impact' upon the makeup of the workforce without being adequately job related can give rise to liability for discrimination under Title VII (*Griggs* v. Duke Power Co., 401 US 424 (1971)). The Civil Rights Act of 1991 codified the Griggs standard into law in response to the Court's narrowing of Griggs in the 1989 decision in *Ward's Cove* v. *Antonio*, 490 US 642 (1989).

Private employers who institute affirmative action programmes seeking to achieve a racially balanced workforce may be subject to 'reverse discrimination' suits under Title VII.[14] However, when governmental entities, such as states, municipalities, public educational institutions and government agencies, seek to achieve balance through preferential hiring, contracting or admissions decisions, they are subject to the additional, and now more strict, constraints of the 14th amendment's equal protection clause. In *Regents of the University of California* v. *Bakke*, 438 US 265 (1978), a qualified but rejected white applicant brought a case against a medical school, owing to its allocation of a certain number of admissions to racial minorities. The court ruled that the medical school's quota system violated the 14th amendment because it used race as an absolutely determinative factor in admissions decisions, but held that race can be one of many factors considered in admissions decisions.

City of Richmond v. *J.A. Croson Co.*, 109 S. Ct. 706, 102 L. Ed. 2d 854 (1989) set additional limits on the use of preferential policies by state and local governments. The city of Richmond's order that 30 per cent of the dollar amount of every city contract be subcontracted to minority businesses was struck by the court. The Croson decision set the precedent that race-conscious measures employed by governmental entities must be 'strictly scrutinized' under the 14th amendment's equal protection clause.[15] Their goal should be only to redress specific histories of past discrimination and not more generally to improve the status of a minority or redress societal discrimination. Finally, race-based preferences should be 'narrowly tailored', or used in the least discriminatory manner and only when other measures will not work.

Another arena of preferential policies is executive orders, particularly those pertaining to federal contracting. In 1965 President Johnson issued Executive Order 11246, which required each federal contract to include an equal opportunity clause to be signed by the contractor. Later regulations required that most federal contractors develop written affirmative action plans involving analysis of minority utilization, goals and timetables, and plans to document progress toward those goals. For those who want federal contracts, 'underutilization' of minorities in relation to their availability necessitates 'result-oriented procedures' (Jones *et al.*, 1987: 598). The executive order is enforced by the Office of Federal Contract Compliance Programs (OFCCP), which oversees compliance reviews and can threaten to terminate federal contracts. Thus executive orders and related regulations also can lead to preferential policies. However, such policies are deemed voluntary since the opportunity to bid for such contracts is made available to all contractors on the same terms, rather than setting aside a number of contracts for minority-owned businesses.

Effectiveness

Jonathan S. Leonard's review of empirical analyses of the effectiveness of equal employment law and affirmative action regulation in the United States comes to the following conclusions. Affirmative action has improved employment opportunities, both low and high skilled, for minorities, especially blacks. One aspect of affirmative action that could be improved is the methods of targeting certain businesses for compliance reviews, since these reviews have tended to miss businesses with the lowest relative proportions of minorities. Business goals and timetables have not been rigidly followed (in a quota-like manner) 'but they are not hollow promises'. Finally, Leonard finds that Title VII litigation has played 'a significant role in increasing black employment' (Leonard, 1987: 319).

A study of affirmative action for African-American and Hispanic faculty in predominantly white colleges highlights the lack of significant increases in minority faculty. The empty threat of federal action resulting from such noncompliance to affirmative action may explain this outcome, since 'no college or university has ever lost federal funds as a result of noncompliance', at least not in a publicized manner (Washington and Harvey, 1989: iii).

In his review of impact studies, J. Faundez notes that the earnings ratio of black males to white males has improved over the last 30 years. Several studies suggest that government anti-discrimination policies played a role in this upswing, in addition to other factors such as improvements in minority education and changing attitudes: 'The confusion among these causes may be confusing as a matter of theory, but it is also evidence of the effectiveness of a broad-based strategy for achieving equal opportunity' (Leonard, 1986: 352).

On the other hand, the effectiveness of affirmative action is limited in several ways. Black females' economic status seems to have lagged behind black males early in the contract compliance programme (Faundez, 1994: 48–51). Black women, between 1960 and 1980, went from holding 2.8 per cent to 4.9 per cent of all professional positions; yet 'they were still the most poorly represented race/gender group in the male-dominated professions' (Sokoloff, 1992: 94). Sokoloff refutes the myth of black women's 'double advantage' under affirmative action due to their targeted gender and race.

Women of colour are not the only ones that disproportionately fail to benefit from preferential policies. The black 'underclass' may be untouched by opportunities opened up by race-based affirmative action, which tends to benefit mostly higher class group members. James E. Jones, Jr notes the increase in minority employment in jobs that are subject to the executive order: 'For those who could possibly benefit from affirmative action – those who are already qualified, able, and available – affirmative action programmes have been both effective and efficient'; however, affirmative action in employment has done little for the unqualified "underclass", although special education and training programmes that may be associated with affirmative action do help them' (Jones, 1993: 353–4). William Julius Wilson has noted that race-specific policies 'although beneficial to more advantaged blacks (i.e. those with higher income, greater education and training, and more prestigious occupations), do little for those who are truly disadvantaged' (Wilson, 1987: 110). Preferential policies did not do much to improve black workers' unemployment rates, which increased relative to whites in the 1970s and did not improve through the 1980s (Badgett, 1994).

Hispanics are another group targeted by affirmative action. Hispanics are under-represented at all levels of federal agencies (Kim, 1993). Hispanics continue to lag behind non-Hispanics in education and have higher unemployment rates (Nicolau and Valdiviesi, 1990). Hispanic professors, as mentioned, have failed to make inroads at white colleges (Washington and Harvey, 1989), and striking levels of discrimination against Hispanic job applicants continue (Cross *et al.*, 1990). Clearly affirmative action has not been enough to counteract the increasing disparity between Hispanics and non-Hispanics.

Longevity

While the intent of US law is to permanently prohibit discrimination, affirmative action measures are only temporary. The Supreme Court case that touches most directly on this issue is *United Steelworkers* v. *Weber*. In this case, a white challenged an affirmative action programme that reserved one half of all trainee spots for blacks. The court found that Title VII invests private sector employers with discretion as to how to correct for past discrimination and that the employer's actions in this particular case were permissible because, in a terribly disparate situation, the measures did not prohibit the advancement of whites and were intended to be only temporary.[16] Justice Brennan notes that 'Preferential selection of craft trainees at the Gramercy plant will end as soon as the percentage of black skilled craftworkers in the Gramercy plant approximates the percentage of blacks in the local labor force' (Jones *et al.*, 1987: 706). Justice Blackmun's concurring opinion also emphasizes that the racially balanced training programme 'operates as a temporary tool for remedying past discrimination' (Jones *et al.*, 1987: 708).

Time-limits on individual preferential policies are preferable to a general halt to all such policies:

> A simple way, for instance, to prevent future preferences from multiplying is to require existing preferences to end. Like more general 'sunset laws' limits on the duration of preferences prevent them from becoming entrenched through the ability of interest groups to block their appeal. (Rutherglen, 1992: 345)

An end to all race-based preferences would be simpler than considering each policy on its merits, 'but at the cost of abandoning any flexibility in considering the need for different preferences in different circumstances' (Rutherglen, 1992: 345). Recent calls to end affirmative action entirely suggest that a more drastic approach may be imminent.

Reception

Much of the controversy over affirmative action revolves around the 'innocent' white or male who may be disadvantaged, as in Justice Scalia's dissent in a 1987 affirmative action case, *Johnson* v. *Transportation Agency, Santa Clara Co.* He makes a fairness argument about the ones left behind as a female or minority is promoted. Many assume that affirmative action results in 'reverse discrimination', or the admission, hiring or promotion of certain groups without regard to merit.[17] Proponents argue that even in cases such as Bakke, which has been touted as an example of reverse discrimination, the ambiguities and subjectivity of admissions decisions means that Bakke's status as a supposedly much more qualified candidate is open to debate. Although he had higher grades and test scores, what is less clear is 'the comparative strength of candidates such as Bakke and those of special admittees in the non-quantifiable areas', such as personal interviews, extracurricular activities and 'overcoming disadvantages' (Fetzer, 1992: 9). Since it is this subjective component in admissions decisions that has so often led to discrimination in the past, many recognize the unfairness of suddenly eradicating subjective considerations when they threaten to work to the disadvantage of their previous beneficiaries.

Disputes over preferential policies have occurred between racial minorities as well. In the 1980s Asians complained of discriminatory university admissions policies, alleging that some major universities were restricting the number of Asians admitted. Over the course of the controversy, the terms of the debate shifted from 'discrimination' to 'reverse discrimination' as some conservatives suggested that the Asians were disadvantaged as a result of affirmative action for blacks and Hispanics (Cooper, 1991: 285; Takagi, 1992).

Other debates over preferential policies emphasize the economic costs of moving away from 'merit' and the threat that integration via preferences will reduce productivity and profits. In practice, however,

> Direct tests of the impact of governmental antidiscrimination and affirmative action regulation on productivity find no significant evidence of a productivity decline. These results suggest that antidiscrimination and affirmative action efforts have helped to reduce discrimination without yet inducing significant and substantial reverse discrimination.   (Leonard, 1986: 347)

Black business leaders supportive of affirmative action rebut critiques based on the economic costs of reverse discrimination with counter-arguments about the costs of discrimination not only to the minorities discriminated against but also to the American economy itself (McCoy, 1994).

Michel Rosenfeld feels that the opposition to affirmative action may appear to be 'a simple political dispute concerning the allocation of scarce social goods. However, something more profound is involved'. He notes that the Bakke case caused a storm of controversy; 'But that the same medical school favored children of friends of high-ranking university officials over more qualified applicants for admission barely provoked any reaction' (Rosenfeld, 1991: 1–2). The societal reaction against affirmative action is tied to its redistributive effects.

Other reactions to affirmative action are rooted in psychology rather than economics. From the point of view of a beneficiary of affirmative action, Stephen L. Carter writes of the often racist reactions to affirmative action and the 'psychological pressure that racial preferences often put on their beneficiaries' due to the 'qualification question' (Carter, 1991: 14).

Public opinion on preferential policies is divided, both among blacks and whites. Respondents were divided in half when a 1989 poll asked blacks, 'Do you believe that, because of past discrimination against black people, qualified blacks should receive preference over equally qualified whites in such matters as getting into college or getting jobs, or not?' (Sigelman and Todd, 1992: 243). Of the whites asked whether 'there should be a law to ensure that a certain number of federal contracts go to minority contractors', 43 per cent supported the setasides. If whites were told that such a programme was the law, support went up to 57 per cent, suggesting that whites' opinions on preferential policies are not set in stone (Sniderman and Piazza, 1993: 128–34).

As in the other cases, there is controversy over who is to be included in the racial categories of affirmative action.

> What ethnic groups should be classified under each category? Are Portuguese and Brazilians to be classified as Hispanics? Should well-educated Chilean and Argentinean refugees be included along with less educated Chicanos and Puerto Ricans? Should African students who recently settled in the United States be included among 'Blacks'?... What constitutes group membership?
> (Weiner, 1983: 50)

The inability of multiracial citizens to fit themselves comfortably into the government's racial categories has implications for preferential policies. Preparations for the 2000 census has sparked lobbying for a 'multiracial' category. Since a high percentage of citizens could tick this box, it has been suggested that a dramatic drop in the number of 'blacks' in the census might undermine affirmative action and even the entire Civil Rights programme, since census information is used to aid monitoring and enforcement (Wright, 1994).

CONCLUSION

First, I shall discuss some of the unique factors in different cases; then I shall turn to some similarities; finally, I propose some policy suggestions drawn out of these cases.

Differences

The different policies used a variety of social categories. Some categories are potentially more fluid than others, with the generally visible racial differences in the United States and Malaysia at one extreme and Northern Ireland's religious differences (invisible and amenable to conversion) at the other. In a relatively fluid social context, the self-identification and classification of group members for the purposes of enforcement and monitoring of preferential policies may be more problematic. Northern Ireland struggled over policies dependent upon making employees reveal their religion. In a worst-case scenario, such information could be used as a basis for discrimination rather than affirmative action. Caste identity in India too is amenable to some degree of symbolic social change, through conversion to non-Hindu religions. However, in spite of the fact that scheduled caste converts to Christianity or Islam continue to suffer from caste-based disadvantages, they are disqualified from preferences for scheduled castes. Regardless of the type of category used, classifying people according to group may obscure or even impede ongoing processes of social change, such as conversion, caste mobility, or ethnic or racial intermarriage. One implication for preferential policies is that they, and the use of social categories, should be frequently reassessed, adjusted, phased out or redirected on a policy by policy basis to respond to such social changes.

The cases of Malaysia and Pakistan demonstrate that this process of adjusting or phasing out preferential policies may be much harder when the policies benefit or ensure the dominance of a majority or politically powerful group. India seems to be moving in this direction, as more and more groups are allowed to qualify for preferences. Politicians may be motivated to promise needy and not so needy groups preferential treatment in order to get new vote blocs. A side-effect of extending preferences to a larger percentage of the population is that this exacerbates the problem of preferences only helping the best-off of this large beneficiary group. A larger pool means that the worst-off are even less likely to feel any effects of preferences. India's attempts to disqualify the 'creamy layer', or upper class, of the beneficiary groups from preferential policies is one way to counter this problem (Das, 1993: 437).

The magnitude of the disparity between rural and urban areas, particularly sharp in the South Asian cases, poses extreme challenges to the effectiveness of preferential policies, which have tended to emphasize opportunities associated with urban, middle-class life. This rural–urban divide is not as major a factor in the United States and Northern Ireland, but, in all cases, preferential policies cannot substitute for broader anti-poverty programmes.

Turning to individual cases, the degree of success of the Malaysian preferential policies is due in part to some unique factors. During the implementation of the NEP, Malaysian economic growth seems to have facilitated progress towards economic equity between ethnic groups and tempered ethnic conflict. Another factor that may have eased the way for Malaysian preferential policies is that the economic disparity they counteracted was due to what Michael L. Wyzan calls 'crowding' rather than discrimination based on ethnic hostility (Wyzan, 1990: 67). Both India and Malaysia are distinct in that preferential policies are specifically allowed in their constitutions. The Indian case stands out owing to its constitutional emphasis on group rights and equality, which, although in conflict with anti-discrimination clauses, provide an unusually firm constitutional footing for preferential policies. Pakistan constitutes an extreme case in that its quota systems have thoroughly permeated higher education and bureaucracies at all levels of government. The Irish case is special due to the international influences on its preferential policies, such as the pressure of the Irish-American lobby and the lessons drawn from similar policies in Canada and United States. By watching this relatively recent development of preferential policies, we may learn about the adaptability of models of preferential policies in new contexts. The US case is characterized by its attempts to achieve more equality for groups while maintaining its traditional emphasis on individual rights. This also may be the case in which the future of preferential policies is most at risk.

Similarities

All cases considered have British colonial experiences. In the Asian cases in particular, colonialism has affected both the social disparities and the policies designed to combat these inequalities. Often there was 'an incipient policy of preference' during colonial periods, when 'British colonial administrators recruited differently from particular segments of the colonized population' (Nevitte and Kennedy, 1986: 10). Later, British colonial administrators initiated other preferential policies to compensate for the inequalities that they had exacerbated.

One important process that effects all cases is the role of migration, which contributes to the ethnic diversity and stratification that sparked preferential policies. Cases of group migration, such as the forced migration of African slaves into the United States, the importation of Indian plantation workers into the Malay region under the

British, and the influx of Muhajirs into Pakistan after partition, seem particularly apt to result in stratification along ethnic lines, setting the stage for preferential policies. The movement of people between countries or regions and from rural to urban areas not only sparked preferential policies, but continues to cause tensions and demands for adjustments in these policies. Particularly salient in all three Asian cases is rural–urban migration which has contributed to tensions over preferential policies as competition for urban jobs tightens.

To various degrees in the different countries, importance and prestige is associated with government jobs, ranging from Pakistan, where 'meaningful input into the policymaking process can only be ensured by securing representation in the civilian bureaucracy' (Kennedy, 1986: 68), to India, where the 'psychological spin-off ' of a bureaucratic job may help one's whole community, to Northern Ireland, where public sector jobs are an especially large proportion of total employment. Thus government jobs seem an apt focal point for preferential policies. In the United States, in addition to public sector jobs, the percentage of private sector employees affected by the executive order programme is substantial, owing to the wide reach of government contracts.

It will be interesting to watch the effect of increasing global trends towards liberalization on preferential policies. The shrinking of the public sector and the dominance of ideologies emphasizing the primacy of the market may bode ill for states' preferential policies. The unfettered allocation of new private sector opportunities may reinforce old patters of ethnic dominance; however, these new opportunities may also alleviate some of the tense competition for scarce government jobs, which has contributed to the unpopularity of some preferential policies. The growing role of multinational corporations means that employment opportunities for disadvantaged groups may depend on the spread of policies such as the MacBride principles, applied in Northern Ireland.

Many of the problems associated with preferential policies can be seen in all cases considered here. The perennial problem is the use of the very social categories the country is trying to eradicate. In Malaysia, for instance, 'Although the ethnic preference system was designed to resolve some of the problems created by ethnicity, it also reinforces ethnicity by defining more and more issues in ethnic terms' (Means, 1986: 113). Similarly, 'Pakistan's redistributional policies at least have made ethnic allegiance more salient in the political process' (Kennedy, 1986: 87). In India the use of caste categories affects 'central issues of personal identity' through 'eligibility requirements that penalize those who would solve the problem of degraded identity by converting to a non-Hindu religion' (Galanter, 1986: 138). These requirements some-time cause scheduled caste converts to continue to publicly identify themselves with a caste.

On the other hand, the argument that preferential policies can be blamed for perpetuating identities such as caste should be viewed with 'some skepticism' (Galanter, 1986: 148–9). Subrata Mitra argues that, 'Far from strengthening caste consciousness, reservation thus weakens it' by breaking the association of caste with an occupational group (Mitra, 1987: 307). In the United States, policy-makers have tried to avoid the problems associated with giving preferences to a category of people by focusing on individuals as much as possible. Yet, as Cormack and Osborne note in their discussion of the Northern Irish case,

> discrimination, by its very nature, is based on the application of a collective label, e.g. black, Catholic, female. The individual is not primarily treated as an individual but as an imputed member of a group.... This suggests that the problem may well have to be treated using collective rather than individual solutions.
>
> (Cormack and Osborne, 1991: 44)

In all the cases considered here, the policies themselves may play some role, but there are many other social, economic and political forces that are responsible for the continuing salience of the categories of citizens benefiting from preferential policies. Moreover, the bound-aries of all of these categories are contested in various ways, ranging from the multiracial movement in the United States to the question of who is an 'indigenous' Bumiputra in Malaysia, to the recently ima-gined Muhajir community's demands to be declared Pakistan's fifth subnational group, to contestation over who is 'backward' in India, to the increasingly blank religion boxes in Northern Ireland's census.

Even if the categories could be neatly defined there remains another common challenge; often those helped by these remedial policies are already the most well-off in each category. As Kennedy notes in the case of the Pakistani system, 'the quota system, rather than weakening class distinctions in the state, actually serves to reinforce such distinc-tions' (Kennedy, 1986: 81). Whatever the type of category used, dis-parities remain within that category. For example, regional categories are clearly a blunt tool in Pakistan's policies; likewise religious cat-egories leave regional disparities in Northern Ireland. In the various cases, lower classes, women, rural-dwellers and those unqualified for many jobs or inadequately prepared for higher education often fail to benefit directly from preferential policies, although they sometimes gain vicariously.

Finally, Kennedy's generalizations from the Pakistani case are apt: 'Policies of preference tend to spread.... are hard to terminate.... [and] create vested interests' (Kennedy, 1986: 86). Weiner, drawing on the example of India to speculate about the future of such policies in places like the United States, is also pessimistic about their 'temporary' nature. 'If preferential policies are adopted, how, if at all, can they ever be terminated?' (Weiner, 1983: 51). While specific programmes, such as that in the United States' Weber case, may have a finite ending point, among the countries examined here, a general, national policy of preferences has never been terminated completely. This is not only due to the political momentum of these policies, but also to the continuity of the disparities that the policies are intended to alleviate. The sheer cumulation of historical disadvantage and the entrenchment of discriminatory practices, which may never be adequately addressed by preferences alone, contribute greatly to the longevity of these policies.

Policy Recommendations

Given the tendency of preferential policies to fail to touch most of the neediest members of disadvantaged groups, Malaysia's dual commitment, in its second economic plan, to uplift the Malays and alleviate poverty more generally, is worth emulating.[18] Although emulating India's exclusion of the 'creamy layer' from the groups targeted for special benefits is an option for countries which have had long-term preferential policy, switching completely to a class-based system of preference is problematic in contexts in which ethnicity, race or caste are still salient (Takagi, 1992; Morton, 1993). Examining the effects of various types of policy on all social groups (including the various segments within each group) is necessary to decide which policies or combination of policies to use. Abstractly dichotomizing policies into those that take account of ethnicity and those that do not, and arguing exclusively along these lines, politicizes policy debates and obscures possible policy combinations.

Constructive debate would be facilitated by a regularly scheduled preferential policy review, along the lines of India's national reconsideration of certain preferential policies every ten years. This would avoid the scheduling of comprehensive reviews only when the policies are under attack, as has happened in the United States. Heated attacks and defences of affirmative action produce few indepth and frank discussions of preferential policies. In such situations preferential policies may be seen in zero-sum terms, which leads to policy deadlock (Horowitz, 1985: 672). Such regular reviews would also address Mark Galanter's admonition that 'A serious programme of compensatory preference must include measures for self-assessment and a design for dismantling itself' (Galanter, 1991: xxii). Scheduled review allows policy-makers to adjust preferential policies in the light of social and economic changes and to phase out or redirect certain policies that have either met their goals or utterly failed. Publicizing the results of these reviews may reduce the misperceptions about preferential policies that have too often sparked protests against them. Moreover, awareness that these policies are not eternal or unchanging will facilitate public acceptance.

Preferential policies can be very useful to achieve ethnic balance in certain sensitive spheres of employment, such as the police and the military. Where the stakes are high owing to the concentration of coercive power, ethnic tensions can flare if one group has privileged access. Moreover, abuses of police or military power along ethnic lines is more likely with an ethnically homogeneous police or military force. The ultimate irony of the seemingly comprehensive Pakistani quota system is that in these key spheres, quotas are conspicuously absent. The military is primarily Punjabi, with some Pathan. In the province of Sindh, the Punjabi-dominated police have been accused of persecuting the Muhajirs, so contributing to ethnic tensions (Wright, 1991: 305).

Turning to the issue of 'quotas', the cases examined here suggest that there may be a happy medium between the Pakistani demands for quotas and Northern Ireland's paranoia of quotas. Taken to an extreme, quotas may compartmentalize society. As the empty slots in India's quotas for scheduled castes and tribes in higher education attest, quotas are not necessarily a more decisive way to alleviate inequalities. Yet the Indian case also demonstrates that quotas are not as pernicious and unchanging as one might expect, but rather are constantly adjusted due to various pressures (Parikh, 1990: 332). In cases of egregious discrimination in the United States, temporary quotas for a limited number of people for a limited purpose have been very effective.[19] The use of 'goals', although fraught with ambiguity in the American context, implies a looser objective that can coexist with a merit system. The use of goals where possible rather than strict quotas may quell the anxiety of dominant groups and make preferential policies more politically palatable. Countries considering eventually phasing out quotas might find the alternative of 'goals' to be a useful notion for transitional policies.

Given the limitations of the preferential policies discussed above, are there alternative ways to achieve these policies' goals of uplifting disadvantaged ethnic groups? A package of policies to deal with inequalities may involve some that downplay group identities and others that offer preferences based on group identity, as in the efforts to both integrate schools and increase Catholic employment in Northern Ireland. More sweeping remedial policies can complement preferential policies and may be necessary to reach their objectives and allow them to be phased out. Thomas Sowell points out the need to start policies to aid disadvantaged groups at the earliest stages of their lives, advocating good primary educations for all groups over preferences for a few individuals at the university level (Sowell, 1990: 183). Sowell feels that 'Preferential policies allow large promises about the future to be made by politicians at small immediate cost to the government' (Sowell, 1990: 181–2). In contrast, programmes involving more fundamental changes are more costly, time-consuming and politically risky. For example, William C. Thiesenhusen advocates land reform as the only truly effective form of affirmative action for Latin America (Thiesenhusen, 1990: 39, 41). Clearly, in contexts of extreme ethnic disparity, more radical policies may be necessary to achieve the goal of equality of opportunity.

NOTES

1. Preferential policies in the economic realm also include training programmes, capital assistance and even granting a group preferential access to the stock market (Rothchild, 1986; Wyzan, 1990).
2. These categories are oversimplified. For example, Malays may be considered 'indigenous' in relation to descendants of immigrants, but other indigenous groups have perhaps older claims; India uses some criteria in addition to caste, etc. Similar policies have been used to advance other groups, such as women, but the focus here is on disadvantaged ethnic groups, 'ethnic' in this case being defined broadly to include race, religion, and caste, similar to Donald L. Horowitz's (1985) usage.
3. Sowell (1990) discusses some 'preferential policies' to aid the privileged.

4. An example of Malay cultural dominance is the use of Malay language in education, as mentioned in the chapter in this volume by Jagdish Gundara and Crispin Jones.

5. Another type of preferential policy in India is for 'sons of the soil' concerned about competition from migrants, a justification for preferences that parallels Malaysia's policies (Weiner and Katzenstein, 1981).

6. Constitution (First Amendment) Act of 1951, section 2 (added Article 15 (4) to (Constitution) (see Galanter, 1984: 164–5; and Tripathi, 1989: 44–7).

7. One factor that may contribute to this changed reaction is the more diverse opportunities for advancement accompanying liberalization, which lessen perceptions of zero-sum competition over scarce public service jobs.

8. 'In August 1973, the quota re-emerged in its present form: 10 per cent merit; 50 per cent Punjab; 7.6 per cent urban Sindh (Karachi, Hyderabad and Sukkur); 11.4 per cent rural Sindh; 11.5 per cent NWFP [Northwest Frontier Province]; 3.5 per cent Balochistan; 4 per cent Northern Areas and Centrally Administered Tribal Areas; and 2 per cent Azad Kashmir' (Kennedy, 1994: 26).

9. 'Special interest' quotas for school admissions have included 'seats for children of medical doctors, attorneys, central government servants, military officers, engineers, university employees, and recipients of military decorations ... for "sportsmen" (usually field hockey or cricket players), widows, destitutes, foreigners, and non-Muslim minorities', etc. (Kennedy, 1986: 73–74). These quotas often do not increase opportunities for disadvantaged groups.

10. The label 'religious' is an oversimplification, since 'In Northern Ireland, as in the emerging ethnic conflicts in a number of other European societies, ethnicity and religiosity are closely intertwined' (Cormack and Osborne, 1991: 6).

11. In the United States this is known as 'impact discrimination', which was held to be illegal in *Griggs* v. *Duke Power* (1971). This decision was later adopted by Congress in 1991, when it amended Title VII of the Civil Rights Act of 1964.

12. 'As with many philosophical debates, code words became a shorthand way of expressing deeper philosophical positions'. Quotas are associated with group rights and goals with an individual rights emphasis (Weiner, 1983: 41).

13. This act, passed only a few weeks after the 14th amendment, suggests that the 14th amendment's equal protection clause, later used to criticize affirmative action, was probably intended to provide a constitutional underpinning for such race-specific programmes (Jones, 1993: 347–9).

14. One example is *United Steelworkers* v. *Weber*, 443 US 193 (1979), in which a 50 per cent minority setaside was challenged under Title VII by a white employee. The Court approved the plan because it was designed to correct a marked disparity and did not 'unnecessarily trammel' the interests of non-minorities or create an absolute bar to non-minority

employment and because it was temporary. See discussion of this case in the section on 'longevity'.

15. For a time, congressionally approved preferential policies were less strictly scrutinized owing to congressional authority under section 5 of the 14th amendment. See *Metro Broadcasting* v. *FCC*, 110 S.Ct. 3002 (1990). However, the Supreme Court recently unified the standard to be applied to such public contract minority set-aside programmes in *Adarand Constructors, Inc.* v. *Pena*, 115 S. Ct. 2097 (1995), so that federal set-aside programmes will be 'strictly scrutinized' under the standard announced in *Croson*.

16. In his opinion, Justice Brennan mentions several criteria for an acceptable affirmative action programme: It should be temporary and participatory (not barring the advancement of white employees), should not 'trammel' whites' rights, should open employment opportunities for Negroes in occupations which have been traditionally closed to them' and 'eliminate conspicuous racial imbalance'.

17. Fetzer (1992) rejects the term 'reverse discrimination' as political and ideological rhetoric. An example of a perspective that emphasizes the 'victimization' of white males due to affirmative action is Lynch (1992).

18. The anti-poverty programmes put in place have been criticized for their 'top-down' approach (Wyzan, 1990, 62–3). Emulating the dual nature of this approach rather than the finer points may be best.

19. Contrary to what the political rhetoric surrounding the Civil Rights Act of 1991 might suggest, 'quotas' have been carefully circumscribed by the courts in American affirmative action.

REFERENCES

Ahmed, Firoz, 1989. 'The Rise of Muhajir Separatism in Pakistan', *Pakistan Progressive* 10, 2/3 (Summer/Fall): 6–52.
Alavi, Hamza, 1987. 'Politics of Ethnicity in Pakistan,' *Pakistan Progressive* 9, 1 (Summer): 4–25.
Allred, Stephen, 1992. 'The Civil Rights Act of 1991: An Overview', *Popular Government* 57, 3 (Winter): 17–21.
Armstrong, David, 1994. 'Unemployment in Northern Ireland: Causes, Characteristics and Cures'. In Michael White (ed.), *Unemployment and Public Policy in a Changing Labour Market*. London: Policy Studies Institute.
Backward Classes Commission, 1980. B. P. Mandal, Chair. *Report*. New Delhi.
Badgett, M. V. Lee. 1994. 'Rising Black Unemployment: Changes in Job Stability or in Employment?' *Review of Black Political Economy* 22 (Winter): 55–75.
Bertsch, Kenneth A., 1991. *The MacBride Principles and US Companies in Northern Ireland 1991*. Washington, D.C.: The Investor Responsibility Research Center.
Brown, David, 1994. *The State and Ethnic Politics in Southeast Asia*. London and New York: Routledge.
Carter, Stephen L., 1991. *Reflections of an Affirmative Action Baby*. New York: Basic Books.
Case, William, 1994. 'The UNMO Party Election in Malaysia: One for the Money', *Asian Survey* 34, 10 (October): 916–30.
Chitnis, Suma, 1984. 'Positive Discrimination in India with Reference to Education'. In Robert B. Goldmann and A. Jeyaratnam Wilson (eds.), *From Independence to Statehood: Managing Ethnic Conflict in Five African and Asian States*. London: Frances Pinter: 31–43.
Cooper, Mary H., 1991. 'Racial Quotas', *CQ Researcher* 1, 217 (May): 279–94.
Cormack, Robert J. and Robert D. Osborne, 1991. *Discrimination and Public Policy in Northern Ireland*. Oxford: Clarendon Press.
Cross, Harry, Genevieve Kenney, Jane Mell and Wendy Zimmerman, 1990. *Employer Hiring Practices: Differential Treatment of Hispanic and Anglo Job Seekers*. Washington, D.C.: The Urban Institute Press.
Das, Bhagwan, 1993. 'The Reservation Policy and the Mandal Judgement', *Social Action* 43, 4 (October–December): 427–38.
Department of Economic Development, 1989. *Fair Employment in Northern Ireland: Key Details of the Act*. Belfast: DED.
Dunn, Dana, 1993. 'Gender Inequality in Education and Employment in the Scheduled Castes and Tribes of India', *Population Research and Policy Review* 12, 1: 53–70.
Faundez, J., 1994. *Affirmative Action: International Perspectives*. Geneva: International Labour Office.
Fetzer, Philip L., 1992. '"Reverse Discrimination": The Political Use of Language', *Thurgood Marshall Law Review* (Spring).
Frankel, Francine, 1988. 'Middle Classes and Castes'. In Atul Kohli (ed.), *India's Democracy: An Analysis of Changing State-Society Relations*. Princeton: Princeton University Press.

Fuchs, Lawrence H., 1990. *The American Kaleidoscope: Race, Ethnicity and the Civic Culture*. Hanover, N.H.: Univerisity Press of New England.

Galanter, Marc., 1984. *Competing Equalities: Law and the Backward Classes in India*. Delhi: Oxford University Press.

Galanter, Marc, 1986. 'Pursuing Equality: An Assessment of India's Policy of Compensatory Discrimination for Disadvantaged Groups'. In Dilip K. Basu and Richard Sisson (eds.), *Social and Economic Development in India: A Reassessment*. University of California: Sage Publications.

Galanter, Marc, 1991. Preface to the paperback edition of *Competing Equalities*. 1991.

Heaton, Norma, Gillian Robinson and Celia Davies. 1993. 'Women in the Northern Ireland Labour Market'. In Paul Teague (ed.), *The Economy of Northern Ireland: Perspectives for Structural Change*. London: Lawrence and Wishart: 170–89.

Hepple, Bob, 1990. 'Discrimination and Equality of Opportunity – Northern Irish Lessons', *Oxford Journal of Legal Studies* 10, 3: 408–21.

Horowitz, Donald L., 1985. *Ethnic Groups in Conflict*. Berkeley: University of California Press.

Hubbell, L. Kenneth, 1990. 'Political and Economic Discrimination in Sri Lanka', In Michael Wyzan (ed.), *The Political Economy of Ethnic Discrimination and Affirmative Action: A Comparative Perspective*. New York: Praeger: 115–39.

Jalali, Rita, 1993. 'Preferential Policies and the Movement of the Disadvantaged: The Case of the Scheduled Castes in India', *Ethnic and Racial Studies* 16, 1: 95–120.

Jesudason, James V., 1995. 'Statist Democracy and the Limits to Civil Society in Malaysia', *Journal of Commonwealth and Comparative Politics* 33, 3 (November): 335–56.

Jones, James E. Jr, 1993. 'The Rise and Fall of Affirmative Action'. In Herbert Hill and James E. Jones, Jr (eds.), *Race in America: The Struggle for Equality*. Madison: University of Wisconsin Press.

Jones, James E. Jr, William P. Murphy and Robert Belton, 1987. *Cases and Materials on Discrimination in Employment*. St. Paul: West Publishing Co., 5th edition.

Kennedy, Charles H., 1986. 'Policies of Redistributional Preference in Pakistan'. In Neil Nevitte and Charles H. Kennedy (eds.), *Ethnic Preference and Public Policy in Developing States*. Boulder: Lynne Rienner Publishers, Inc.: 63–93.

Kennedy, Charles H., 1994. 'Policies of Ethnic Preference in Pakistan'. Paper prepared for the UNRISD/UNDP Project on Ethnic Diversity and Public Policies.

Kim, Pan Suk, 1993. 'Racial Integration in the American Federal Government: With Special Reference to Asian-Americans', *Review of Public Personnel Administration* 13, 1 (Winter): 52–66.

Kumar, Dharma, 1994. 'The Backward Classes: Affirmative Action and Ethnicity'. Paper prepared for the Seminar on Ethnicity and Nation Building organized by the US Educational Foundation in India and the Centre for South and Southeast Asian Studies, University of Madras, 21–23 March.

Leonard, Jonathan S., 1986. 'The Effectiveness of Equal Employment Law and Affirmative Action Regulation', *Research in Labor Economics* 8: 319–50.

Lim, Mah Hui, 1985. 'Affirmative Action, Ethnicity, and Integration: The Case of Malaysia', *Ethnic and Racial Studies* 8, 2 (April): 250–76.

Lynch, Frederick R., 1992. 'Race Unconsciousness and the White Male', *Society* 29, 2 (January/February): 30–5.

Malik, Iftikhar H., 1994. 'Pakistan's National Security and Regional Issues', *Asian Survey* 34, 2 (December): 1077–92.

Mauzy, Diane, 1993. 'Malaysia: Malay Political Hegemony and "Coercive Consociationalism". In John McGarry and Brendon O'Leary (eds.), *The Politics of Ethnic Conflict Regulation: Case Studies of Protracted Ethnic Conflicts*. New York: Routledge: 106–27.

McCoy, Frank, 1994. 'Rethinking the Cost of Discrimination', *Black Enterprise* 24 (January): 54–9.

Means, Gordon P., 1986. 'Ethnic Preference in Malaysia'. In Neil Nevitte and Charles H. Kennedy (eds.), *Ethnic Preference and Public Policy in Developing States*. Boulder: Lynne Rienner Publishers, Inc.: 95–118.

Milne, R. S., 1986. 'Ethnic Aspects of Privatization in Malaysia'. In Neil Nevitte and Charles H. Kennedy (eds.), *Ethnic Preference and Public Policy in Developing States*. Boulder: Lynne Rienner Publishers, Inc.: 119–34.

Mitra, Subrata, 1987. 'The Perils of Promoting Equality: The Latent Significance of the Anti-Reservation Movement in India', *Journal of Commonwealth and Comparative Politics* 25, 3 (November): 292–312.

Mitra, Subrata, 1994. 'Caste, Democracy and the Politics of Community Formation in India', In Mary Searle-Chatterjee and Ursula Sharma (eds.), *Contextualizing Caste: Post Dumontian Approaches*. Oxford: Blackwell.

Morton, Frederick A. Jr, 1993. 'Class-based Affirmative Action: Another Illustration of America Denying the Impact of Race', *Rutgers Law Review*: 1089–141.

Nevitte, Neil and Kennedy, Charles H.L. (eds.), 1986. *Ethnic Preference and Public Policy in Developing States*. Boulder: Lynne Rienner Publishers, Inc.

Nicolau, Siobhan and Refac/Valdivieso, 1990. *A More Perfect Union: Achieving Hispaxic Parity by the Year 2000*. Queenstown, Md.: Aspen Institute.

Oberst, Robert, 1986. 'Policies of Ethnic Preference in Sri Lanka'. In Neil Nevitte and Charles H. Kennedy (eds.), *Ethnic Preference and Public Policy in Developing States*. Boulder: Lynne Rienner Publishers, Inc.: 135–54.

O'Duffy, Brendan, 1993. 'Containment or Regulation? The British Approach to Ethnic Conflict in Northern Ireland'. In John McGarry and Brendon O'Leary (eds.), *The Politics of Ethnic Conflict Regulation: Case Studies of Protracted Ethnic Conflicts*. New York: Routledge: 128–50.

Osborne, Robert. D., 1992. 'Fair Employment Equity: Policy Learning in a Comparative Context', *Public Money and Management* 12, 4 (October–December): 11–18.

Parikh, Sunita, 1990. 'Preferences for Equality: A Comparative Analysis of Higher Education Policy in the United States and India'. PhD diss., University of Chicago.

Raman, C. K., 1994. 'Inequities in Society and Compensatory Discrimination: The Story of the Vanniars of Tamil Nadu'. Paper prepared for the Seminar on Ethnicity and Nation Building organized by the US Educational Foundation in India and the Centre for South and Southeast Asian Studies, University of Madras, 21–23 March.

Raman, Kannamma, 1995. 'Dynamics of the Reservation Policy: An Overview', *Social Action* 45, 4 (October–December): 405–20.

Rosenfeld, Michel, 1991. *Affirmative Action and Justice: A Philosophical and Constitutional Inquiry*. New Haven: Yale University Press.

Rothchild, Donald, 1986. 'State and Ethnicity in Africa'. In Neil Nevitte and Charles H. Kennedy (eds.), *Ethnic Preference and Public Policy in Developing States*. Boulder: Lynne Rienner Publishers, Inc.: 15–61.

Rutherglen, George, 1992. 'After Affirmative Action: Conditions and Consequences of Ending Preferences in Employment', *University of Illinois Law Review*: 339–66.

Shah, Hemant, 1994. 'News and the "Self Production of Society": Times of India Coverage of Caste Conflict and Job Reservations in India', *Journalism Monographs* 144 (April).

Sidanius, Jim and Felicia Pratto, 1993. 'The Inevitability of Oppression and the Dynamics of Social Dominance'. In Paul M. Sniderman, Philip E. Tetlock and Edward G. Carmines (eds.), *Prejudice, Politics, and the American Dilemma*. Stanford: Stanford University Press: 173–211.

Sinnadurai, Visu, 1989. 'Unity and Diversity: The Constitution of Malaysia'. In Robert A. Goldwin, Art Kaufman and William A. Schambra (eds.), *Forging Unity Out of Diversity*. Washington, D.C.: American Enterprise Institute for Public Policy Research.

Sniderman, Paul M. and Thomas Piazza, 1993. *The Scar of Race*. Cambridge, MA and London: Belknap Press of Harvard University Press.

Sokoloff, Natalie, J., 1992. *Black Women and White Women in the Professions*. New York: Routledge.

Sowell, Thomas, 1990. *Preferential Policies: An International Perspective*. New York: W. Morrow.

Sudarsen, V., 1994. 'Scheduled Castes and Scheduled Tribes of India: Constitutional Safeguards and Ground Realities'. Paper prepared for the Seminar on Ethnicity and Nation Building organized by the US Educational Foundation in India and the Centre for South and Southeast Asian Studies, University of Madras, 21–23 March.

Sigelman, Lee and James S. Todd, 1992. 'Clarence Thomas, Black Pluralism, and Civil Rights Policy', *Political Science Quarterly*, 107, 2: 231–48.

Takagi, Dana Y., 1992. *Retreat from Race: Asian-American Admissions and Racial Politics*. New Brunswick: Rutgers University Press.

Taylor, Charles, 1992. 'Multiculturalism and the Politics of Recognition'. In Amy Gutman (ed.), *Multiculturalism and the Politics of Recognition, an Essay*. Princeton: Princeton University Press.

Teague, Paul, 1993. 'Discrimination and Fair Employment in Northern Ireland'. In Paul Teague (ed.), *The Economy of Northern Ireland: Perspectives for Structural Change*. London: Lawrence and Wishart: 141–69.

Thiesenhusen, William C., 1990. 'Human Rights, Affirmative Action, and Land Reform in Latin America'. In Michael Wyzan (ed.), *The Political*

Economy of Ethnic Discrimination and Affirmative Action: A Comparative Perspective. New York: Praeger.

Tripathi, P. K., 1989. 'Commentary'. In Robert A. Goldwin, Art Kaufman and William A. Schambra (eds.), *Forging Unity out of Diversity*. Washington, D.C.: American Enterprise Institute for Public Policy Research: 38–47.

Washington, Valora and William Harvey, 1989. *Affirmative Rhetoric, Negative Action: African-American and Hispanic Faculty at Predominantly White Institutions*. Report No. 2. Washington, D.C.: School of Education and Human Development, The George Washington University.

Weiner, Myron, 1983. 'The Political Consequences of Preferential Policies: A Comparative Perspective', *Comparative Politics* 16, 1 (October): 35–52.

Weiner, Myron and Mary Fainsod Katzenstein, 1981. *India's Preferential Policies*. Chicago and London: University of Chicago Press.

Wilson, William Julius, 1987. *The Truly Disadvantaged: The Inner City, the Underclass, and Public Policy*. Chicago and London: University of Chicago Press.

Wright, Lawrence, 1994. 'One Drop of Blood', *The New Yorker* (25 July): 46–55.

Wright, Theodore P. Jr, 1991. 'Center–Periphery Relations and Ethnic Conflict in Pakistan: Sindhis, Muhajirs, and Punjabis', *Comparative Politics* 23, 3 (April): 299–312.

Wyzan, Michael, 1990. *The Political Economy of Ethnic Discrimination and Affirmative Action: A Comparative Perspective*. New York: Praeger.

Index